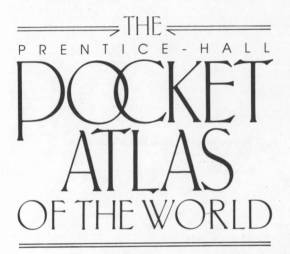

# THE
## PRENTICE-HALL
# POCKET
# ATLAS
## OF THE WORLD

Edited by
**Harold Fullard, MSc**
Director of Cartography

**Prentice-Hall, Inc.**
ENGLEWOOD CLIFFS, NEW JERSEY 07632

**Library of Congress Cataloging in Publication Data**
Main entry under title:

Prentice-Hall pocket atlas of the world.

Includes index.
1. Atlases. I. Fullard, Harold. II. Prentice-Hall,
inc. III. Title. IV. Title: Pocket atlas of the world.
G1021.P686  1983          912          83-675890
ISBN 0-13-697045-1

1 2 3 4 5 6 7 8 9 10

# ISBN 0-13-697045-1

Cover Photographs: Richard Hawthorne; Bill Voss/West Light
Cover Design: Suzanne Beck

Prentice-Hall International, London
Prentice Hall of Australia Pty. Limited, Sydney
Prentice Hall Canada Inc., Toronto
Prentice Hall of India Private Limited, New Delhi
Prentice Hall of Japan, Inc. Tokyo
Prentice Hall of Southeast Asia Pte. Ltd., Singapore
Whitehall Books Limited, Wellington, New Zealand
Editora Prentice-Hall do Brazil Ltda., Rio de Janeiro

# Contents

M=Millions

**World Maps**
1      The World: Air Routes 1 : 250M.
2-3    The World 1 : 175M.

**Europe**
4-5    Europe 1 : 27½M.
6-7    England and Wales 1 : 3½M.
8      Scotland 1 : 3½M.
9      Ireland 1 : 3½M.
10-11  Scandinavia and Finland 1 : 9M.
       Inset: Iceland 1 : 9M.
12     Denmark 1 : 3½M.
13     Switzerland 1 : 2½M.
14-15  France and the Low Countries 1 : 6M.
16-17  Germany and Austria 1 : 5M.
18-19  West Germany, Benelux and North
       East France 1 : 3½M.
20-21  East France, Switzerland and North
       West Italy 1 : 3½M.
22-23  Poland and Czechoslovakia 1 : 5M.
24-25  Mediterranean Lands 1 : 20M.
26     Spain and Portugal 1 : 9M.
27     Greece, Turkey and Cyprus 1 : 9M.
28-29  Italy 1 : 6M.
30-31  Hungary and the Balkan States 1 : 6M.
32-33  Russia in Europe 1 : 18M.
34-35  USSR 1 : 40M.

**Asia**
36-37  Asia 1 : 60M.
38-39  South West Asia and the Nile Valley
       1 : 25M.
40     The Levant 1 : 4M.
41     Suez Canal 1 : 1M.
42-43  Central Middle East Countries 1 : 17½M.
44-45  India, Pakistan, Ceylon and Burma
       1 : 20M.
46-47  Indo-Gangetic Plain 1 : 12M.
48-49  East Indies and Further India 1 : 25M.
50-51  China 1 : 25M.
52-53  Korea and Japan 1 : 12½M.
54-55  Japan 1 : 8½M.

## Pacific Ocean
56-57    Pacific Ocean 1 : 100M.

## Australasia
58-59    Australia 1 : 22½M.
60-61    South East Australia 1 : 8M.
          Inset : Tasmania 1 : 8M.
62-63    Australia : East 1 : 15M.
          Inset : New Guinea 1 : 20M.
64-65    Australia : West 1 : 15M.
66-67    New Zealand : 1 : 7M.
          Inset :
          (a) Fiji and Tonga Islands 1 : 15M.
          (b) Samoa 1 : 15M.
          (c) New Zealand and its Antipodes

## Africa
68-69    Africa 1 : 45M.
70-71    West and North West Africa 1 : 20M.
72-73    Central and East Africa 1 : 18M.
74-75    South Africa 1 : 12½M.

## N. America
76-77    North America 1 : 40M.
78-79    Canada 1 : 27½M.
80        Western Canada 1 : 17½M.
81        Eastern Canada 1 : 17½M.
82-83    United States 1 : 25M.
          Inset :
          (a) Alaska 1 : 25M.
          (b) Hawaiian Islands 1 : 10M.
          (c) Aleutian Islands 1 : 25M.
84-85    Western United States 1 : 15M.
86-87    Eastern United States 1 : 15M.
88-89    North Eastern United States 1 : 7½M.
90        Mexico 1 : 20M.

## Central America
91        West Indies 1 : 20M.

## South America
92-93    South America 1 : 40M.
94-95    South America : Central 1 : 16M.

## Polar Regions
96        Polar Regions 1 : 80M.

## Index

# THE WORLD: AIR ROUTES

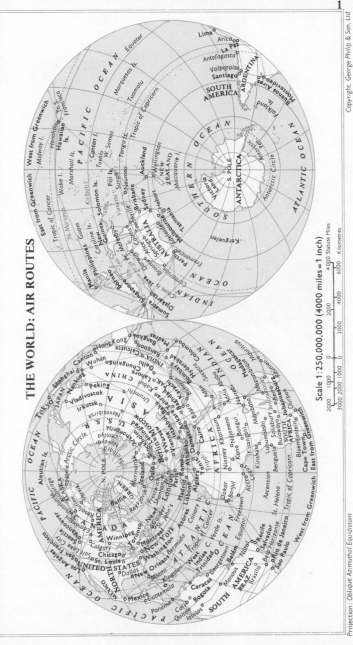

Scale 1:250,000,000 (4000 miles = 1 inch)

Projection: Oblique Azimuthal Equidistant

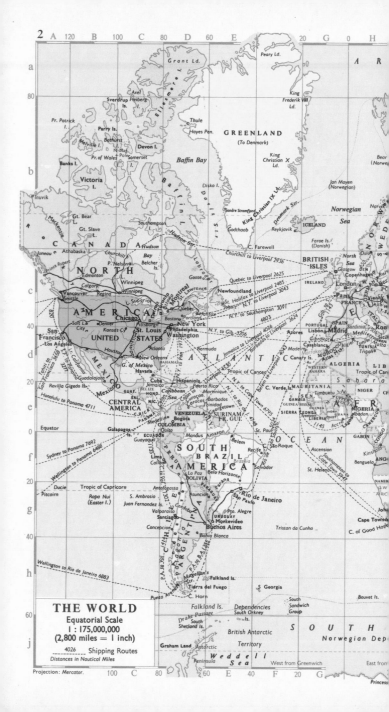

# THE WORLD
## Equatorial Scale
### 1 : 175,000,000
(2,800 miles = 1 inch)

———— 4026 Shipping Routes
Distances in Nautical Miles

Projection: Mercator.

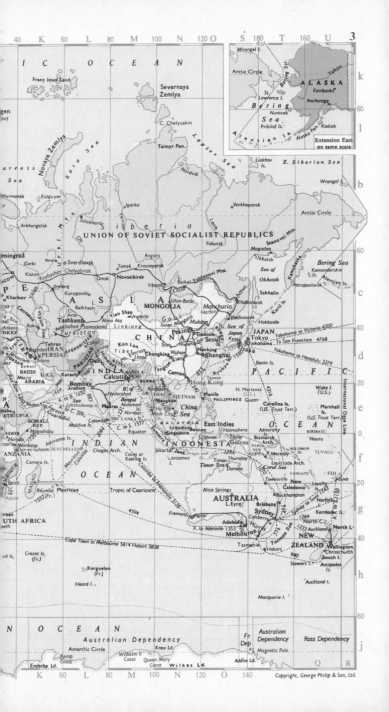

# EUROPE

Scale 1 : 27,500,000 (440 miles = 1 inch)

100 50 0 100 200 300 400 500 Statute Miles

100 0 100 200 300 400 500 600 700 800 Kilometres

—— Railways ········ Canals

Projection: Bonne

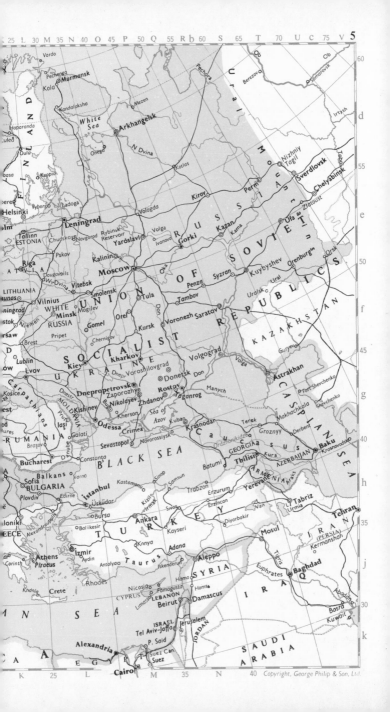

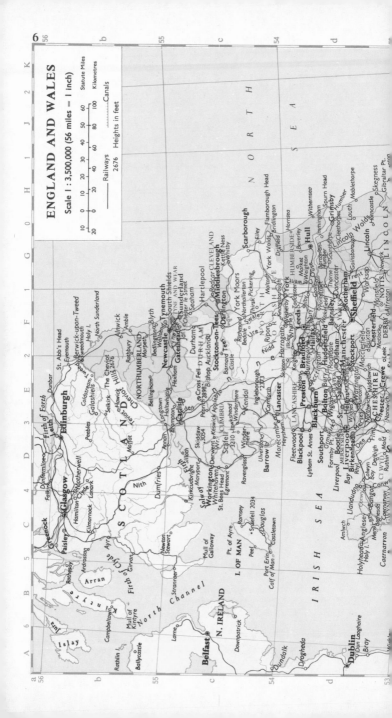

# ENGLAND AND WALES

Scale 1 : 3,500,000 (56 miles = 1 inch)

Statute Miles
Kilometres
Canals

Railways
2676 Heights in feet

# SCOTLAND

Scale 1 : 3,500,000 (56 miles = 1 inch)

Statute Miles
20  10  0        20        40
0    20   40   60
Kilometres

—— Railways ........ Canals   3547 Heights in feet

Projection: Conical
with two standard parallels.

Copyright, George Philip & Son, Ltd

**9**

## IRELAND

Scale 1 : 3,500,000 (56 miles = 1 inch)

Railways ⸱⸱⸱⸱⸱ Canals  2466 Heights in feet

### DISTRICTS OF NORTHERN IRELAND

| | | |
|---|---|---|
| 1 Londonderry | 10 Strabane | 19 Lisburn |
| 2 Limavady | 11 Omagh | 20 Antrim |
| 3 Coleraine | 12 Fermanagh | 21 Newtownabbey |
| 4 Ballymoney | 13 Dungannon | 22 Carrickfergus |
| 5 Moyle | 14 Craigavon | 23 North Down |
| 6 Larne | 15 Armagh | 24 Ards |
| 7 Ballymena | 16 Newry & Mourne | 25 Castlereagh |
| 8 Magherafelt | 17 Banbridge | 26 Belfast |
| 9 Cookstown | 18 Down | |

Projection: Conical with two standard parallels

West from Greenwich

Copyright, George Philip & Son, Ltd

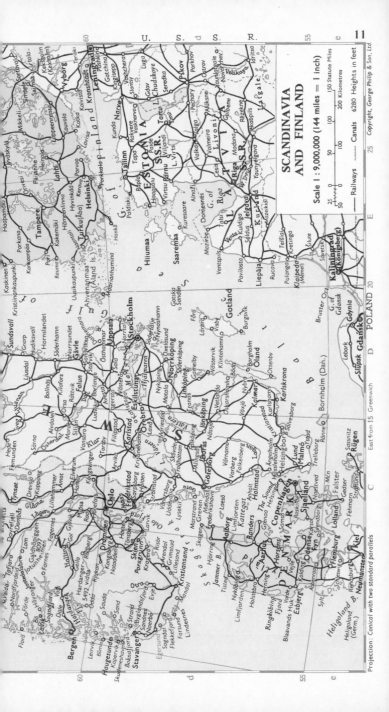

**11**

## SCANDINAVIA AND FINLAND

Scale 1 : 9,000,000 (144 miles = 1 inch)

Statute Miles
25 0 50 100 150
Kilometres
50 0 100 200

6280 Heights in feet

—— Railways  - - - - Canals

Copyright, George Philip & Son, Ltd.

Projection: Conical with two standard parallels

East from 15 Greenwich

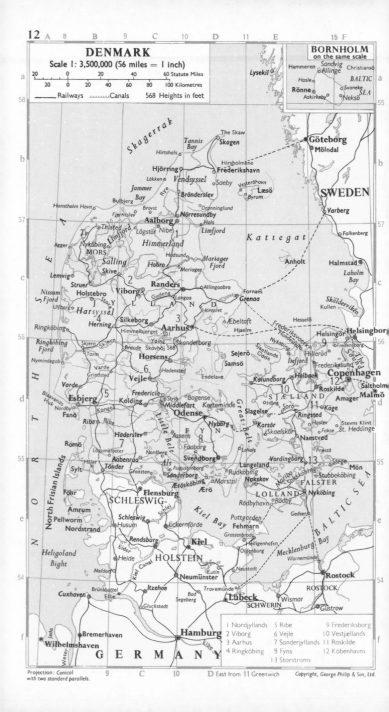

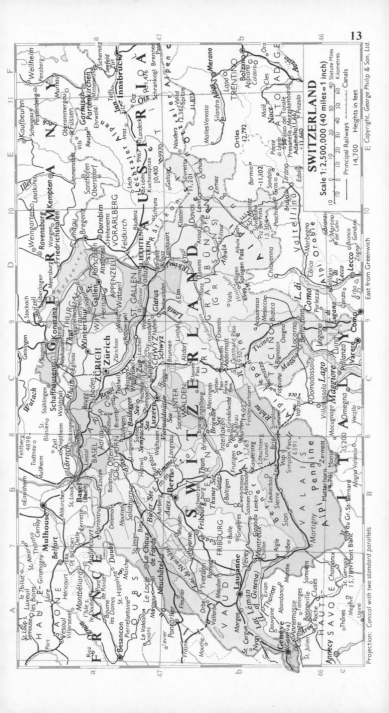

**13**

### SWITZERLAND

Scale 1:2,500,000 (40 miles = 1 inch)

10   0   10   20   30   40   50   60   Statute Miles

10   0   10   20   30   40   50   60   Kilometres

Principal Railways ————   Canals

Heights in feet

E Copyright, George Philip & Son. Ltd.

Projection: Conical with two standard parallels

East from Greenwich

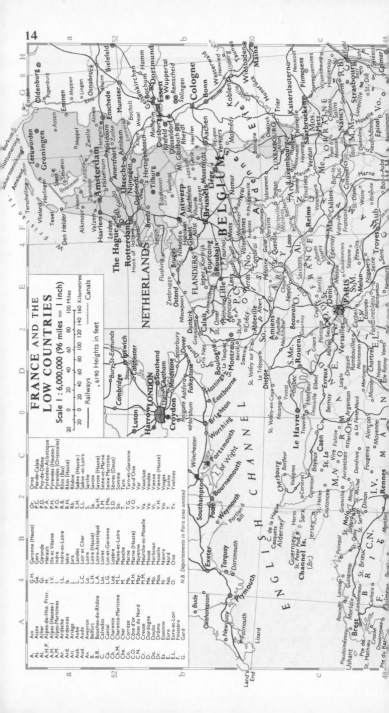

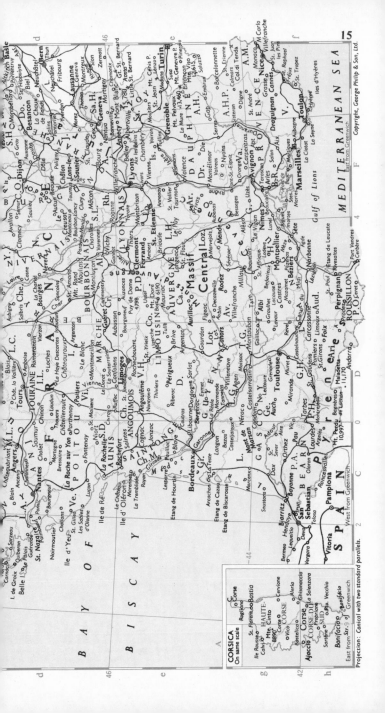

# GERMANY AND AUSTRIA

Scale 1:5,000,000 (80 miles=1 inch)

Statute Miles
25 0 25 50 75 100 125 150

Kilometres
25 0 25 50 75 100

Railways ———— Canals

.4887 Heights in feet

SWEDEN

Ystad
Trelleborg
Falsterbo
Rönne

NORTH SEA

N.

Frisian Islands
Heligoland
Wangerooge
Longeoog
Norderney
Juist
Borkum
Schiermonnikoog
Ameland

NETH.
Groningen
Leeuwarden
Sneek
Zwolle
Meppel
Apeldoorn
Deventer
Almelo
Enschede
Arnhem
Nijmegen
Kleve

DENMARK
Esbjerg
Fanø
Rømø
Sylt
Amrum
Föhr
Pellworm
Nordstrand
Kolding
Ribe
Haderslev
Åbenrå
Flensburg
Tønder
Sønderborg
Als
Alsen
Fyen
Odense
Svendborg
Ærø
Lolland
Falster
Gedser
Nysted
Møn
Sjælland (Zealand)
Korsør
Slagelse
Næstved
Køge
Gt. Belt
Little Belt
Rødbyhavn
Gedser

Kiel Bay
Fehmarn
Fehmarn Belt
Grossenbrode
Warnemünde
Rostock
Wismar
Rügen
Sassnitz
Greifswald
Stralsund
Zingst
Güstrow

Kiel
Neumünster
Rendsburg
Schleswig
Heide
Brunsbüttelkoog
Glückstadt
Cuxhaven
Lehe
Bremerhaven
Wilhelmshaven
Emden
Papenburg
Oldenburg
Leer

HAMBURG
Lübeck
Travemünde
Lauenburg
Schwerin
Parchim
Harburg
Lüneburg
Lüneburg Heath
Celle
Verden
Nienburg
BREMEN
Osnabrück
Münster
Rheine
Lingen
Meppen

Usedom
Swinoujscie
Wolin
Kolobrzeg
Koszalin
Darlowo
Bialogard
Szczecinek
Czersk
Brda
Chojnice
Tuchola

Neubrandenburg
Neustrelitz
Prenzlau
Anklam
Demmin
Pasewalk
Szczecin (Stettin)
Gryfice
Kamien
Goleniów
Stargard
Drawsko
Szczecinek
Walcz
Pila
Chodziez
Wagrowiec

L. Müritz
Wittstock
Oranienburg
Angermünde
Neuruppin
Havel
Rathenow
Wittenberge
Havel
Fürstenwalde
BERLIN
Potsdam
Spree
Oder
Eberswalde
Frankfurt
Kostrzyn
Gorzów
Myslibórz
Pyrzyce
Choszczno
Drawsko
Miedzychód
Miedzyrzecz
Nowy Tomysl
Skwierzyna
Warta
Swiebodzin
Sulechów
Krosno
Zielona Góra
Zagan
Zary
Zary

POLAND
Wałcz
Czarnków
Oborniki
Szamotuly
POZNAŃ
Gniezno
Wrzesnia
Wagrowiec
Gostyn
Kórnik
Srem
Sroda
Koscian
Leszno
Gostyn
Rawicz
Glogów
Odolanów
Olesnica
Gubin
Forst
Spremberg
Sorau

Salzwedel
Stendal
Brandenburg
Burg
MAGDEBURG
Bernburg
Zerbst
Dessau
Zeitz
Wittenberg
Luckenwalde
Jüterbog
Finsterwalde
Luckau
Lübben
Cottbus
Senftenberg
Grossenhain
Bautzen

Osnabrück
Bielefeld
Detmold
Lippstadt
Paderborn
Minden
Hameln
Hildesheim
HANOVER
Braunschweig (Brunswick)
Salzgitter
Goslar
Brocken 3747
Clausthal-Zellerfeld
Göttingen
Münden
Mühlhausen
Kassel
Nordhausen
Eisleben
Halberstadt

DORTMUND
BOCHUM
ESSEN
DUISBURG
Gelsenkirchen
Hagen
Wuppertal
DÜSSELDORF
Wesel
Bocholt
Krefeld
M.Gladbach
M'Gladbach
Bottrop
Hamm
Dortmund
2760

L. Dümmer
Hunte
Weser
Jade
Jade Bay
Weser
Ems
Vechte

HALLE
LEIPZIG
Merseburg
Torgau
Wurzen
Mulde
Saale
Eisenhüttenstadt

Oder
Neisse
Bobr
Bautzen

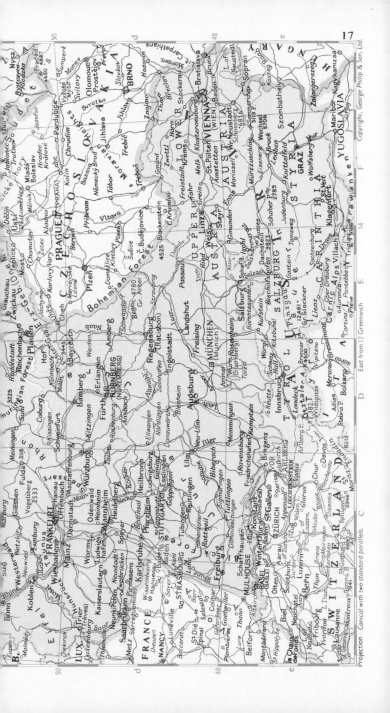

**17**

Projection : Conical with two standard parallels.

East from 12 Greenwich

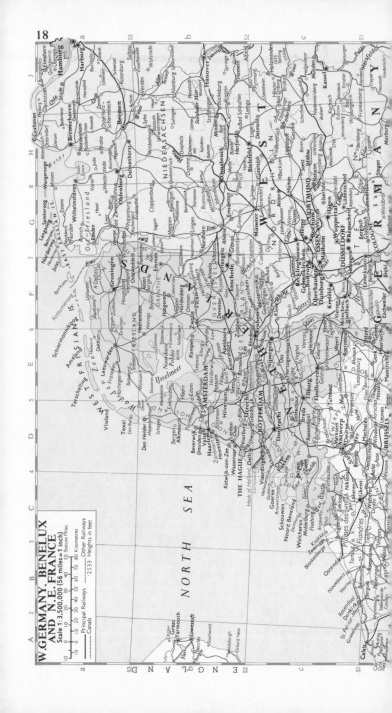

**18**

## W. GERMANY, BENELUX AND N.E. FRANCE

Scale 1:3,500,000 (56 miles = 1 inch)

Principal Railways
Other Railways
Canals
Heights in feet

2533

East from 6 Greenwich

Projection: Conical with two standard parallels.

Projection: Conical with two standard parallels.

POLAND AND
CZECHOSLOVAKIA
Scale 1 : 5,000,000 (80 miles = 1 inch)

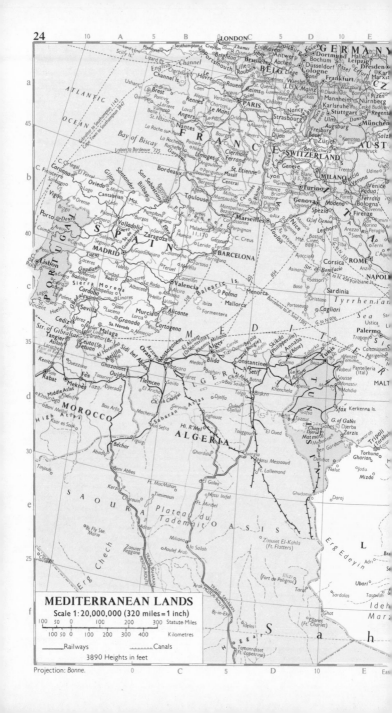

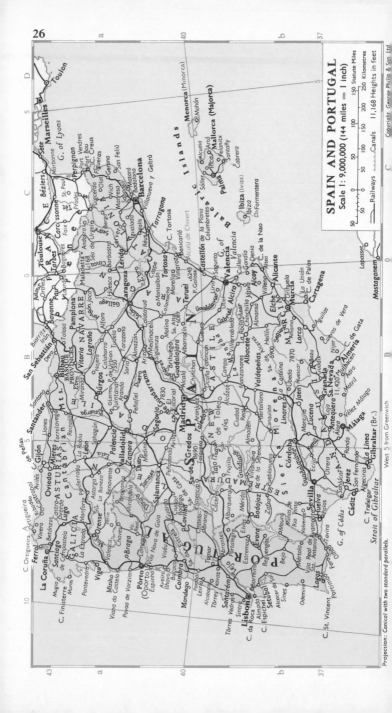

**26**

**SPAIN AND PORTUGAL**
Scale 1: 9,000,000 (144 miles = 1 inch)

| 50 | 0 | 50 | 100 | 150 Statute Miles |

| 50 | 0 | 50 | 100 | 150 | 200 | 250 Kilometres |

Railways ...... Canals 11,168 Heights in feet

Projection: Conical with two standard parallels.

West 5 from Greenwich

Copyright George Philip & Son Ltd.

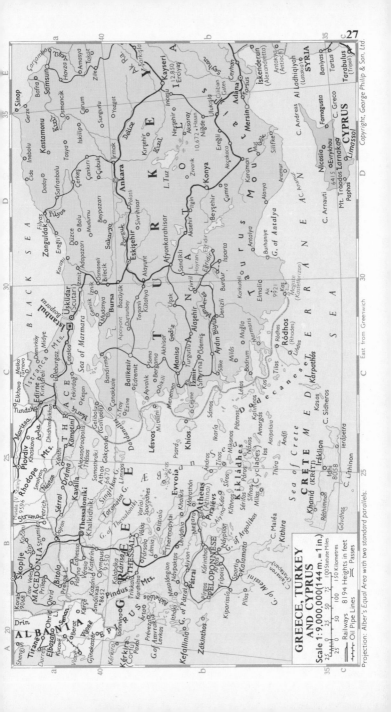

# GREECE, TURKEY AND CYPRUS

Scale 1:9,000,000(144 m.=1 in.)

25 0 25 50 75 100 150 Kilometres
25 0 25 50 75 100 Statute Miles

—— Railways   8194 Heights in feet
++++ Oil Pipe Lines   ⤬ Passes

Projection: Alber's Equal Area with two standard parallels.

Copyright, George Philip & Son, Ltd.

**27**

C   East from Greenwich   C

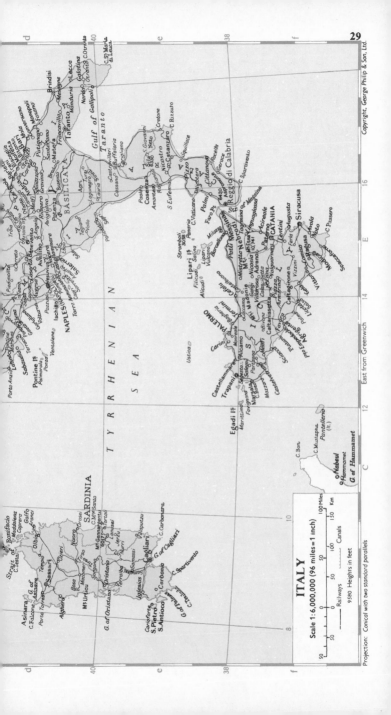

**29**

## ITALY

Scale 1:6,000,000 (96 miles=1 inch)

0   50   100 Miles

0   50   100   150 Km

——— Railways   ⊢⊣⊢⊣ Canals

9580 Heights in feet

Projection: Conical with two standard parallels

East from Greenwich

TYRRHENIAN SEA

SARDINIA

Gulf of Taranto

Gulf of Gallipoli

BASILICATA

NAPLES

Lipari Is.

PALERMO

CATANIA

G. of Hammamet

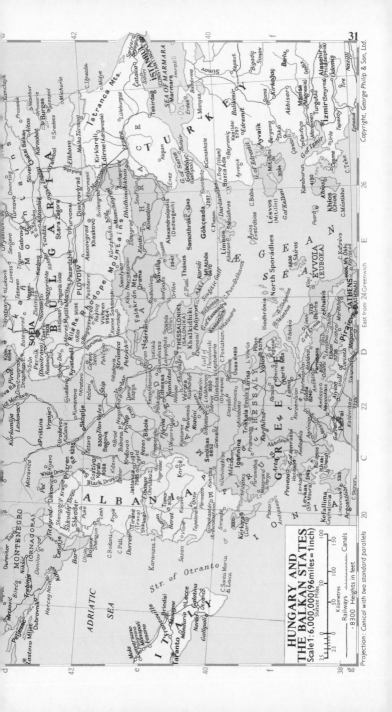

**31**

## HUNGARY AND THE BALKAN STATES

Scale 1:6,000,000 (96 miles=1inch)

Statute Miles

Kilometres

—— Railways ......... Canals

· 8300 Heights in feet

Projection: Conical with two standard parallels

East from Greenwich

Copyright, George Philip & Son, Ltd.

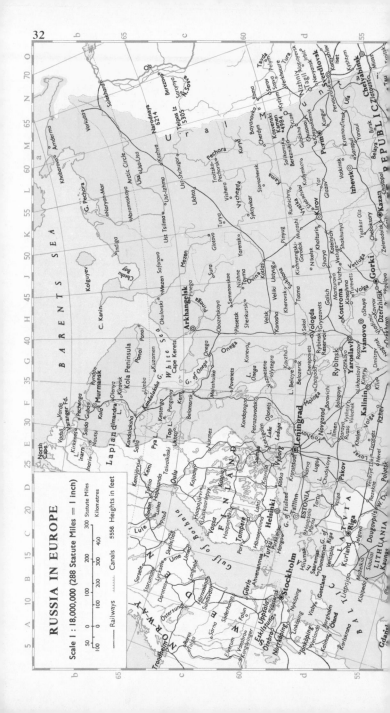

# RUSSIA IN EUROPE

## Scale 1 : 18,000,000 (288 Statute Miles = 1 inch)

```
50   0      100        200        300 Statute Miles
100  0     100    200    300    400
                    Kilometres
```

—— Railways    ······ Canals    5558 Heights in feet

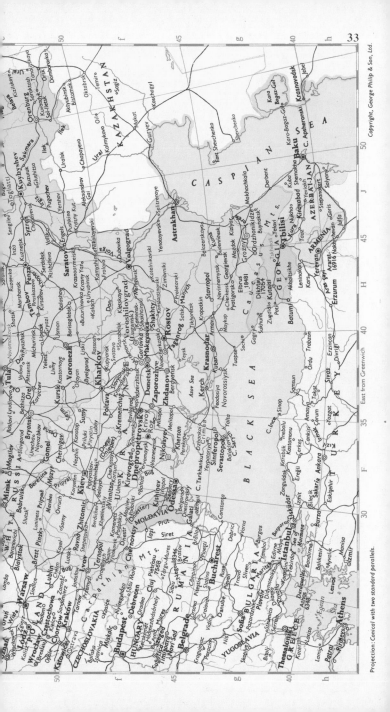

East from Greenwich

Projection: Conical with two standard parallels.

Projection: Conical Orthomorphic with two standard parallels.

West from Greenwich

a  80  b  70  c  60

Bering Strait

Wrangel I.

Chukot Sea

Anadyr Range

Gulf of Anadyr

St. Lawrence I. (U.S.A.)

OCEAN

Komsomolets I.
October Revolution I.
Bolshevik I.

De Long Is.
New Siberian Is.

Lyakhov Is.

East Siberian Sea

d

Bering

Anadyr

Anadir

Anadyrchik

Bering Sea

-rang Mts.

Laptev Sea

Taimyr
Nordvik

Iksi

Buluna

Yana

Nizhne Kolymsk

Srednekolymsk

Kolyma

Gizhiga

Kamchatka

Komandorskiye Is.

Khatanga
Khatanga

Zhigansk

Verkhoyansk

Verkhoyansk Range

Magadan

Shelekhov Gulf

Okhotsk

Klyuchevsk. Vol. 15012

-za

-sk

oviIyuysk

Yakutsk

Lena

Aldan

SOCIALIST     REPUBLIC

Okhotsk

Sea of Okhotsk

Ust Kamchatsk

Petropavlovsk

Circle

50

ower Tunguska

oginsk

Stony Tunguska

Olekminsk

Aldan

R.

Dzhugadzhur Ra.

Shantar Is.
Okha

Sakhalin

Nikolayevsk

Aleksandrovsk

-eniseysk

Angara

Kirensk

Bodaibo

Lena

Stanovoi Ra.

Skovorodino

Belgorsk

Komsomolsk

Sovetskoye Gavan

Gulf of Tartary

Karsakov

Kuril Is.

sk

Krasnoyarsk

Kansk

Nizhneudinsk

Taishet

L. Baikal

Yablonovy Ra.

Amur

Belgorsk

Birobidzhan

Khabarovsk

Sikhote Alin Range

S.

-vo

Kuznetski

Tulun

Cheremkhovo

Ulan

Ude

Chita

Sretensk

Nerchinsk

Blagoveshchensk

Algun

Sapporo

Otaru

Minusinsk

Munku-Sarbyk 11,457

Irkutsk

Petrovsk

Khilok

Oloyyannaya

Hailar

Sungari

Sikhote

Hakodate

Vladivostok

JAPAN

40

Yenisey

Kyakhta

Selenga

Harbin

Ussuri

JAPAN

Ulyasutay

Ulan Bator
(Urga)

Changchun

Mukden
(Shenyang)

Antung

N.

Wonsan

Sea of Japan

-yd

MONGOLIA

INNER MONGOLIA

Yingkow

Seoul

KOREA

Pyongyang

Inchon

S.

Puson

-mchi

Gobi Desert

Paotow

Peking

Lü-ta

Kunsan

Masan

Hiroshima

-urfan

Hami

REPUBLIC

WALL

Tatung

Tientsin

Tsingtao

Mokpo

Nagasaki

JAPAN

30

G-

Chengting

Nor

Suchow

Kanchow

GREAT

CHINESE     CHINGHAI     Lanchow

U.S.S.R.

Scale 1 : 40,000,000 (640 miles = 1 inch)

200  0  200  400  600 Statute Miles

200  0  200  400  600  800  1000 Kilometres

Railways     Canals

90  East from Greenv.  100  N  110  O  120  P

East from Greenwich

Copyright, George Philip and Son, Ltd.

C 70 A b B 80 C D E F G H J K L M N

60

d

GREENLAND
Svalbard
ARCTIC
Severnaya
Zemlya
Bear I.
Barents
Sea
Novaya Zemlya
Dickson I.
Ust Port
ICELAND
Arctic Circle
North Cape
Sea
Kara
Sea
Murmansk
Vorkuta
Novy Port
Salekhard
Turukhansk
Yenisey

BRITISH
ISLES
IRELAND
Edinburgh
Belfast
Dublin
Liverpool
London
Brussels
Paris

Norwegian
Sea
White
Sea
Arkhangelsk
Ob
Berezovo
Tobolsk

Oslo
Stockholm
Helsinki
North
Sea
Hamburg
Berlin
Baltic
Sea
Gdansk
Riga
Kaliningrad
Leningrad
Moscow
Vitebsk
Gorki
Perm
Tyumen
Sverdlovsk
Ishim
Novosibirsk
Omsk

50

e

U. S. S. R.
Kazan
Ufa
Chelyabinsk
Tselinograd
Semip

Vienna
Budapest
Belgrade
Warsaw
Kiev
Voronezh
Saratov
Kuybyshev
Orenburg
Orsk
Magnitogorsk
Uralsk
Karaganda
Kounradski
Bc

Rome
Thessaloníki
Odessa
Kharkov
Rostov
Volga
Astrakhan
KAZAKHSTAN
Balkhash L.

40

f

Mediterranean
Sea
Athens
Izmir
Bursa
Istanbul
Black Sea
Sinop
Samsun
Batumi
Trabzon
Erzurum
TURKEY
Ankara
Kurdistan
GEORGIA
Tbilisi
Yerevan
ARM.
AZER.
Baku
Rasht
Krasnovodsk
Caspian Sea
Khiva
Bukhara
Aral Sea
Syr Darya
Kokand
Balkhash
Ili
Tashkent
Kuldja
Alma Ata
FERGIZIA
SIN
Kashgar
Yarkand
Khotan
Kuldi

30

LIBYA
Alexandria
Cairo
CYPRUS
Beirut
LEB.
Tel Aviv-Jaffa
ISRAEL
Damascus
Aleppo
SYRIA
Euphrates
Tabriz
Mosul
IRAQ
Baghdad
Tehran
Mashhad
Dushanbe
TADZHIK.
ISTAN
UZBEKISTAN
TURKMENISTAN
Ashkhabad
Mary
Amu Darya
Kushka
Herat
Kabul
Peshawar
AFGHANISTAN
Ghazni
Kandahar
Srinagar
Kashmir
Rawalpindi
Simla
Lahore
Gartok

g

EGYPT
Suez
Jerusalem
JORDAN
Basra
Shustar
Abadan
Shiraz
Esfahan
IRAN
Kerman
Zahidan
Quetta
Kalat
Multan
PAKISTAN
Delhi
Jaipur
Agra
NE

20

h

SAUDI
ARABIA
Medina
Hail
Kuwait
The Gulf
Bahrain
Riyadh
Bushire
Bandar Abbas
Gwadar
UNITED ARAB
EMIRATES
G. of Oman
Muscat
Karachi
Ajmér
Kanpur
Lucknow
Allahabad
Indore
Vadodara
Surat
INDIA

Port Sudan
Medina
Jiddah
Mecca
Red Sea
Asir
OMAN
Ahmádabad
Diu
Daman
Bombay
Nagpur
Pune
Hyderabad
Goddari

10

i

Khartoum
El Obeid
Kamaran
YEMEN
Sana
Mukalla
Hadhramaut
Kuria Muria Is.
Arabian
Sea
Goa

j

Addis Ababa
Djibouti
Zeila
Berbera
G. of Aden
Perim
SOUTH YEMEN
Obak
Dire Dawa
Harer
Socotra
(South Yemen)
C. Guardafui
Ras Hafun
SOMALI
Bangalore
Mahé
Kozhikode
(Calicut)
Lakshadweep Is.
(India)
Madra
Pondicherry
Tiruchira
SR
LA

0

ETHIOPIA
UGANDA
Entebbe
KENYA
Nairobi
REP.
Obbia
Cochin
Trivandrum
C. Comorin
Madurai
Colombo

TANZANIA
Mogadishu
Equator
INDIAN
OC
Maldive Is.

k

SEYCHELLES

l
10

### ASIA

1 : 60,000,000 (960 miles = 1 inch)

200 0 200 400 600 800 Statute Miles
200 0 200 400 600 800 1000 1200 Kilometres

—— Railways ········ Canals

Amirantes

| ARM. | Armenia |
| AZER. | Azerbaijan |
| BHU. | Bhutan |
| LEB. | Lebanon |
| SIK. | Sikkim |

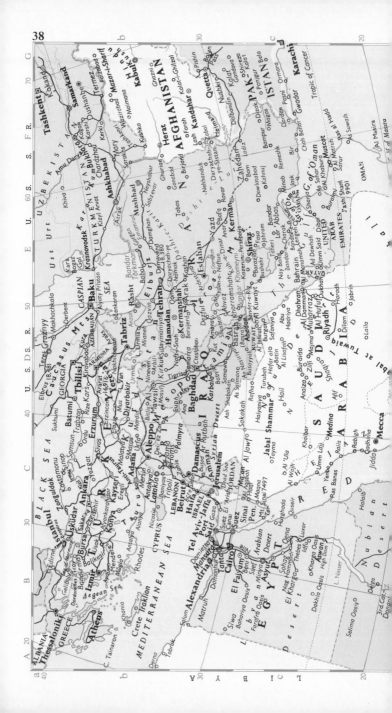

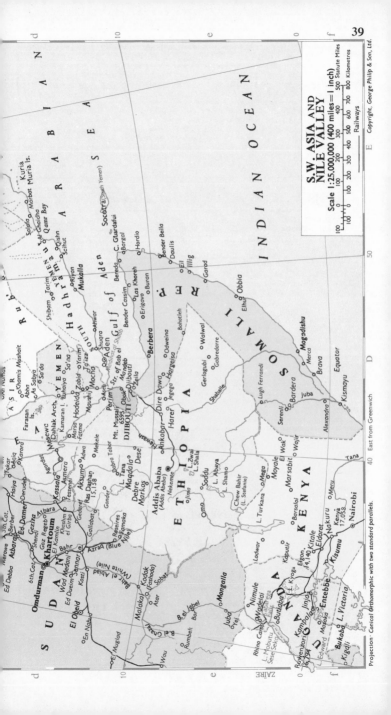

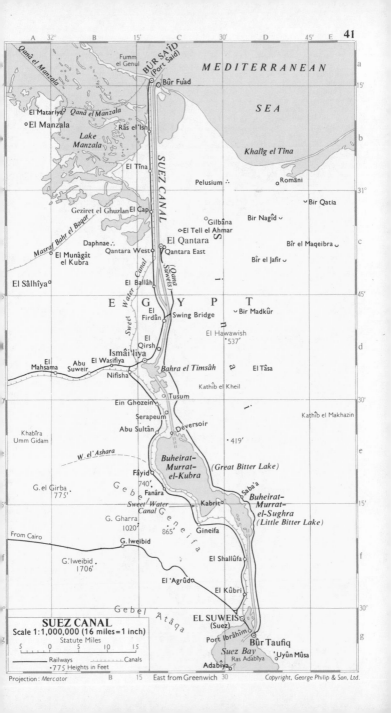

**41**

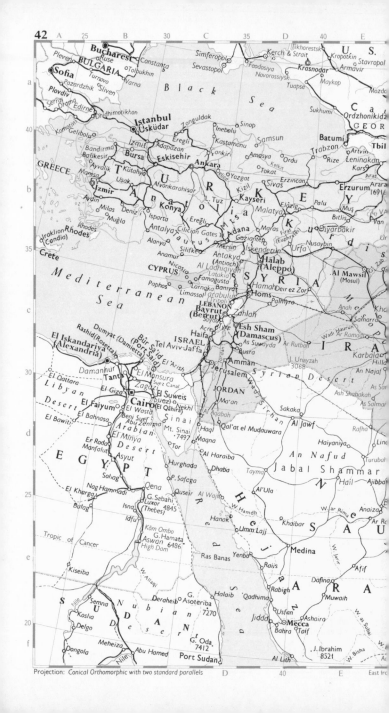

A  25  B  30  C  35  D  40  E

**Bucharest**
Ploiești
Cahușe
**BULGARIA**
Constanța
Tolbukhin
Turnovo
Pleven
**Sofia**
Pazardzhik
Sliven
Plovdiv
Varna

Simferopol
Kerch & Strait
Likhorestsk
Kropotkin
Stavropol
U.S.

Feodosiya
Sevastopol
Krasnodar
Armavir
Tuapse
Mozdo

Serta
Drama
Edirne
Komotin
Gelibolu
Ondhimotikhon

**Istanbul**
Üsküdar
Zonguldak
Inebolu
Sinop
Samsun
Ordu
Trabzon
Rize
Sukhumi
Ordzhonikidze
GEOR
Batumi
**Tbil**

Black    Sea

Kastamonu
Çankırı
Amasya
Kelkit
Erzincan
Artvin
Leninakan
Kars

**GREECE**
Bandirma
**Bursa**
**Eskisehir**
**Ankara**
Yozgat
Tokat
Sivas
Erzurum
Ararat
1691

Balikesir
Ayvalik
Kütahya
Afyonkarahisar
L. Tuz
Kizil
Kayseri
Elazig
Palu
Bitlis
**Izmir**
Usak
**Konya**
Eregli
Malatya
Diyarbakir
Nusaybin
Van

Aydin
Milas
Denizli
Isparta
Antalya
Taurus
Cilician Gates
Adana
Gaziantep
Urfa

Mugla
Alanya
Silifke
Mersin
Iskenderun
Al Mawsil
(Mosul)

Iraklion
(Candia)
Rhodes
Anamur
Antakya
(Antioch)
**Halab**
(Aleppo)

Crete
Nicosia
Al Ladhiqiyah
Latakia
Deir ez Zor
Anah
Kho

Mediterranean
Sea
**CYPRUS**
Famagusta
Larnaka
Baniyas
**SYRIA**
Palmyra
Samar

Paphos
Limassol
arabulus
Hama
Homs
Deir ez Zor
Wadi Hauran
Ar Ramadi

LEBANON
**Bayrut**
(Beirut)
Zahlah
Ar Rutban
IRA

Dumyat (Damietta)
Rashid (Rosetta)
Acre
Haifa
**Esh Sham**
(Damascus)
As Suwayda

**El Iskandariya**
(Alexandria)
Bur Said
(Port Said)
El 'Arish
Tel Aviv-Jaffa
**ISRAEL**
Busra
**Amman**
Ar Rutbah
Karbala

Damanhur
El Mansura
Suez Canal
Jerusalem
Syrian   Desert
An Najaf

El Qattara
**Tanta**
Zagazig
**JORDAN**
J. Unayzah
3068
As Sar

Libyan
El Giza
El Suweis
(Suez)
Ma'an
Sakaka
Ash Shabakah
As Salman

Desert
El Faiyum
**Cairo**
El Nekhl
Wadi Sirhan
Al Jawf
Rafha

El Bahnasa
Beni Suef
Abu Zenima
Sinai
Al Aqabah
Qal'at el Mudauwara

El Bawiti
El Minya
Mt. Sinai
7497
Haql
Magna
Haiyaniya
Turubah

Arabian
Manfalut
Tor
Dhaba
An  Nafud
Hail
Ajibbah

Er Roda
Asyut
Al Haraiba
Tayma
Jabal   Shammar

**EGYPT**
Desert
Sohag
Hurghada
P. Safaga
Al'Ula
Anaiza

El Kharga
Nag Hammadi
Qena
Quseir
Al Wajh
Khaibar
Ar Ru

Butag
Isna
Luxor
(Thebes)
G. Sabahi
4845
W. Hamdh
**Medina**

Idfu
Hanok
Umm Lajj

Tropic of Cancer
Kom Ombo
G. Hamata
Aswan
6486
High Dam
Ras Banas
Yenbo
Raiis
Afif

Kiseiba
Wadi Allaqi
Dafina
Muwaih

Semna
Derahieb
G. Asoteriba
7270
Halaib
Qadhima
Rabigh
**ARA**

**SUDAN**
Koshia
Delgo
Nubian
Desert
Usfan
Ashaira
Jidda
**Mecca**
Bahra
Taif

Meheiza
Abu Hamed
G. Oda
7412
Al Lith
J. Ibrahim
8521

Dongola
Nile
Port Sudan

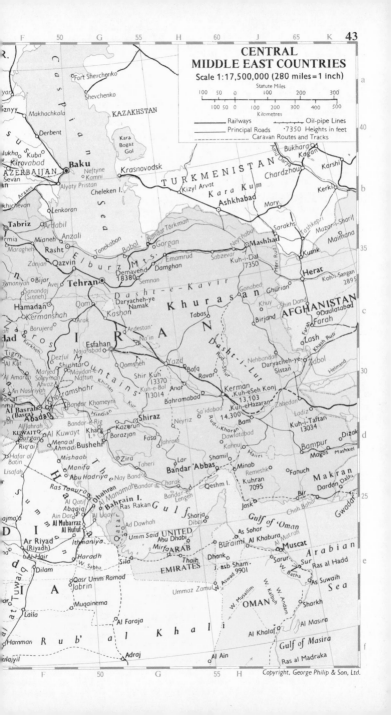

# CENTRAL
# MIDDLE EAST COUNTRIES

Scale 1:17,500,000 (280 miles = 1 inch)

Statute Miles
100  50  0        100        200        300
Kilometres
100  0  100  200  300  400  500

—————— Railways          ·········· Oil-pipe Lines
—————— Principal Roads    ·7350 Heights in feet
- - - - - Caravan Routes and Tracks

KAZAKHSTAN

Fort Shevchenko
Shevchenko
Makhachkala
Derbent
Kuba
Jukha
Kirovabad
AZERBAIJAN
Sevan
Baku
Neftnye
Kamni
Alyaty Pristan
Krasnovodsk
Cheleken I.
Kizyl Arvat
TURKMENISTAN
Kara Kum
Ashkhabad
Mary
Chardzhou
Bukhara
Kagan
Karshi
Kerki
Lenkoran
Tabriz
Ardabil
Anzali
Mianeh
Maragheh
Rasht
Tonekabon
Bandar Torkman
Gorgan
Babol
Kashabut
Neyshabur
Mashhad
Sarakhs
Kusht
Mazar-i-Sharif
Maimana
Zanjan
Qazvin
Elburz Mts.
Emamrud
Damghan
Sabzevar
Kuh-i-Dal
7350
Herat
Koh-i-Sangan
2895
Avej
Demavend
18380
Semnan
Ghurian
AFGHANISTAN
Tehran
Dasht-e-Kavir
Daryacheh-ye
Namak
Qom
Khurasan
Khuy
Shin Dand
Hamadan
Kermanshah
Arak
Kashan
Ardestan
Na'in
Tabas
Gonabad
Birjand
Daulatabad
Farah
Borujerd
Esfahan
I    R    A    N
Dasht-i-Lut
Nehbandan
Lash
Khash Rud
Dezful
Najafabad
Qomsheh
Yazd
Bafq
Shin Dand
Daryacheh-ye
Sistan
Zabol
Helmand
Shushtar
Maydan
Naftun
Shir Kuh
13370
Kuh-e-Bol
13014
Anar
Ravar
Rud-i-Shur
Ahvaz
Khorramshahr
Bandar Khomeyni
Hindian
Bahramabad
Kerman
Kuh-eSeh Konj
13,103
Kuh-eHazaran
14,300
Zahedan
Kuh-i-Taftan
13034
Dizak
Al Amarah
An Nasiriyah
Al Basrah
Abadan
Bandar-e-Rig
Kharg
Shiraz
Kazerun
Borazjan
Fasa
Sa'idabad
Rud-i-Khoran
Dawlatabad
Kahnuj
Bampur
Makran
Dardan Dasht
KUWAIT
Al Jahrah
Burgan
Mena al
Ahmadi
Riq'ai
Al Kuwayt
Mishaab
Manifa
Abu Hadriya
Zira
Taheri
Nay Band
Jahrom
Lar
Neyriz
Shamil
Hailri
Minab
Remeshk
Fanuch
Magas
Hafar al
Batin
Lisafah
Ras Tanura
Dhahran
Al Qatif
Ras Rakan
Charak
Bandar-e-
Lengeh
Bandar 'Abbas
Qeshm I.
Kuhran
7095
Jask
Bir
Chah Bahar
Gwadar
Ajman
Abqaiq
Ain Dar
Al Uqayr
Al Mubarraz
Al Hufuf
Bahrain I.
Al Manamah
Ad Dawhah
Umm Said
Abu Dhabi
Sharja
Dibai
Gulf
Gulf of 'Oman
As Sohar
Al Khabura
Matrah
Muscat
Arabian
Ithmaniya
Ummaz Zamul
Buraimi
Sarur
Sur
Ras al Hadd
Ar Riyad
(Riyadh)
Al-Hair
Haradh
W. Sabha
Sila
UNITED
ARAB
EMIRATES
Mirfa
Thaih
Dhank
J. asb Sham
Awad Sham
9901
As Suwaih
Sharkh
Dilam
Qasr Umm Ramad
Jabrin
Muqainema
OMAN
W. Musallim
W. Andan
W. Kalbuh
W. Batha
Al Khalaf
Al Masira
Laila
Harman
Rub' al Khali
Al Faraja
Ummaz Zamul
Gulf of Masira
Ras al Madraka
Adraj
Al Ain
Ras al Madraka

Copyright, George Philip & Son, Ltd.

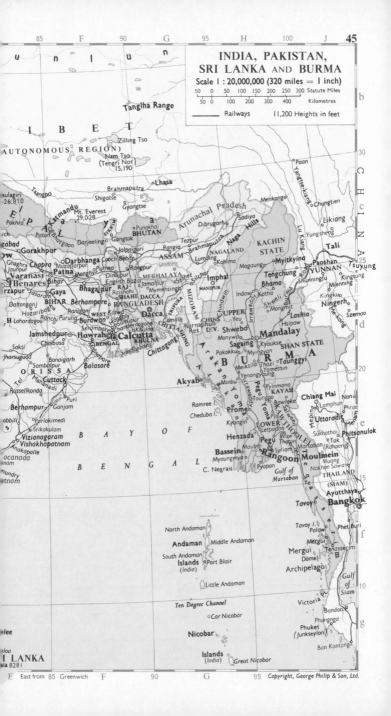

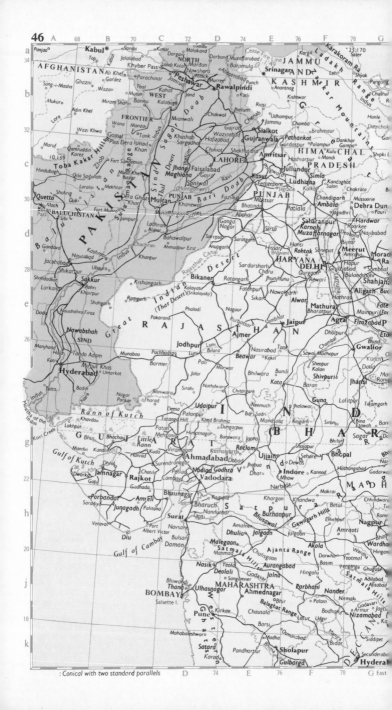

**46**

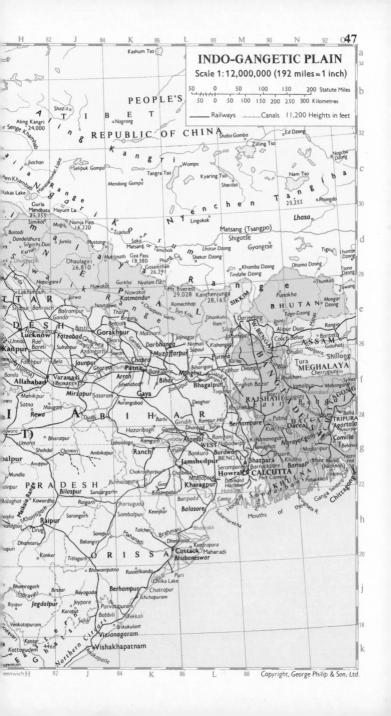

## INDO-GANGETIC PLAIN
### Scale 1:12,000,000 (192 miles = 1 inch)

50    0    50    100    150    200 Statute Miles
50    0   50  100  150  200  250  300 Kilometres

—— Railways  ····· Canals  11,200 Heights in feet

PEOPLE'S
REPUBLIC OF CHINA

Kangri

Aling Kangri
24,000

Senge Khambab
hen Khambab
Rakas Lake

Gurla
Mandhata
25,355

Simikot

Baitadi
Dandeldhura
Silgarhi-Doti
Dhangarhi

Unnao
Jumla

Mugu

Namja Pass
16,220

Mustang

Tripdan
Saka

Mendong Gompa

Selipuk Gompa

Mansarowar Lake

Jiachan

Shaziang

Nogrong

Shaba Gomba

Ed Dzong

Zilling Tso

Tangra Tso

Wampo

Kyaring Tso

Sheritsa

Nam Tso

Nagchu
Dzong

Phongda

Matsang (Tsangpo)

Shigatse

Lhasa

Lingokok

Nyenchen Tanglha
23,255

Muktinath
Gya Pass
18,380

Phung Chu

Lhotse Dzong

Shekar Dzong

Gyangtse

Tiguo

Jhuntse
Dzong

Dhaulagiri
26,810

Gosainthan
26,291

Mt. Everest
29,028

Kanchenjunga
28,165

Khamba Dzong

Tindzhe Dzong

Dhama Dzong

Tsona
Dzong

Thunkal

Jawang

Nuwakot

Nawakot

Gurkha

Namche
Sun Kosi

Dhankuta

Ilam

Darjeeling

Jaintí

Punakha

Tögo-Dzong

Mongar
Dzong

UTTAR

Lakhimpur

Bahraich

Balrampur

Gonda

Nepalgunj

Thori

Bettiah

Birganj

Motihari

SIKKIM

Siliguri

Jalpaiguri

Alipur Duar

Cooch Behar

BHUTAN

Rangia

Barpeta

Gauhati

ASSAM

DESH

Lucknow

Faizabad

Bareli

Sultanpur

Gorakhpur

Deoria

Darbhanga

Nirmali

Supaul

Kishanganj

Purnea

Barsoi

Dhubri

Tura

MEGHALAYA

Shillong

Cherrapunji

Kanpur

Rae
Bareli

Jaunpur

Azamgarh

Ghazipur

Siwan

Chapra

Muzaffarpur

Bihariganj

Katihar

Dinajpur

Bogra

Jamalpur

Mohanganj

Sylhet

Fatehpur

Bela

Allahabad
Benares

Varanasi
Benares

Mirzapur

Sasaram

Arrah

Bankipore

Patna

Bihar

Monghyr

Bhagalpur

English Bazar

RAJSHAHI

Pabna

DACCA

Jamalpur

Narsingdi

Mohanganj

TRIPURA

Agartala

Mahiha

Satna

Rewa

BIHAR

Maugani

Jahanabad

Gaya

Deoghar

Tinpahar

Rajshahi

Kushtia

Narayanganj

Comilla

Belonia

Amarpur

Umaria

Bharatpur

Dudhi

Lohardaga

Hazaribagh

Giridih

Rampur Hat

Dhanbad

Ranigunj

Berhampore

Krishnanagar

Ranaghat

Madaripur

Balia

Shahdol

Anuppur

Chirmiri

Ambikapur

Ramgarh

Ranchi

Asansol

Purulia

WEST

Nabadwip

Burdwan

Serampore

Barrackpore

Jessore

Khulna

Bhola

Majuli
(Nadkhali)

Haria

PRADESH

Bilaspur

Kawardha

Jharsuguda

Chakradharpur

Jamshedpur

Chaibasa

BENGAL

Midnapore

Howrah

CALCUTTA

Bhatpara

Port Canning

Diamond
Harbour

KHULNA

Patuakhali

Balaghat

Khairlanji

Raigarh

Sarangarh

Sambalpur

Baripada

Balasore

Contai

Haldia

Sundarbans

Mouths of

Ganga

Chittagong

Raipur

Drug

Sonepur

Talcher

Keonjhar

Bhadrakh

Mahanadi

Subarnarekha

 Hooghly

the Ganga R.

Dhamtari

Balangir

Mahanadi

Dhenkanal

Kendrapara

Brahmani

Kanker

Titlagarh

ORISSA

Cuttack

Bhubaneswar

Mahanadi

Bhamragarh

Bestar

Rayagada

Bhawanipatna

Russellkonda

Chilka Lake

Puri

Indravati

Jeypore

Parvatipuram

Chatrapur

Ichchapuram

Jagdalpur

Karaput

Bobbili

Tekkali

Salur

Srikakulam

Venkatapuram

Kontar
4466

Kottagudem

Northern Circars

Vizianagaram

Vishakhapatnam

Anakapalle

Greenwich

Copyright, George Philip & Son, Ltd.

# EAST INDIES
# AND
# FURTHER INDIA
### Scale 1:25,000,000
(400 miles=1 inch)

100 50 0  100   200   300 Statute Miles
100 50 0 100 200 300 400 500 Kilometres
━━━ Railways   ━━━ Canals
━━━ Oil Pipe Lines  9612 Heights in feet

Projection: Conical

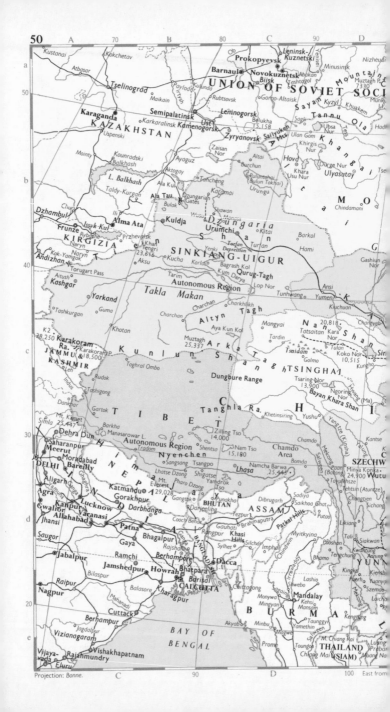

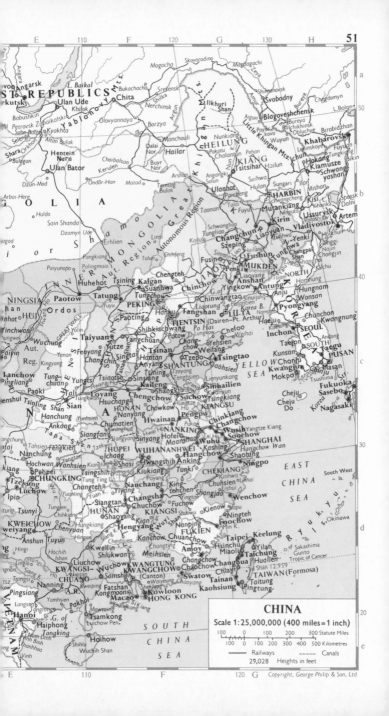

**51**

**CHINA**

Scale 1:25,000,000 (400 miles=1 inch)

```
100   0        100        200        300 Statute Miles
100   0   100  200  300  400  500 Kilometres
```

——— Railways    ∿∿∿ Canals

29,028   Heights in feet

Copyright, George Philip & Son, Ltd.

A 120 B 130

INNER

MONGOLIA
(Autonomous Region)

Lins

Wengniu

Chihfeng

Lunghwa   Chienping

Chengteh

HOPEI

Tangshan

Hanku

Weifang

SHANTUNG

Chuhsien

Tsingkiang

Sinhailien

Kwanyun

Hwaian

KIANGSU

Kaoyu

Yangchow   Taichow

Chinkiang

Changchow   Nantung

Wusih   Soochow   Yangtze-Kiang

Huchow   Sunkiang

SHANGHAI

Hangchow

Shaohing   Fenghwa   Ningpo

Kinhwa

CHEKIANG

Lishui   Linhai

Wenchow

Taichintala   Paicheng

Taonan   Talai

Kcitung

Nungan

Kailu   Changchun   Kirin

Kulunkai   Changwu   Szeping   Kungchuling

Sinmin   Tiehling   Liaoyuan   Hailung

Fusin   Fushun   Tunghwa

Chinchow   LIAONING   Liaoyang   Penki

Suichung   Anshan

Chinwangtao   Yingkow   G. of Liaotung

Tsunhua   Tashihkiao

Chongli   Kaiping

Fuchow   Antung

Pulantien   Kushan

Lungkow

(Dairen)   Korea B.

LÜ-TA   Anju

(Port Arthur)   Pyongyang

Yehsien   Nampo

Chefoo   Weihai

Mowping   Haiju

Kiaohsien   Sariwon

Haiyang   Shihtao

Shwangcheng   HARBIN

Fuyu   Wuchang   Shulan

HEILUNGKIA

Hulan   Payen   Ilan

Fangcheng

Imienpo   Mutankiang

Ninguta   Tungning

Sungari Res.   Tunhwa   Wanching

Hweinan   Yenki   Hunchun

Changpai Shan   Hoeryong

Linkiang   Musan   1   Unggi   Najin

Changjin   Nanam   Chongjin

Talan   3

NORTH   4   2   Kilchu

Hwanjen   Tanchon

Kwanchien   Yalu

Fengcheng   5   Hamhung   Wonsan

Sinuiju   6

Anju   Hungnam

10   Wonsan

Kosong   Cease Fire Line

7   9   July 27, 1953

11   Chorwon

Kaesong   Chunchon   Samchok

Kuksong   21   SEOUL   13

Inchon   12   Yongwol

Sawon   14   Chungju   Andong

15   Taejon   16

Chonan   Kunchon   Yongchon   Kyongju

Kunsan   18   Chonju   Yongchon   17

Kwangju   Miryang   PUSAN

Mokpo   Chinju   Masan

19   Iri

Tsushima   Shimonoseki   Hiros

Cheju   KITAKYŪSHŪ   Yamaguchi

Cheju Do   20   Fukuoka   Bofu

(Quelpart)   Kurume   Beppu

Sasebo   Omuta   Kumamo

Nagasaki   Yatsushiro

Kyushu

Sendai   Kobayashi   Miye

Kagoshima   Miyako

Kanoya   Tanega S

YELLOW

SEA

Po Hai
(G. of Chihli)

Huang Ho

KOREA

SOUTH

Korea

EAST   CHINA

SEA

South-West Islands

Amami O Shima

Projection: Bonne

B 130

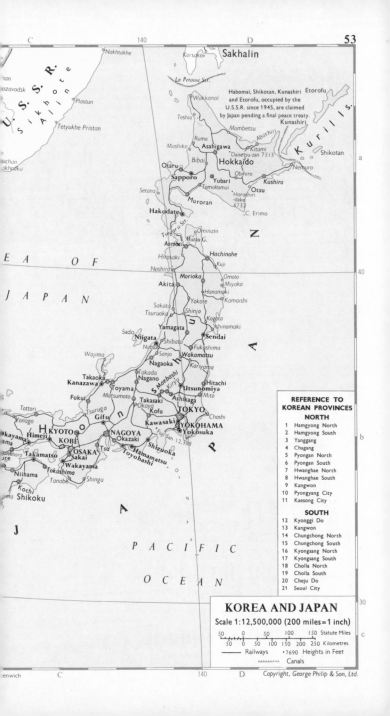

**Sakhalin**

Habomai, Shikotan, Kunashiri Etorofu
and Etorofu, occupied by the
U.S.S.R. since 1945, are claimed
by Japan pending a final peace treaty.

Kunashiri

**Hokkaido**

Sapporo

Hakodate

Aomori

Morioka

Akita

Yamagata

Niigata Sendai

Nagaoka Wakamatsu

Takaoka Maebashi Hitachi
Kanazawa Nagano Utsunomiya
Toyama Takasaki
Fukui Matsumoto Ashikaga Mito

Gifu Takasaki
Kofu **TOKYO**
NAGOYA Kawasaki
KYOTO Okazaki YOKOHAMA
KOBE Shizuoka Yokosuka
OSAKA Hamamatsu
Sakai Toyohashi
Wakayama

Takamatsu

Tokushima

Kochi **Shikoku**

**PACIFIC**

**OCEAN**

**SEA OF JAPAN**

**U.S.S.R.**

### REFERENCE TO KOREAN PROVINCES
#### NORTH
1 Hamgyong North
2 Hamgyong South
3 Yanggang
4 Chagang
5 Pyongan North
6 Pyongan South
7 Hwanghae North
8 Hwanghae South
9 Kangwon
10 Pyongyang City
11 Kaesong City

#### SOUTH
12 Kyonggi Do
13 Kangwon
14 Chungchong North
15 Chungchong South
16 Kyongsang North
17 Kyongsang South
18 Cholla North
19 Cholla South
20 Cheju Do
21 Seoul City

## KOREA AND JAPAN
### Scale 1:12,500,000 (200 miles=1 inch)

50   0          50        100        150 Statute Miles
50   0    50   100   150   200   250 Kilometres
— Railways    •7690 Heights in Feet
⌒⌒⌒ Canals

Copyright, George Philip & Son, Ltd.

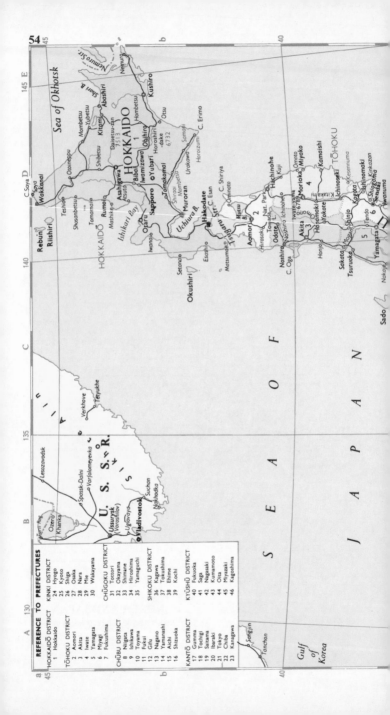

**54**

## REFERENCE TO PREFECTURES

**HOKKAIDŌ DISTRICT**
1 Hokkaido

**TŌHOKU DISTRICT**
2 Aomori
3 Akita
4 Iwate
5 Yamagata
6 Miyagi
7 Fukushima

**CHŪBU DISTRICT**
8 Niigata
9 Ishikawa
10 Toyama
11 Fukui
12 Gifu
13 Nagano
14 Yamanashi
15 Aichi
16 Shizuoka

**KANTŌ DISTRICT**
17 Gumma
18 Tochigi
19 Saitama
20 Ibaraki
21 Tokyo
22 Chiba
23 Kanagawa

**KINKI DISTRICT**
24 Hyogo
25 Kyoto
26 Osaka
27 Shiga
28 Nara
29 Mie
30 Wakayama

**CHŪGOKU DISTRICT**
31 Tottori
32 Okayama
33 Shimane
34 Hiroshima
35 Yamaguchi

**SHIKOKU DISTRICT**
36 Kagawa
37 Tokushima
38 Ehime
39 Kochi

**KYŪSHŪ DISTRICT**
40 Fukuoka
41 Saga
42 Nagasaki
43 Kumamoto
44 Oita
45 Miyazaki
46 Kagoshima

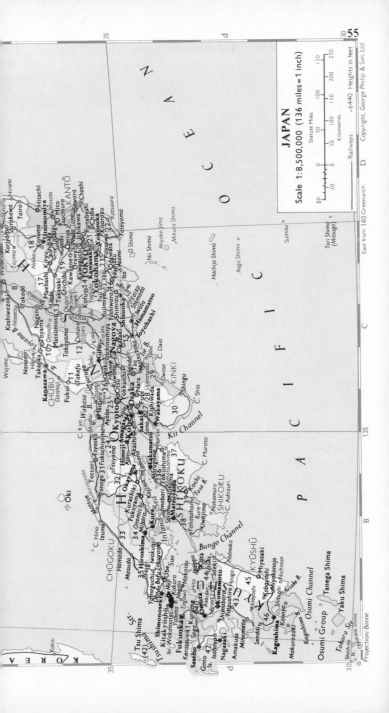

**55**

**JAPAN**

Scale 1:8,500,000 (136 miles=1 inch)

Statute Miles

Kilometres

Railways · 6440 Heights in feet

East from 140 Greenwich

Copyright, George Philip & Son, Ltd.

Projection: Bonne

P A C I F I C    O C E A N

KOREA

HONSHŪ

CHŪBU

KINKI

CHŪGOKU

SHIKOKU

KYŪSHŪ

ANTŌ

Oki

Tsushima

Goto Is.

Osumi Group    Tanega Shima    Yaku Shima

Tokara-to

Koshiki

Iki

Hachijo Shima

Aoga Shima

Mikura Shima

Miyake Jima

Ō Shima

Nii Shima

Miyako Jima

Tori Shima (Mitsugo)

Sumisu

**UNION OF SOVIET SOCIALIST REPUBLICS**

_Bering Sea_

Lena
Kirensk
L. Baikal
Yablonovy Range
Stanovoi Range
Chita
Sretensk
Blagoveshchensk
Khabarovsk
Nikolayevsk
Ust Botsheretsk
Mt. Klyuchevsk 15,912
Komandorskiye Is.
Andreanof Is. Dutch Harbor
Bristol

_Sea of Okhotsk_
Kamchatka
Near I. (U.S.)
Kiska I. (U.S.)
Aleutian Islands

Uda B.
Udan B.
Aleksandrovsk
Sakhalin
Petropavlovsk-Kamchatski
C. Lopatka

MONGOLIA
Gobi or Shamo
Inner Mongolia
Manchuria
Tsitsihar
Harbin
Changchun
Sikhote Range
Tartary
La Perouse Strait
Kuril Islands

Mukden
Peking
Antung
Vladivostok
Tsugaru Strait
Hokkaido
Hakodate

TIENTSIN
CHINESE REP.
Tsinan
Seoul
Wonsan
Tsingtao
Korea Strait
_Sea of Japan_
Sendai

Sian
Nanking
Kaifeng
Yellow Sea
Kyoto
Osaka
Nagoya
**TOKYO**
Yokohama

_Yokohama to Honolulu 3379_

Wuhan
Yangtze Kiang
SHANGHAI
East China Sea
Shikoku
Kyushu
Nagasaki

Hangchow
Changsha
Wenchow
Foochow
_Yap to Yokohama 1660_

Bonin Is.
Midway I. U.S.
Lisianski I. (U.S.)
Laysan I. (U.S.)

Wuchow
Amoy
Taipeh
Marcus I.

Canton
Macao
Taiwan (Formosa)
HONG KONG
Bashee Channel

Hainan
C. Engano
Luzon
Quezon City
Wake I. (U.S.)

VIETNAM
Hue
Manila
PHILIPPINES

_P A C_

N. Marianas (U.S.)
Guam (U.S.)
U.S. Trust Territory of the Pacific Islands

International Date Line

_Suva to Honolulu 3726_

Mindoro
Panay
Samar
MALAYSIA
Palawan
Negros
Mindanao
Apo Vol 9690
Yap I.
Belau
Truk I.
Ponape
Caroline Islands
Jaluit
Marshall Islands (U.S. Trust Territory)

Makin
Baker I. (U.S.)
Canton I.
Enderbury
Phoenix Islands

Celebes Sea
Borneo
Halmahera
Manado
Dampier Strait
Schouten Is.
Admiralty
Equator
KIRIBATI
NAURU

Java Sea
Celebes
Buru
Amboina
New Guinea
New Ireland
Rabaul
New Britain
SOLOMON ISLANDS

INDONESIA
Banda Sea
Ceram
PAPUA NEW GUINEA
Madang
Lae
Salamaua
Port Moresby
Guadalcanal
Santa Cruz

Semarang
Surabaya
Bali
Lombok
Sumbawa
Flores
Flores Sea
Tanimbar
Aru Is.
Duff Is.
TUVALU
Funafuti
Rotuma
Vanua Levu
SAMOA
Tutuila (U.S.)

Timor
Arafura Sea
Torres Strait
Thursday I.
C. York
VANUATU
Viti Levu
Suva
FIJI
Palmerston I.

Ashmore Is.
Darwin
Arnhem Land
G. of Carpentaria
Great Barrier Reef
Coral Sea
Loyalty Is.
TONGA
Niue

C. Leveque
Wyndham
NORTHERN TERRITORY
Cairns
Townsville
Chesterfield (Fr.)
New Caledonia
Tongatabu

North West Cape
Onslow
Mt. Isa
Rockhampton
Brisbane to Suva
1321

Shark Bay
Steep Pt.
Nannine
WESTERN AUSTRALIA
Alice Springs
Longreach
QUEENSLAND
Maryborough
Brisbane
Ipswich
C. Byron
Sydney to Suva 1743
1098
Norfolk I.
1150
Sydney to Tahiti 3299

Geraldton
Kalgoorlie
SOUTH AUSTRALIA
A U S T R A L I A
Eyre
Toowoomba
Darling
Lord Howe I.
Auckland to Rarotonga
1638
Wellington to Rarotonga 1815

Perth
Fremantle
Geographic B.
C. Leeuwin
K. George Sd.
Albany
Great Australian Bight
_Fremantle to A. 1353_
Port Pirie
Murray
Bendigo
NEW SOUTH WALES
Blue Mountains
Newcastle
Wollongong
Canberra
_S. to A.1264_
Kermadec Is.

Encounter Bay
Adelaide
Geelong
Ballarat
Melbourne
Bass Strait
Sydney
Howe
_Tasman Sea_
Auckland
North I.
Hamilton
Ruapehu 9175
Manukau
Palmerston N.
Wellington

VICTORIA
_M. to Cape Town 5814_
_H. to C.T. 5838_
Launceston
Hobart
_H. to W. 1293_
TASMANIA
_H. to B. 940_
Nelson
Mt. Cook 12,349
Christchurch
Dunedin
NEW ZEALAND
Chatham Is.

South I.
Damaru
Invercargill
Stewart I.
Bounty Is.
Antipodes I.

Auckland I.
Campbell I.

---

**PACIFIC OCEAN**
Equatorial Scale 1:100,000,000 (1600 miles = 1 inch)
Railways ---- 4570 Shipping Routes (Dist. in Naut. Miles)

Projection: Mercator 140 C 160 East from Greenwich 180 West from Greenwich

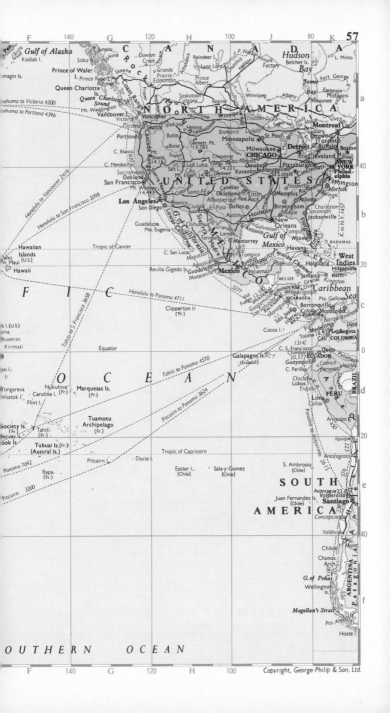

115  East from B Greenwich  120    C    125    D    130    E

*Timor Sea*

INDIAN

OCEAN

Ashmore I.

Melville I.
Bathurst I.
P. Darwin  **Darwin**
Pt. Blaze
C. Ford

Van
Diemen
Gulf

C. Londonderry
C. Bougainville
York Sound
Buccaneer
Archipelago
C. Leveque
Yampi Sound
**Kimberley**
*Leopold Ras.*
Wyndham
Mt. Cockburn
1593

Victoria
Victoria River
Downs
Wave Hill

Arnhe
Rum Jungle
Pine Cr
Kath

Dampier
Land
**Broome**
C. Baskerville
C. Bossut
La Grange
Derby
Fitzroy
Crossing
Hall's Creek

Newcastl
Waters
L.
Woods

NOR

Tennant

Larrey Pt. Eighty Mile Beach
P. Hedland
Mount Goldsworthy

Joanna
Spring

Da

TERR

Dampier Arch.
Dampier
Barrow I.
Onslow
Exmouth Gulf
Fortescue
**Hamersley Ra.**
Mt. Brockman
3654
Cossack
Roebourne
Pilbara
Marble Bar
Wittenoom Gorge
Nullagine

L.
Mackay

Reynolds

WESTERN

Pt. Cloates
Learmonth
Ashburton
Mt. Bruce
4024
**Ophthalmia**
Ra.
Mt Whaleback
**Robertson**
**Ra.**

L.
Disappointment

L.
Macdonald

Macdon
Hermannsburg
**James R**
Amadeus

C. Cuvier
Geographic
Channel
Gascoyne
**Carnarvon**
Mt.
Gould
2300
Mt. Augustus
3627
Barlee Ra.

Weld Spring

L. Carnegie

Rewlinson
Ranges

Mt. Squires
2270•

**Musgrave R**
Mt.
**Woodroffe** 497

Shark B.
Dirk
Hartog I.
Steep
Point
Wooramel
**Robinson Ras.**
Mt. Hale
2400
Murchison
•Peak Hill
Wiluna
Meekatharra

AUSTRALIA

Freycinet Est.
Nannine
Big Bello
L. Austin
Sandstone
Cue
Mt. Sir Samuel
Lawlers

Ajana
Northampton
Mt. Magnet
Yalgoo
Mullewa
L. Barlee
Leonora
Mt. Morgans
Malcolm
Laverton

Maral

**Geraldton**
Dongarra
Mingenew
Yunndaga
Menzies
**Kalgoorlie**
**Boulder**
Loongana
Deakin
Ooldea
Watson

Miling
Coolamling
Bonnie Rock
Bencubbin
Southern
Cross
Coolgardie
Zanthus Naretha

**Nullarbor**

Deakin
*Plain*
Penong

Gingin
**Midland Junc.**
**Perth**
**Fremantle**
Pinjarra
Northam
Merredin
Hyden
York
Pingelly
Newdegate
Norseman
The Johnston Lakes
Eyre
Eucla
C. Adieu
Thever

Darling
Ranges
**Collie**
**Bunbury**
Geographe B.
C. Naturaliste
Busselton
Augusta
Boyup
Pemberton
Brook
town
Narrogin
Wagin
Ongerup
Katanning
**Mt. Barker**
Kojonup
Cranbrook
Gnowangerup
Ravensthorpe
Hopetoun
C.
Knob
Esperance
C. Arid
Archipelago of
the Recherche

Great Australian

Bight

Nuyts Arch

Inve

C. Leeuwin
Pt. D'Entrecasteaux
Pt. Nuyts
Denmark
West C. Howe
**Albany**

SOUT

Projection: Bonne.    A    115    B    120    C    125    D    130    E

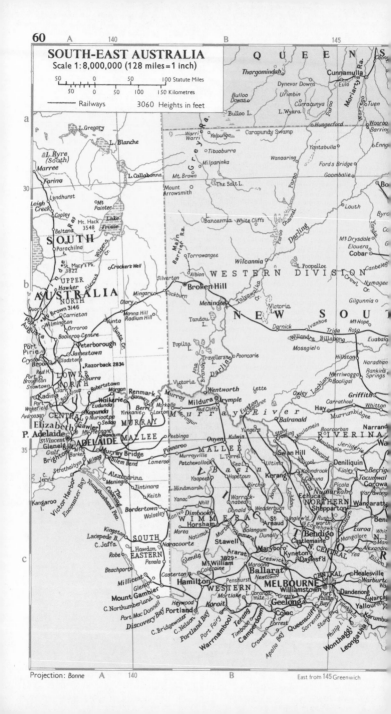

**60**

## SOUTH-EAST AUSTRALIA
Scale 1:8,000,000 (128 miles=1 inch)

50   0   50   100 Statute Miles

50   0   50   100   150 Kilometres

—— Railways     3060 Heights in feet

QUEENS

Thargomindah    Cunnamulla

Dynevor Downs   Eulo

Bulloo   Urimbin   Tuen   Wooroo
Downs    Curracunya    Barring

Bulloo L.    L. Wyara    Hungerford    Enng

**a**

L.Gregory    Warri   Yalpunga   Carapundy Swamp

Warri    Yantabulla

L. Blanche    Tibooburra

L. Eyre    Milparinka    Wanaaring    Ford's Bridge

(South)    Goombalie   Bo

Marree    Mt. Brown

Farina    L.Callabonna    Mount   The Salt L.    Louth   Byr

**30**   Lyndhurst    Arrowsmith

Leigh   Copley    Mt Drysdale   Co

Creek   Beltana   Mt   Bancannia   White Cliffs    Elouera   G

  Painter   Lake     Cobar

Mt. Hack   Frome   Main   Darling

SOUTH   3548    Barrier Ra.   Wilcannia   L.Poopaloe    Canbele

Parachilna    Torrowangee    WESTERN DIVISION   Nymage

St. Mary's Pk.   Crockers Well    Crowl Cr.   Gilgunnia

AUSTRALIA   3822    Silverton   Albion    Menindee    Mt Hope

**b**   UPPER   Hawker   3146    Broken Hill

NORTH   Mingary   Cockburn    NEW SOU

Quorn   Carrieton   Olary    Talyawalka Cr.   Victoria    Ivanhoe

P. Augusta   Wilmington   Manna Hill   Menindee    Darnick   Trida   Roto   Euabalo

Orroroo   Radium Hill   Tandou    Willandra Billabong

Port   Booleroo Centre   Yunta   L.    Mossgiel   Hillston   Naradhan

Pirie   Peterborough   Popilta    Rankins

Crystal   Jamestown   L.    Merriwagga   Springs

Brook   Gladstone   Razorback 2834    Travellers   Pooncarie   Oxley Lachlan   Booligal

Red Hill   LOWER   Burra    Carrathool   Whitton

Port   Snowtown   NORTH   Clare   L.Victoria    Lette    Hay   Murrumbidgee   Griffith

Broughton   Robertstown   Wentworth    RIVERINA

Kadina   CENTRAL   Morgan   Renmark   Murray   Mildura   Irymple    Narrand

Port   Wakefield   Eudunda   Berri    Euston   Balranald    Wa

Ardrossan   Kapunda   Waikerie   Morkalla   Red Cliffs   River    Jerilde

  Nuriootpa   Yinkanie   Loxton    Moulamein   Deniliquin

MURRAY   Sedan    Yungera   Stony   Crossing

P. Adelaide   Gawler   Mt Pleasant    MALLEE    Boordoorban   Edward

Elizabeth    Peebinga   Ouyen   Kulwin    Swan Hill   Koondrook   Finley

St.Vincent   Glenelg   Barossa    Wakool   Picola   Tocumwal

Gulf   Brighton   Birdwood   Pinnaroo   Murrayville   L.Tyrrell   Ultima   Kerang   Cohuna   Nunurkah   Corowa

**35**   Strathalbyn   Murray Bridge   Lameroo   Patchewollock   Sea L.    Koondrook   Yarrawonga

Jervis   Barker   Tailem Bend    Birchip   Loddon   Echuca   NORTHERN   Wangaratta

  Milang   Yaapeet   Hopetoun    Shepparton   Ben

C. Jervis   Meningie   Tintinara   Yanac   Warrack-   Wedderburn    N CENTRAL

Kangaroo   L.Alexandrina   Keith   Nhill   nabeal   Donald   Inglew'd   Rush-   Euroa   Whit

Island   Victor Harbor    Kaniva   Dimboola   Morea   St   worth   Mangalore   N I Man

  Encounter Bay   Bordertown   Horsham   Arnaud   Dunolly   Eaglehawk   OR

  Youngshusband Pen.   Wolseley   WIMMERA   Natimuk   Bolangum   Castlemaine   Yea   Eildon

   SOUTH    Bendigo   Kyneton   Daylesf'd

Kingston   L.Hindmarsh   Stawell   Maryboro   CENTRAL   Healesville

Lacepede B.    EASTERN   Glenelg   Maroona   Creswick   Kyneton   Warburt

C. Jaffa   Robe   Naracoorte   Penola    Ararat   Newtown    MELBOURNE

**c**    Beachport    Casterton   Mt William   Daylesf'd   Williamstown   Dandenong

  Millicent    3829   Coleraine    Ballarat   Port   Warraga

  Glenelg   Hamilton   Penshurst    Phillip   Yallourn

Mount Gambier    Mortlake   Coran-   Cressy   Bay

C. Northumberland   Koroit   dite   Geelong   Korumb

Port Mac Donnell   Heywood    Colac   Queenscliff   Wonth

Discovery Bay   Portland   C.Nelson    Sorrento   Phillip Isl   Leonga

C.Bridgewater   Port Fairy   Forrest   Apollo Bay

  Portland Bay   Warrnambool   Timboo   Camperdown    Crowes   Sorrento

A N D

C · 150 · D

Bindle
Binda
Bendena
Ballon
Moonie
Flinton
St George
Millmerran
Mt Domville 2106
Toowoomba
Pittsworth
Oakey
MORETON
Jimbour
Dalby
Jondaryan
BRISBANE
Dunwich
Stradbroke I.
Southport
South Coast
Coolangatta
Pt Danger
Murwillumbah
Mullumbimby
C.Byron
Byron Bay
Bangalow
Ballina
Evans Head

Nindigully
Thallon
Weir
Inglewood
Yelarbon
Warwick
Killarney
Amiens
Texas
Clifton
Laidley
Rosewood
Ipswich
Boonah
Kyogle
Casino

Mungallala
Cunnamulla
Hebel
Angledool
Goodooga
Dirranbandi
Dareel
Boggabilla
Yetman
Stanthorpe
Deepwater
Tenterfield
England Ra. 4955
Drake
Rappville
Lismore

Goondiwindi
Moree
Camurra
Wariabda
Bingara
Bellata
Emmaville
Glen Innes
Inverell
Tingha
Guyra
B.Lomond 4987
Mt Hyland
Glenreagh
Maclean
Ulmarra
Grafton

NORTH
CENTRAL
PLAIN
NORTHERN
TABLELAND
Coff's Harbour
Dorrigo
Urunya
Bellingen
Nambucca Heads
Macksville

Collarenebri
Walgett
Burren
Junc.
Wee Waa
Narrabri
Barraba
Bundarra
Barraba
Manilla
Armidale
Uralla
Walcha
Macleay Ra.
Smoky C.
Smithton & Gladstone

Pilliga
Namoi
Baan Baa
Boggabri
Gunnedah
N. WEST
SLOPE
Tamworth
Werris Cr.
Hastings
Wanchope
Kempsey
Port Macquarie
& Hastings R.

Coonamble
Baradine
Coonabara-bran
Binnaway
Liverpool
Plains
Quirindi
Nundle
Comboyne
Wingham
Taree

Gilgandra
Dunedoo
Coolah 4500
Scone
Merriwa
Murrurundi
Gloucester
Forster
C.Hawke
Manning
Tuncurry
Sugarloaf Pt

Dubbo
Wellington
Gulgong
Mudgee
HUNTER & MANNING
Muswellbrook
Dungog
Stroud

Wz A L E S
Peak Hill
Eton
Cudgegong
Rylstone
Singleton
Kurri Kurri
Cessnock
Wallsend
Maitland
Port Stephens

Parkes
Molong
Orange
CENTRAL
Hunter Ra. 4180
Newnes
NEWCASTLE & Port Hunter
Toronto

Forbes
Eugowra
Bathurst
TABLE
Portland
Lithgow
Wind-
sor
Gosford
Broken Bay & Hawkesbury R.

Grenfell
Cowra
Canowindra
LAND
Katoomba
Penrith
Hornsby
Manly
Campden
Parramatta
Liverpool
SYDNEY
& Port Jackson
M METROPOLITAN

Young
Temora
Koorawatha
Grong
Crook
Camden 3678
Picton
Cronulla & Botany B.
Campbelltown

Cootamundra
Junee
Murrumburrah
Burrinjuck Res.
Goulburn
Mittagong
Moss
Vale
Wollongong
Shellharbour
Kiama

WESTERN
Yass
Gunning
Cullarin
Berry
Nowra
Ulladulla
Jervis Bay
(COMMONWEALTH TERR.)

SLOPE
CANBERRA
CAP.
TER.
Queanbeyan
Bungendore
Braidwood
Batemans
Bay
Moruya

Holbrook
Tumbarumba
Cooma
Nimmitabel
Narooma

Hume Res.
Cudgewa
Australian Alps
Kosciusko 7316
Bega

Corryong
Bowen Mts
Bombala
Delegate
Eden
Twofold Bay

Mt Ellery 4255
Orbost
Green C.
Disaster B.
C.Howe
Mallacoota Inlet

Bruthen
Lakes Entrance
C.Everard

Bairnsdale
Mt Wellington

C · 150 · D

Narracoopa
Currie
King I.
Flinders I.
Bass Strait
Furneaux
Whitemark
40

Stokes Pt
Three Hummock I.
Robbins I.
Hunter I.
Group
C. Barren I.
C.Portland
Banks Strait
Gladstone
Herrick

Smithton
Stanley
Wynyard
Penguin
Devonport
Mayfield Bay
Bridport
Scott's C.
Avoca
St Marys

Arthur
Trowutta
Burnie
N.W.Ulverstone
Sheffield
Latrobe
Launceston
Ben Lomond 5160

Waratah
Cradle Mt 5116
Mole Cr.
Deloraine
Westbury
Longford
Campbell
Avoca

Zeehan
Mt Ossa
Great
L.
Cressy
Oatlands
MID

Queenstown
W.
Tarraleah
Bothwell
Apsley
Brighton
Oyster B.
Maria I.

C.Sorell
Macquarie
Harb.
Pt Hibbs
Gordon
Derwent
New Norfolk
Glenorchy
Bellevue
Sorell
S E

Port Davey
Huonville
HOBART
Geeveston
Storm Bay
C.Pillar
Dover
Bruny I.
S.E.Cape

TASMANIA
On the same scale

B · 145 · C

## TERRITORY OF
## PAPUA NEW GUINEA
### Scale 1:20,000,000 (320 miles=1 inch)

*PAPUA NEW GUINEA*

*SOLOMON SEA*

*Bismarck Archipelago*

*Bismarck Sea*

New Hanover

Manus I.
Admiralty Is.

Schouten Is.

New Ireland

Rabaul

New Britain

Buka I.
Kieta
Toroking
Green Is.
Solomon Is.

Woodlark I.

Trobriand or Kiriwina Is.
D'Entrecasteaux Is.
Normanby I.
Tagula I.
Louisiade Arch.
Samarai

Wewak
Aitape
Yaimo
Moprik
Mopril
Marienburg
Manam
Karkar I.
Medang
Bogadzim
Madang
Umboi I.
Finschhafen
Morobe
Lae
Wau
Bulolo
Salamaua
Buna
Fofo Fofo
Kerema
Delena
Port Moresby
Abau

*Owen Stanley Ra.*

*Gulf of Papua*

Kikori
Kerema

*Muller Ra.*

*Stickland*

Fly

Aburo

*CORAL SEA*

*Great Barrier Reef*

*Gulf of Carpentaria*

Wessel Is.
Melville Bay
C. Arnhem
Caledon Bay
Blue Mud Bay
Groote Eylandt

Sir Edward Pellew Group
Vanderlin I.

Mornington
Wellesley Is.

Thursday I.
Prince of Wales I.
Endeavour Str.
C. York

Cape York Peninsula

P. Musgrave
Shelburne Bay
C. Grenville
Duifken Pt.
Weipa
C. Direction
Princess Charlotte B.
C. Melville
C. Flattery
Cooktown
C. York
Archer
Holroyd
Keerweer

*QUEENSLAND*

Barkly Tableland

Camooweal
Australia Downs
Burketown
Leichhardt
McCubbin
Cloncurry
Mt. Isa
Duchess
Dajarra
Boulia
Georgina
Marshall
L. Philippi
Hay
Selwyn
Burke
Hamilton
Diamantina
Opalton

Normanton
Croydon
Georgetown
Einasleigh
Forsyth
Gilbert
Staaten
Mitchell
Lynd
Palmer
Laura
Normanby
Mt. Mulligan
Mareeba
Atherton
Herberton
Dimbulah
Cairns
P. Douglas
C. Grafton
Innisfail
5287

Mt. Bartle Frere
Cardwell
Hinchinbrook I.
Ingham
Halifax Bay
C. Cleveland
Townsville
Ayr
Charters Towers
Ravenswood
Burdekin
Leichhardt Ra.
Bowen
C. Upstart
R. Denison
Proserpine
Whitsunday I.
Mackay
Broad Sd.
C. Palmerston
Sarina
St. Lawrence
Shoalwater Bay
C. Townshend
Swain Reefs
Northumberland Is.
Curtis I.
Port Curtis
Keppel Bay
Ernot Park
C. Capricorn Capricorn Chan.
Rockhampton

Hughenden
Richmond
Prairie
Pentland
Torrens Cr.
Buchanan
L. Galilee
Aramac
Barcaldine
Jericho
Clermont
Peak Ra.
Blair Athol Ra.
Nebo
Eton
Netherdale
Ravens Ck.

Woolgar
Gregory Ra.
Muttaburra
Winton
Longreach
Ilfracombe
Isisford
Barcoo
Blackall
Tambo

Flinders
Cloncurry
Winton
Kynuna

*G*

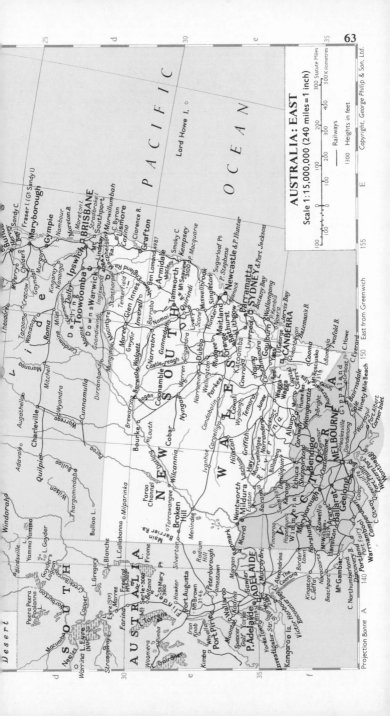

### AUSTRALIA: EAST

Scale 1:15,000,000 (240 miles=1 inch)

| | | | | | | |
|---|---|---|---|---|---|---|
| 100 | 0 | 100 | 200 | 300 | 400 | 500 Statute Miles |

300 Kilometres

—— Railways

1300 Heights in feet

Copyright, George Philip & Son. Ltd.

Projection Bonne

East from Greenwich

PACIFIC OCEAN

Lord Howe I.

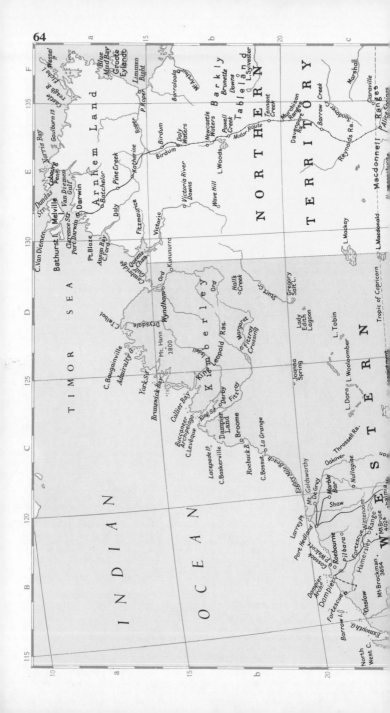

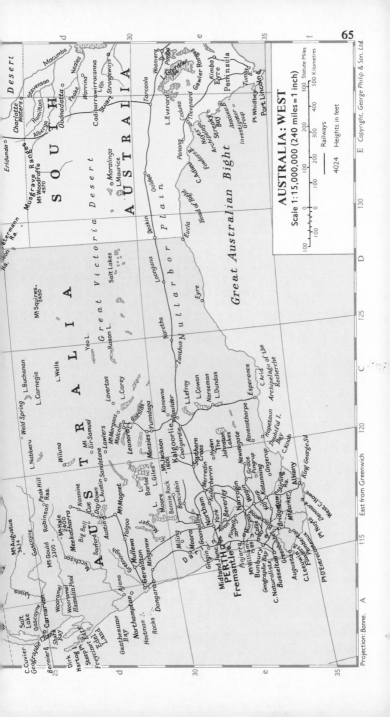

**65**

## AUSTRALIA: WEST

Scale 1:15,000,000 (240 miles=1 inch)

Railways
4024 Heights in feet

Statute Miles
Kilometres

Projection: Bonne.    East from Greenwich    E  Copyright, George Philip & Son, Ltd.

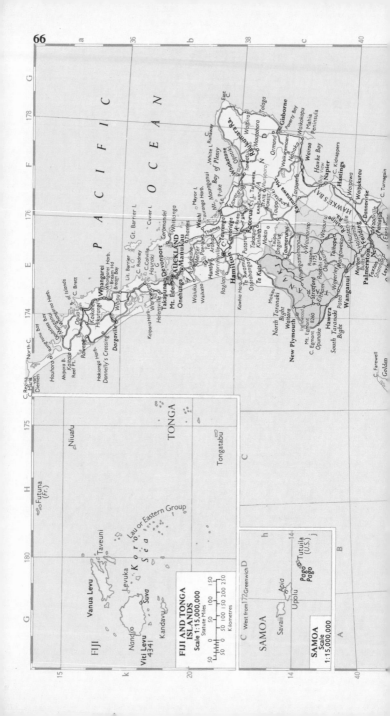

PACIFIC OCEAN

North C.
C. Regina
Muri
Van Diemen
Ahipara B.
Houhora B.
Kaitaia
Reef Pt.
Houhora Harb.
Hokianga Harb.
Donnelly's Crossing
Rawene
Kaikohe
Kaeo
Mangonui
Whangaroa Harb.
Doubtless Bay
Bay of Islands
C. Brett
Whangaruru Harb.
Hikurangi
Opua
Dargaville
Kokohe
Waipu
Whangarei
Bream Hd.
Bream Bay
Lit. Barrier I.
Gt. Barrier I.
C. Rodney
Helensville
Kaipara Harb.
Warkworth
C.Colville
Coromandel
Thames
Mt. Eden AUCKLAND
Takapuna Devonport
Onehunga Manukau
Hauraki
Gulf
Cuvier I.
Mayor I.
Whitianga
Waiuku
Woukou
Mercer
Paeroa
Te Aroha
Waihi
Tauranga
Te Puke
Maketu
Whakatane
White I.
East C.
Bay of Plenty
Waihou
Morrinsville
Huntly
Ngaruawahia
Raglan
HAMILTON
Cambridge
Matamata
Putaruru
Rotorua
Tarawera
Kawhia Harb.
Te Awamutu
Kihikihi
Kawhia
Otorohanga
Te Kuiti
Waikato
Mt. Moangunui
Te Puke
L. Taupo
Tongariro
L. Rotorua
KAINGAROA
STATE
FOREST
Murupara
Waikaremoana
Wairoa
Gisborne
Ormond
Tolaga
Te Karaka
Waipiro
Waiapu
Tokomaru Bay
RAUKUMARA RANGE
Mt. Ruapehu 9175
Raetihi
Ohakune
Taihape
Taumarunui
Ongarue
Mokau
New Plymouth
Waitara
Inglewood
Stratford
Eltham
Mt. Egmont
C. Egmont 8260
Opunake
Hawera
Patea
Waverley
North Taranaki Bight
South Taranaki Bight
Wanganui
Marton
Bulls
Feilding
PALMERSTON N.
Foxton
Hunterville
Raetihi
Ngamatapouri
Woodville
Dannevirke
Waipukurau
Waipawa
Hastings
HAWKE'S BAY
Napier
C. Kidnappers
Hawke Bay
Mohaka
Wairoa
Mahia Peninsula
Mt. Edgecumbe
C. Turnagain
C. Farewell
Golden

TONGA

Niuafu

Tongatabu

Futuna (Fr.)

Taveuni

Lau or Eastern Group

Koro Sea

FIJI

Vanua Levu

Levuka

Suva

Viti Levu 4341

Nandjo

Kandavu

### FIJI AND TONGA ISLANDS
Scale 1:15,000,000

50  0  50  100  150  200  250
Statute Miles

50  0  50  100  150
Kilometres

West from 172 Greenwich

SAMOA

Savaii

Apia

Upolu

Pago Pago
Tutuila (U.S.)

### SAMOA
Scale 1:15,000,000

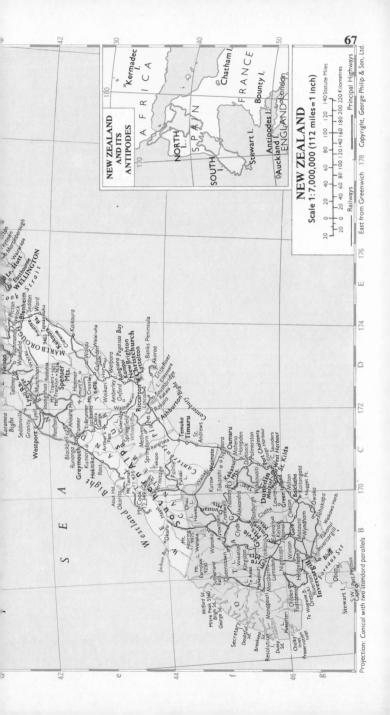

**67**

**NEW ZEALAND AND ITS ANTIPODES**

Kermadec I.

AFRICA

NORTH I.

SPAIN

SOUTH I.

FRANCE

Stewart I.

Antipodes I.

Auckland I.

Bounty I.

Chatham I.

ENGLAND London

**NEW ZEALAND**

Scale 1:7,000,000 (112 miles = 1 inch)

20  0  20  40  60  80  100  120  140 Statute Miles

20  0  20  40  60  80 100 120 140 160 180 200 220 Kilometres

Railways ———— Principal Highways

East from Greenwich

Projection: Conical with two standard parallels

**WELLINGTON**

Hutt

Eastbourne

Blenheim

Seddon

Picton

Havelock

Richmond

Nelson

Tadmor

Wakefield

Motueka

Murchison

Lyell

Spenser Mts.

Mt. Travers 9965

Mt. Franklin 7671

Hanmer

Waiau-uha

Rotoiti

Inangahua

Reefton

Mt. Cossie

Oxford

Kaiapoi

Rangiora

Pegasus Bay

New Brighton

Riccarton **Christchurch**

Lyttelton

Lincoln

Banks Peninsula

Akaroa

Little River

Southbridge

Rakaia

Leeston

MARLBOROUGH

Wairau

Seddonville

Granity

Westport

Charleston

Buller

Karamea Bight

Karamea

Mokihinui

Blackball

Grey

Greymouth

Brunner

Runanga

Kumara

Hokitika

Ross

Arthur's Pass

Mt. Rolleston

Otira

Lake Brunner

Kanieri

Mt. Tasman 11,475

Mt. Cook 12,349

Westland

Okarito

Abut Hd.

Waimakariri R.

Springfield

Sheffield

Coalgate

Methven

Ashburton (Canterbury)

Rangitata (R.)

Temuka

**Timaru**

St. Andrews

Geraldine

Fairlie

Burke's Pass

L. Tekapo

L. Pukaki

Mt. Aspiring 9975

L. Ohau

Waimate

Kurow

Duntroon

Oamaru

Hampden

Moeraki

Palmerston

Waikouaiti

Port Chalmers

West Harbour

St. Kilda

**Dunedin**

Mosgiel

Saddle Hill

Greenisland

Milton

Balclutha

Kaitangata

Clinton

Owaka

Nugget Pt.

Tokomairiro

Lawrence

Roxburgh

Alexandra

Clyde

Cromwell

Wanaka

L. Wanaka

L. Hawea

Arrowtown

Queenstown

Frankton

L. Wakatipu

Kingston

Athol

Lumsden

Gore

Mataura

Edendale

Wyndham

Tokonui

Waikawa Harb.

Catlins

Kaitangata

Tapanui

Clutha

Heriot

Tuapeka

Waipahi

Balfour

Winton

Riverton

Colac

Otautau

Nightcaps

Ohai

Orepuki

Waiau

Te Waewae B.

Invercargill

Bluff

Foveaux Str.

Stewart I.

S.W. Cape

Port Pegasus

Manapouri

L. Manapouri

Mossburn

Te Anau

L. Te Anau

Sutherland Falls

Milford Sd.

Mitre Peak 5560

Bligh Sd.

George Sd.

Secretary I.

Doubtful Sd.

Breaksea Sd.

Resolution

Dusky Sd.

Chalky Inlet

Preservation Inlet

Te Waewae B.

Dunrobin

Tuatapere

Clifden

Lillburn

Hollyford

Big Bay

Jackson Bay

Haast

Mt. Earnslaw 9250

Glenorchy

SEA

WESTLAND

CANTERBURY PLAINS

SOUTHERN ALPS

SOUTH ISLAND

OTAGO

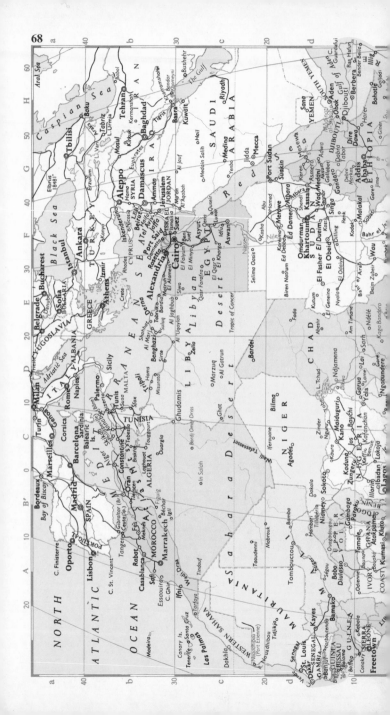

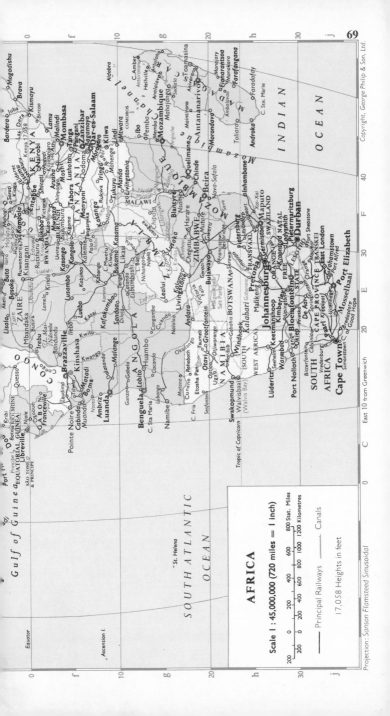

**69**

AFRICA

Scale 1 : 45,000,000 (720 miles = 1 inch)

——— Principal Railways   Canals

17,058 Heights in feet

Projection: Sanson Flamsteed Sinusoidal

Copyright, George Philip & Son, Ltd.

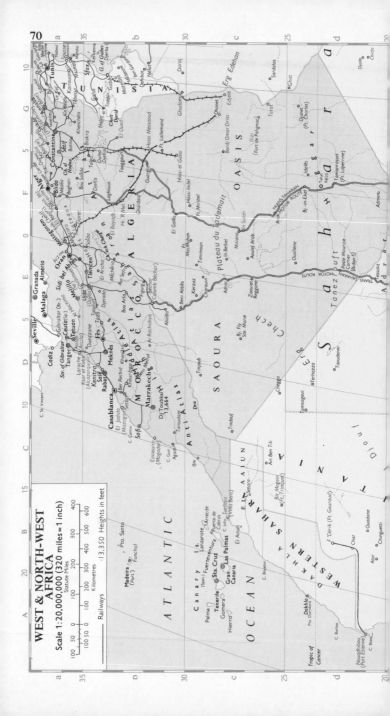

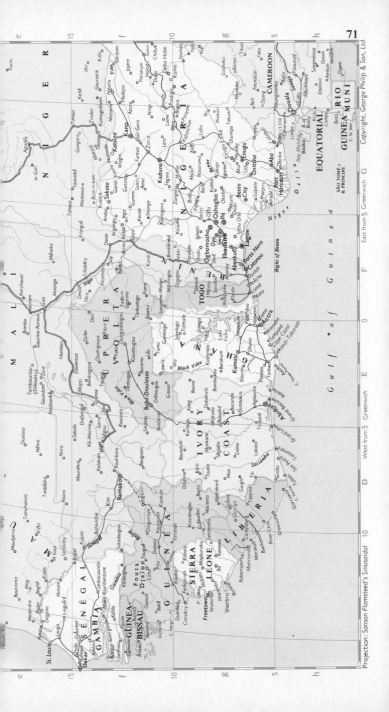

# CENTRAL AND EAST AFRICA
## Scale 1:18,000,000 (288 miles = 1 inch)

Statute Miles
100  50  0        100        200        300        400

100 50 0   100   200   300   400   500   600
Kilometres

_____ Railways        ·17,040  Heights in feet

72

A    15    B    20    C    25

**CHAD**

Am Dam · Am Guereda · Mogororo · Nyola · Tawersha · N. DARFUR
Goz Beida · SOUTHERN · Idd el Ghnnam · DARFUR
Hagar Banga · Rahad el Berdi · Buram · Abu Ma
Am Timan · Mangueigne · Birao · Songo · Kafia Kingi · Bah... el

Numan · Yola · Garoua · Pala · De Behagle · Kyabe · Sah · Kouga · Ouanda Djalé
Poli · Rei Bouba · Moundou · Doba · Koumra · Ndélé · Ouadda · Salif Bundas · Raga · BAHR
Gashaka · Ngaoundéré · Baibokoum · Paoua · Batangafo · Kaga Bandoro · Mouka · Mérékè · Delm Zuber · EL GHAZ
Banya · Meiyganga · Boécaranga · Bossangoa · **CENTRAL AFRICA** · Bouca · Bakala · Ippy · Yalinga · Sokobo · Djema
Tibati · Bébua · Bouar · Bozoum · Bossembélé · Sibut · Grimari · Bambari · Bakouma · O
Yoko · Bétaré Oya · Carnot · Kouango · Bangassou · M'Bomu · Zémio · Doru

**CAMEROON** · Berfoua · Batouri · Berberati · Boda · Bangui · Zongo · Bosobola · Mobaye · Ouanga · Bondo · Ulere · Ango
Yaoundé · Doumé · Abong Mbang · Nola · Mbaïki · Libenge · Mobayi · Yakoma · Likati · Bambili · Titule
Mbalmayo · Yokadouma · Bayanga · Businga · Monveda · Aketi · Buta
Sangmelima · Lomié · Moloundou · Dongou · Impfondo · Bomongo · Bongandanga · Lisala · Bumba · Busu-Djanoa · **HAUT ZA**
Akoafim · Djoum · Souanke · Ouesso · Oubangui · Bolomba · Yahuma · Basoko · Arumimi · Banalia · Yangambi · **Kisangani**
Oyem · Myadhi · Mékambo · **G · O** · Lulonga · **EQUATEUR** · Djolu · Isangi · Yangoma
Mitzick · Makokou · Abolo · Makoua · Befale · Opala · Ubundu
**GABON** · Booué · Equator · Kellé · Ft. Rousset · Mbandaka · Bokote · Bokungu · Ikela · Lomami · Lowa · Kirundu
Lastoursville · Okondja · Ewo · Irebu · Bikora · Bokoro · Boende · **Z · A · I · R · E**
Koula Moutou · Mabirou · Mossaka Lukolela · L. Tumba · Monkoto · Lomela · Kindu · Shabur
Franceville · Gamboma · Lukenie · Ikongo · Dekese · Kole · Lodja · Katako · Kibombo
Zanaga · Djambala · Mushie · Kutu · Tolo · Oshwe · Lomela · Kombe · Lubelu
Mossendjo · Komono · Kwamouth · Bandundu · Loto · **KASAI** · Lusambo · Ishofa · Sangwa
Kibangou · Sibiti · Mindouli · **Brazzaville** · Kasongolu · Basongo · Ilebo · Mweka · Dumbelenge · Mbuji Mayi · Kabinda · Katompe · Ankoro
Pointe Noire · Loubomo · Madingou · **Kinshasa** · Kenge · Kikwit · Idiofa · **OCCIDENTAL** · Dembu · **ORIENTAL**
Landana · Tshelao · Mbanza Ngungu · **BAS** · Masi Manimba · Charlesville · Makumbi · **Kananga** · Dibaya · Kanda Kanda · Katombe
Cabinda · Boma · **ZAIRE** · **Matadi** · Popokabaka · Gungu · Tshikapa · Kazumba · Luisa · Kabongo
Muanda · Soyo · Naqui · Maquela · do Zombo · Feshi · Kasongo Lunda · Kahemba · Lauchima · Kabanga · Kamina
Nzeto · Ambriz · Mbanza Congo · Damba · Sanza Pombo · Va. Verissimo · **SHA B**
Carmona · Comabatela · Luremo · Saurimo · Sandoa · Kafakumba · Lubudi
**Luanda** · Caxito · Quibaxi · Monte Verde · Caungula · Capaia · **Kolwezi** · Tenke · Shi
Pta. das Palmeirinhas · Columbo · Ndalatando · Malanje · Lubalo · Kasenga · Dilolo · Mutshatsha · Mwinilunga · Kipus
Muxima · Dondo · Nova Gaia · Cacolo · Mucónda · Luau · Luashi · Solwesi · Z
Gunza · Gabela · Andulo · Luena · Cazombo · Colunda · Macondo · Kasempa · Z
Ngunza · Va Nova · do Seles · Bailundo · Camacupa · **A · N · G · O · L · A** · Lumai · Zambezi
Egita · B.l.é · Kuito · Munhango · Lucusse · Chavuma
**Lobito** · Chinguar · Huambo · Va. de
**Benguela** · Ganda · Caconda · Chitembo · Cangamba
Dombe Grande · **Plateau**

Projection: Sanson Flamsteed's Sinusoidal

B    20    C    25

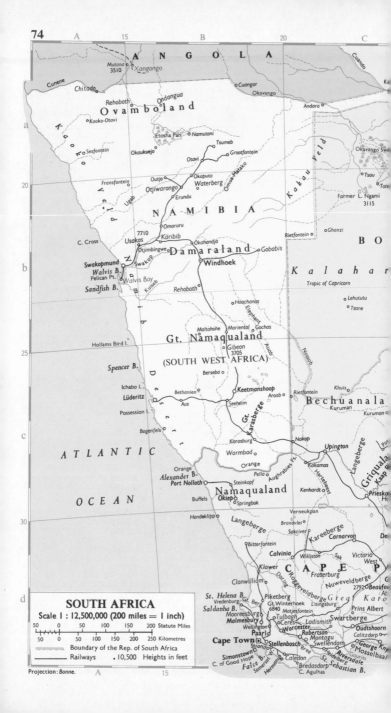

A N G O L A

Mutana
3510
Xangongo

Cunene

Chitado

Kaoko-Otavi

Rehoboth

O v a m b o l a n d

Cuangar
Okavango

Andara

Okavango Sw

Sesfontein

Etosha Pan

Namutoni

Tsumeb

Okaukuejo

Otavi

Grootfontein

Omu-Mako

Tsou

Tote

Fransfontein

Outjo

Okaputa

Waterberg

Otjiwarongo

Erundu

N A M I B I A

Former L. Ngami
3115

Ghanzi

Rietfontein

K a k a u   V e l d

Omaruru

7710

Karibib

Okahandja

Gobabis

B O

Usakos

Otjimbingwe

D a m a r a l a n d

C. Cross

Swakopmund

Walvis B.

Swak°

Windhoek

K a l a h a r

Pelican Pt.

Walvis Bay

Sandfish B.

Rehoboth

Tropic of Capricorn

Hoachanas

Elephant

Lehututu

Tsane

Hollams Bird I.

Maltahohe

Mariental

Gochas

Gt. Namaqualand

Gibeon
3705

Auob

Spencer B.

(SOUTH WEST AFRICA)

Berseba

Khuis

Ichabo I.

Bethanien

Keetmanshoop

Rietfontein

Araob

Bechuanala

Lüderitz

Aus

Seeheim

Kuruman

Kuruman

Possession I.

Gt. Karasberge

Langeberge

Bogenfels

Karasburg

Nakop

Upington

Griqual

Kaap

Warmbad

Orange

Kakamas

Priesk

A T L A N T I C

Orange

Augrabies Fs.

Hartebeest

Pella

Kenhardt

Alexander B.

Steinkopf

Port Nolloth

N a m a q u a l a n d

Buffels

Okiep

Springbok

Verneukpan

O C E A N

Hondeklipp

Brandvlei

Langeberge

Sakriver

Kareeberge

Carnarvon

Calvinia

Williston

Victoria
West

Klawer

Droogeveldberge

Fraserburg

Nuweveldberge

Clanwilliam

C A P E   P

St. Helena B.

Piketberg

Gt. Berg

Greg.

Karo

2792

Beaufor

Vredenburg

Gt. Winterhoek
6840

Laingsburg

Prins Albert

Saldanha B.

Mooreesburg

Matjesfontein

Malmesbury

Tulbagh

Ceres

Ladismith

Swartberge

Oudtshoorn

Wellington

Worcester

Robertson

Montagu

Colitzdorp

George

Paarl

Stellenbosch

Swellendam

Riversdale

Mossel

Cape Town

Simonstown

Strandfontein

Gouritz

C. of Good Hope

Caledon

Bredasdorp

Sebastian B.

False B.

Somerset W.

Hermanus

C. Agulhas

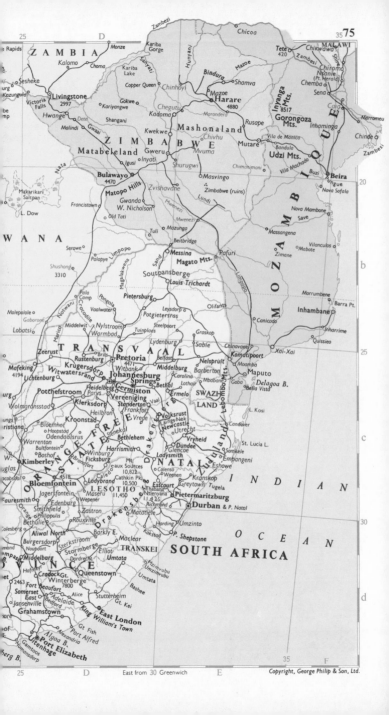

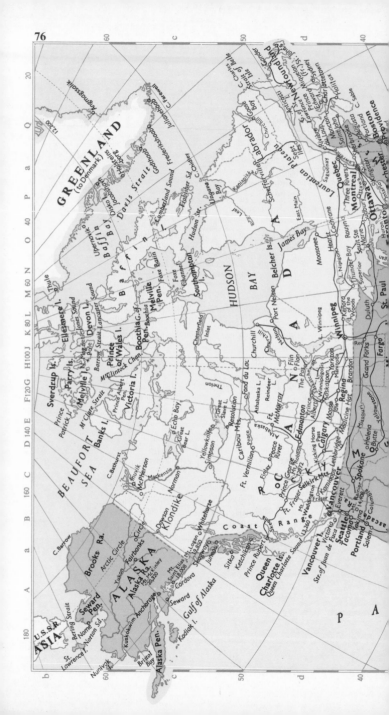

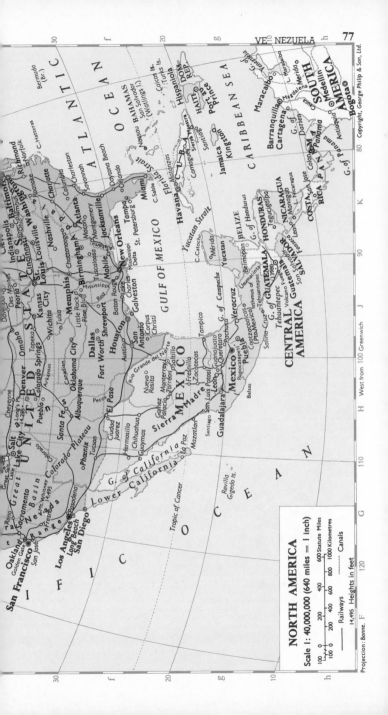

# CANADA

Scale 1 : 27,500,000 (440 miles = 1 inch)

100  0  100  200  300  Statute Miles
100  0  100 200 300 400 500  Kilometres

——— Railways    ········ Canals

10,500  Heights in feet

Projection: Bonne.

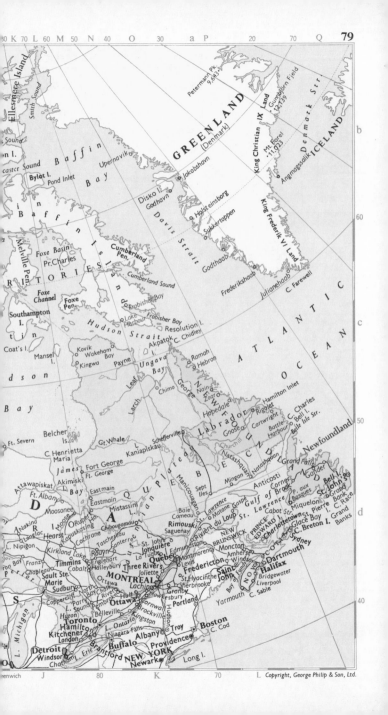

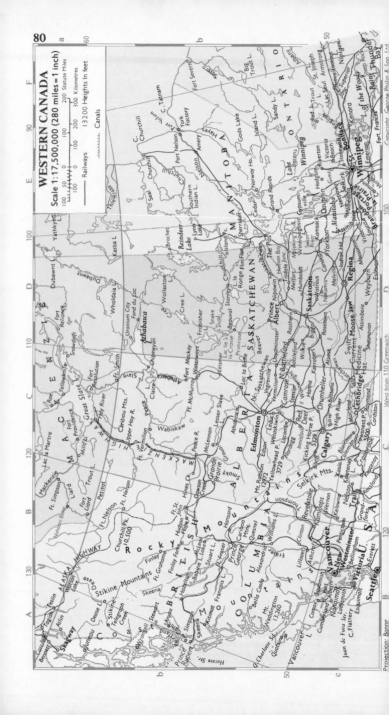

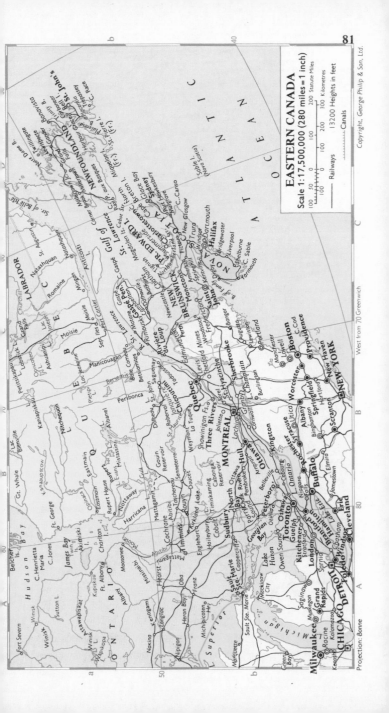

**81**

**EASTERN CANADA**

Scale 1:17,500,000 (280 miles=1 inch)

100 50 0 100 200 Statute Miles

100 0 100 200 300 Kilometres

Railways ——— 13200 Heights in feet

Canals ∙∙∙∙∙∙∙∙

Copyright, George Philip & Son, Ltd.

Projection: Bonne

West from 70° Greenwich

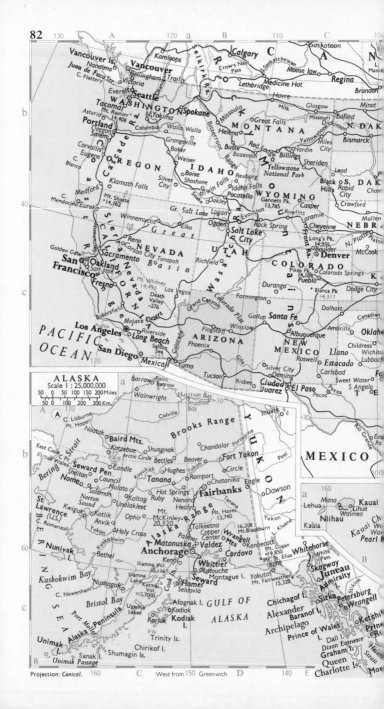

130    A    120    a    B    110    C    10

Saskatoon

Calgary    C    A    N

Kamloops    Crows Nest    S.Saskatchewan    Moose Jaw    Regina

Vancouver Is.    Vancouver    Pass    L.    Mani

Nanaimo    Bellingham    Trail    Medicine Hat    Brandon

Juan de Fuca Str.    Victoria    Lethbridge    Minot

C. Flattery    Everett    Seattle    Havre    Glasgow

Tacoma    Spokane    Missoula    Milk    Buford    N. DAK.

Astoria    WASHINGTON    Great Falls    Missouri    Dickinson

b    Mt.Rainier    Yakima    Bitterroot Ra.    Helena    M O N T A N A

14,408    Columbia    Walla Walla    Red Lodge    Yellowstone    Billings    Bismarck

Portland    Salem    Grangeville    Butte    Bozeman    Hardin    Sheridan

Corvallis    O R E G O N    Baker    Range    Billings

Eugene    Weiser    I D A H O    Rexburg    Yellowstone    Black    S. DAK.

C. Blanco    Silver    Boise    National Park    Hills    Rapid    Cham

Medford    City    Shoshone    Idaho Falls    W Y O M I N G    City

Klamath Falls    Twin Falls    Oakley    Pocatello    Gannett Pk.    Casper    Crawford

40    Eureka    Mt.Shasta    Snake    Gt. Salt Lake    Logan    13,785    Rawlins

C. Mendocino    14,162    Winnemucca    Elko    Ogden    Evanston    Laramie    Cheyenne    NEBR.

Reno    Salt Lake    Rock Spring    Front Ra.    N. Platte    Platte

Golden Gate    Carson City    City    Long's Pk.    McCook

San    Sacramento    N E V A D A    U T A H    14,255    Boulder

Francisco    Oakland    Tonopah    Richfield    C O L O R A D O    Denver

Fresno    San Jose    B a s i n    Las Vegas    Pikes Pk.    Colorado Springs

Mt.Whitney    Death    Grand Canyon    Durango    Pueblo    Dodge City

c    14,495    Valley    Colorado Plat.    Farmington    Blanca Pk.    Dalhart

Bakersfield    -276    14,317    Canadian

Mojave Desert    Gallup    Santa Fe    Amarillo    Oklah

Los Angeles    Riverside    Flagstaff    Winslow    Albuquerque    Childress

Long Beach    Salton    A R I Z O N A    N E W    Llano    Wichita

San Diego    Sea    Phoenix    M E X I C O    Lubboc

PACIFIC    120    -234    Gila    Roswell    Estacado

Mexicali    Yuma    Silver City    Deming    Carlsbad    Sweet Water

OCEAN    Tucson    Bisbee    Ciudad    El Paso    S Angelo

Juarez    Pecos    T

**ALASKA**    Barrow    Point    Harrison Bay    Prudhoe    Inuvik

Scale 1 : 25,000,000    Barrow    Bay    70    -30    E

50  0  50 100 150 200 Miles    Wainwright    MEXICO    Pa

0  100  200  300 Km.    Colville    Y U K O N    Rio Grande

A    170    C. Lisburne    Brooks Range    100

Pt. Hope    Noatak    Chandalar    Porcupine    160

b    East Cape    Cr.    Shungnak    Arctic Circle    Bettles    Beaver    Fort Yukon    Mana    Kauai

Pr. of Wales    Kotzebue    Koyukuk    Hughes    Yukon    Circle    Peel    Lehua    Lihue    Waimea

Bering    Seward Pen.    Candle    Rampart    Eagle    Niihau    Kaula    Wa

Nome    Shelton    Council    Tanana    Chatanika    Dawson    Kauai Ch

Solomon    Nulato    Hot Springs    Fairbanks    Pearl H

Norton    Kaltag    Ruby    Nenana    Tanana

Sound    Unalakleet    Healy    Yukon

St    Kwiguk    Ophir    Mt.    Mt. Hayes

Lawrence    Kotlik    Holy Cross    McKinley    13,740    16,208

(U.S.)    Anvik    Alaska    20,320    Talkeetna    Mt.Blackburn

60    C. Romanzof    Kuskokwim    Copper    Wrangell    Mt. Logan

Nunivak    Bethel    Range    Matanuska    Center    Mes    Kennecott    19,850    Whitehorse

Iliamna Vol.    Palmer    Valdez    Kluane    Mt. St. Elias    White

Kuskokwim Bay    10,116    Anchorage    Cordova    18,008    Pass

Nushagak    Kenai    Whittier    Skagway

C. Newenham    Iliamna    Seward    Yakutat    Juneau

Bristol Bay    Lake    Katmai    Montague I.    Mt. Fairweather    Admiralty

Ugashik    Vol.    Homer    15,320    Sitka    Petersburg

Port Moller    Lakes    ~7000    Seldovia    Chichagof I.    Wrangell

Unimak    Karluk    Afognak I.    GULF OF    Alexander    Prince of Wales    Ketchi

Alaska    Kodiak    ALASKA    Baranof    Archipelago    Prin

Sanak I.    Trinity Is.    Dall I.    OR

Unimak Passage    Chirikof Is.    Prince of Wales    Dixon Entrance    Graham I.

Shumagin Is.    I.    Queen    Str.

Charlotte Is.    Mo

Projection: Conical.    160    C    West from 150 Greenwich    D    140    E

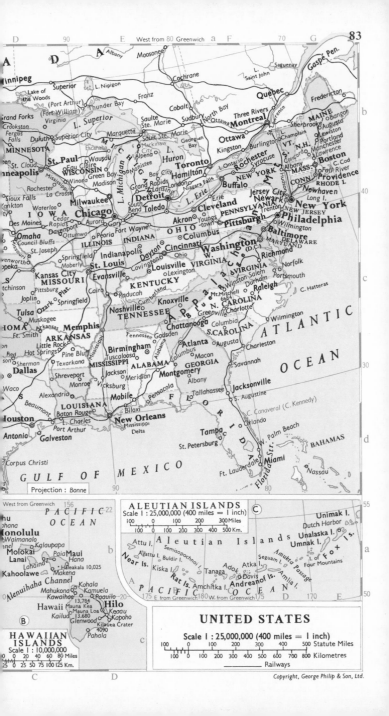

**UNITED STATES**

Scale 1 : 25,000,000 (400 miles = 1 inch)

Railways

**ALEUTIAN ISLANDS**
Scale 1 : 25,000,000 (400 miles = 1 inch)

**HAWAIIAN
ISLANDS**
Scale 1 : 10,000,000

Projection : Bonne

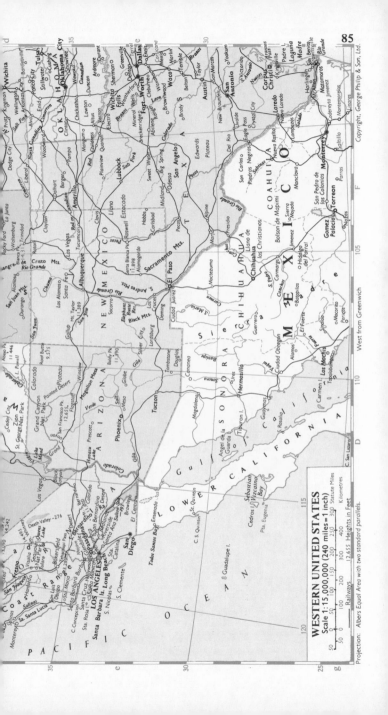

## WESTERN UNITED STATES

Scale 1:15,000,000 (240 miles = 1 inch)

Statute Miles
50  0    50   100   150   200   250   300

Kilometres
50  0   100   200   300   400

Railways          12,655 Heights in Feet

Projection: Albers Equal Area with two standard parallels.

West from Greenwich

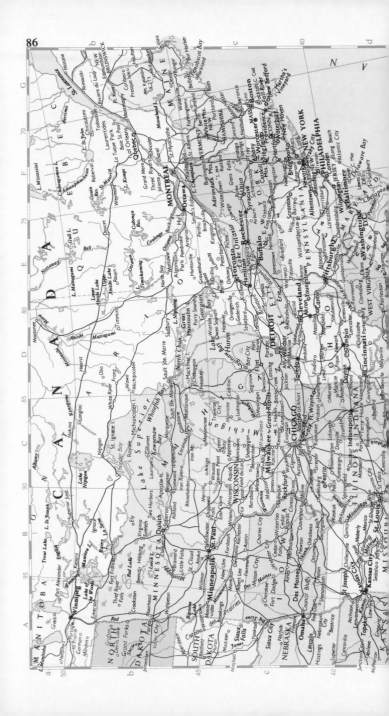

# EASTERN UNITED STATES
Scale 1:15,000,000 (240 miles = 1 inch)

Statute Miles
50 0 50 100 150 200 250 300

Kilometers

12,655   Heights in feet

───── Railways

Projection: Albers Equal Area with two standard parallels

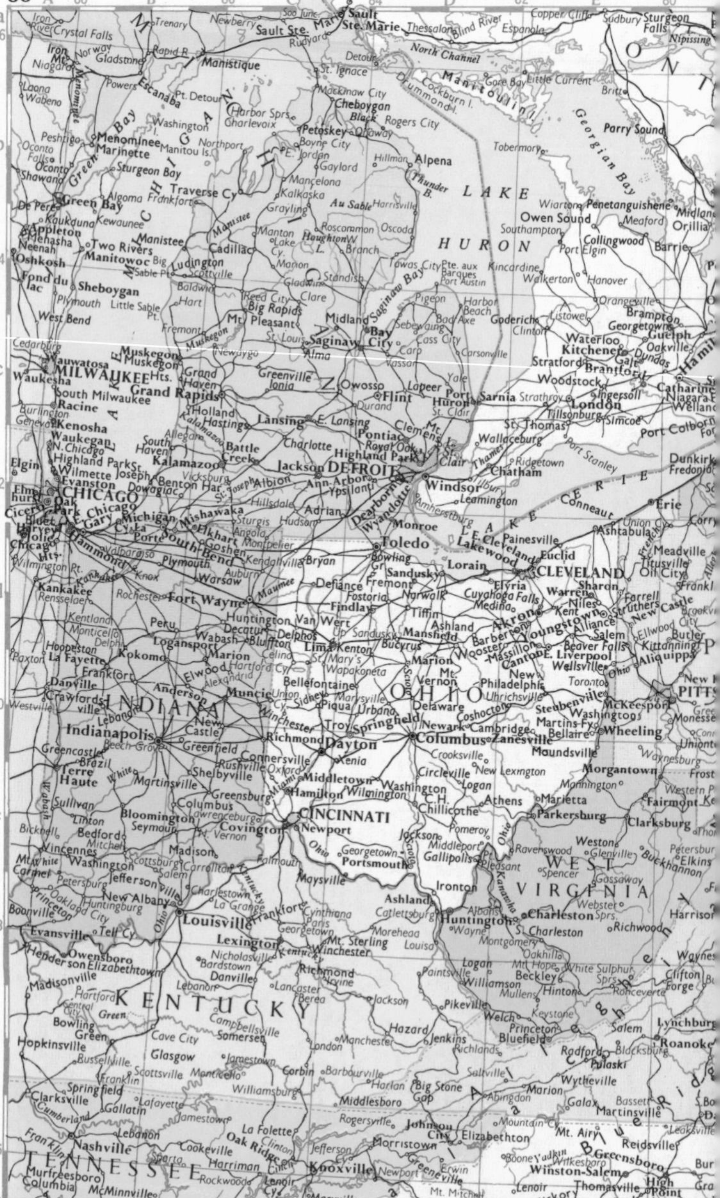

MICHIGAN
LAKE HURON
LAKE ERIE
ONT
Georgian Bay
Manitoulin I.
North Channel
Green Bay
Saginaw Bay
OHIO
INDIANA
KENTUCKY
TENNESSEE
WEST VIRGINIA
Sault Ste. Marie
Manistique
Escanaba
Menominee
Marinette
Green Bay
Traverse Cy
Cheboygan
Petoskey
Alpena
Appleton
Oshkosh
Manitowoc
Sheboygan
Two Rivers
Ludington
Cadillac
Midland
Bay City
Saginaw
Flint
Lansing
Grand Rapids
Muskegon
MILWAUKEE
Racine
Kenosha
Waukegan
Kalamazoo
Battle Creek
Jackson
DETROIT
Ann Arbor
Pontiac
Sarnia
London
Windsor
Chatham
CHICAGO
Gary
Hammond
South Bend
Elkhart
Toledo
Sandusky
Lorain
CLEVELAND
Akron
Youngstown
Canton
Erie
Fort Wayne
Lima
Mansfield
Marion
Columbus
Dayton
Springfield
Hamilton
Middletown
CINCINNATI
Covington
Newport
Zanesville
Wheeling
Steubenville
Parkersburg
Huntington
Charleston
Ashland
Portsmouth
Kokomo
Muncie
Anderson
Indianapolis
Terre Haute
Bloomington
Evansville
Owensboro
Louisville
Lexington
Frankfort
Knoxville
Nashville
Asheville
Winston-Salem
Greensboro
Roanoke
Lynchburg
Bluefield
Kitchener
Waterloo
Brantford
Hamilton
Pittsburgh
Projection: Alber's Equal Area with two standard parallels
West from Greenwich

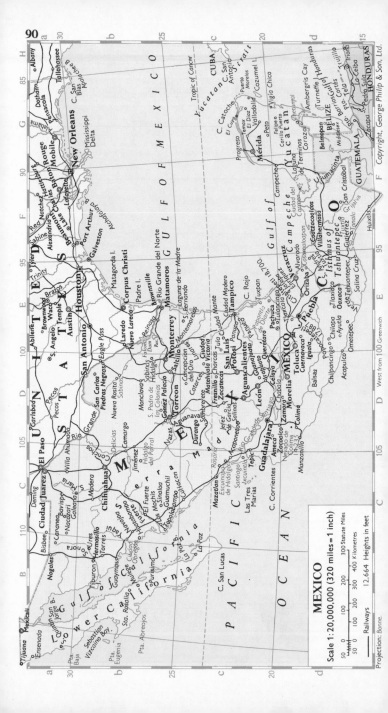

**90**

# MEXICO

Scale 1:20,000,000 (320 miles = 1 inch)

50  0    100    200    300 Statute Miles

50  0  100  200  300  400 Kilometres

Railways ━━━  12,664 Heights in feet

Projection: Bonne.

Copyright, George Philip & Son, Ltd.

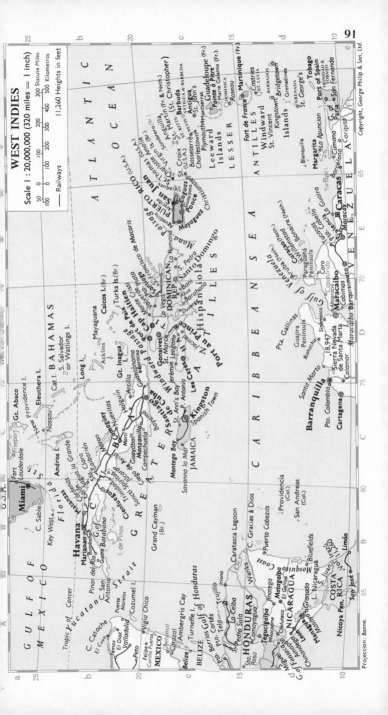

**WEST INDIES**

Scale 1 : 20,000,000 (320 miles = 1 inch)

50    100         200         300 Statute Miles

100    200    300    400    500 Kilometres

—— Railways          11,260 Heights in feet

Copyright, George Philip & Son, Ltd.

**91**

Projection: Bonne.

A T L A N T I C   O C E A N

C A R I B B E A N   S E A

G U L F   O F   M E X I C O

G R E A T E R   A N T I L L E S

L E S S E R   A N T I L L E S

BAHAMAS

B. Cuba

JAMAICA

HAITI

DOMINICAN

PUERTO RICO (U.S.A.)

Leeward Islands

Windward Islands

V E N E Z U E L A

MEXICO

BELIZE

HONDURAS

NICARAGUA

COSTA RICA

Tropic of Cancer

West from Greenwich

Miami
U.S.A.
Florida
Key West
C. Sable
Gt. Abaco
Freeport
Ft. Lauderdale
New Providence I.
Nassau
Eleuthera I.
Cat I.
Andros I.
S. Salvador or Watlings I.
Long I.
Acklins
Mayaguana
Crooked I.
Gt. Inagua
Caicos Is. (Br.)
Turks Is. (Br.)

Havana
Marianao
Pinar del Río
C. San Antonio
Matanzas
Cárdenas
Sagua la Grande
Santa Clara
I. de Pinos
Guane Batabanó
G. of Batabanó
Cienfuegos
Trinidad
Morón
Nuevitas
Camagüey
Manzanillo
Bayamo
Holguín
Antilla
Santiago de Cuba
Guantánamo
St. Ann's Bay
Montego Bay
Savanna la Mar
Spanish Town
Kingston

Grand Cayman (Br.)

Môle St. Nicolas
Port de Paix
Cap Haïtien
Gonaïves
St. Marc
Jérémie
Les Cayes
Port au Prince
Jacmel

Monte Cristi
Santiago
La Vega
Puerto Plata
San Francisco de Macorís
San Pedro de Macorís
Santo Domingo
Baní
Barahona

Mona Passage

Aguadilla
Mayagüez
Ponce
San Juan
Guayama
Arecibo

St. Thomas (U.S.A.)
St. John (U.S.A.)
St. Croix (U.S.A.)
Virgin Is. (Br.)
Anguilla (Fr. & Neth.)
St. Martin (Fr. & Neth.)
St. Christopher (St. Kitts)
Nevis
Antigua
Barbuda
Basseterre
Charlestown
St. John's
Montserrat
Plymouth
Guadeloupe (Fr.)
Pointe à Pitre
Marie Galante (Fr.)
Dominica (Br.)
Roseau
Fort de France
Martinique (Fr.)
St. Lucia
Castries
St. Vincent
Kingstown
Grenadines
Barbados
Bridgetown
Grenada
St. George's
Tobago
Trinidad
Port of Spain
San Fernando

Margarita
Blanquilla
Tortuga I.
Gulf of Paria
Caripito

Caracas
La Guaira
Puerto Cabello
Tucacas
Coro
Maracaibo
L. of Maracaibo
Lagunillas
Gibraltar
Cabimas
Altagracia
Paraguaná Peninsula
Curaçao (Neth.)
Bonaire (Neth.)
Aruba (Neth.)

Barranquilla
Cartagena
Pto. Colombia
Santa Marta
Sierra Nevada de Santa Marta
18,947
Calamar
Ríohacha
Guajira Peninsula
Pta. Gallinas

C. Catoche
El Cuyo
Temax
Río Lagartos
Progreso
Mérida
Valladolid
Peto
Carillo Puerto
Felipe
Chetumal
Cozumel I.
Vigía Chica
Ambergris Cay
Turneffe I.
Belize
Puerto Morelos

C. Gracias a Dios
Cape Gracias a Dios
Puerto Cabezs
Caratasca Lagoon
Bluefields
Mosquito Coast
Puerto Cabezas
El Gallo
Wanks R.
Providencia (Col.)
San Andreas (Col.)

Gulf of Honduras
Puerto Cortés
Pto. Barrios
Tela
La Ceiba
Trujillo
San Pedro Sula
Sta. Rosa
Comayagua
Tegucigalpa
Choluteca
Nacaome
Danlí
Juticalpa
Matagalpa
Jinotega
León
Managua
L. Managua
L. Nicaragua
Granada
Rivas
San Juan del Norte
Limón
Nicoya Pen.
G. of Nicoya
San José

Yucatán Strait

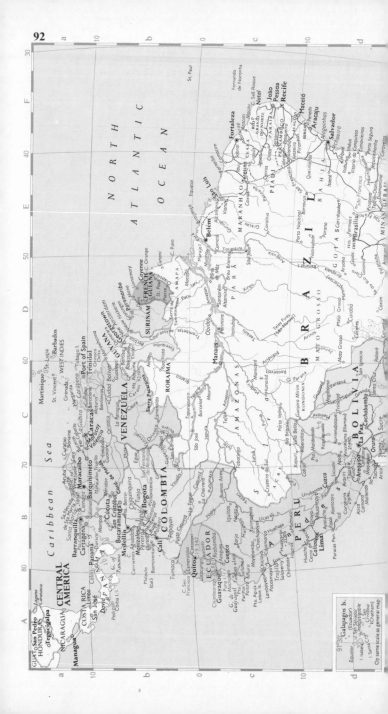

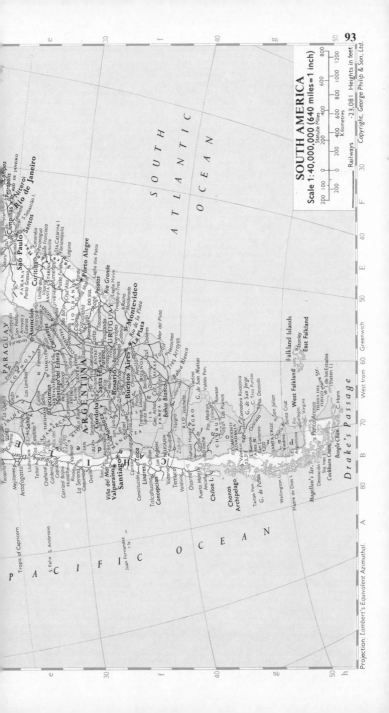

**SOUTH AMERICA**

Scale 1:40,000,000 (640 miles=1 inch)

Statute Miles
200 100 0    200    400    600    800

Kilometres
200 0    200    400    600    800    1000   1200

Railways ――――    Heights in feet    -23,081

Copyright, George Philip & Son, Ltd.

SOUTH

ATLANTIC

OCEAN

PACIFIC OCEAN

Drake's Passage

Falkland Islands
Stanley
East Falkland
West Falkland

Rio de Janeiro
Niteroi
Santos
São Paulo
Campinas
Curitiba
Porto Alegre
Rio Grande
Montevideo
La Plata
Buenos Aires
Rosario
Santa Fé
Córdoba
PARAGUAY
Asunción
URUGUAY
ARGENTINA
Santiago
Valparaiso
Viña del Mar
Concepción
Talca
Linares
Chillán
Temuco
Valdivia
Puerto Montt
Chiloe I.
Chonos Archipelago
Wellington I.
Magellan's Str.
Punta Arenas
C. Horn
Beagle Chan.
Tropic of Capricorn
Antofagasta
S. Felix  S. Ambrosio
Juan Fernandez Is.

Projection: Lambert's Equivalent Azimuthal.

West from    Greenwich

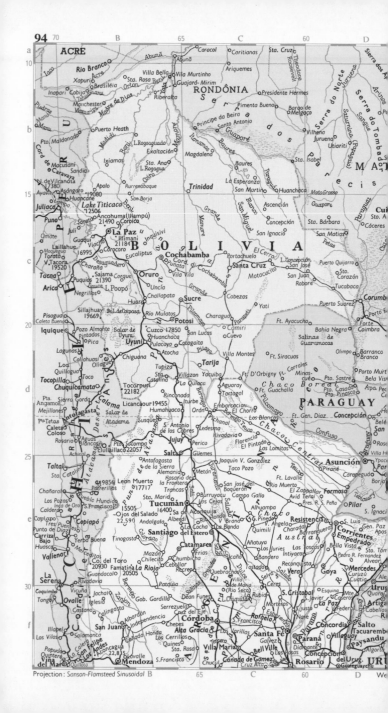

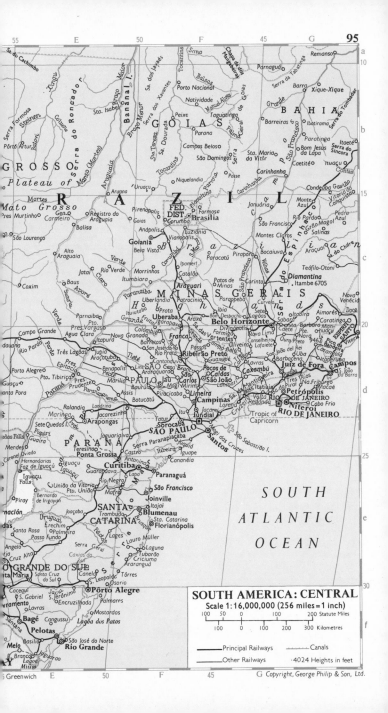

SOUTH AMERICA: CENTRAL
Scale 1:16,000,000 (256 miles=1 inch)

Principal Railways — Canals
Other Railways · 4024 Heights in feet

G Copyright, George Philip & Son, Ltd.

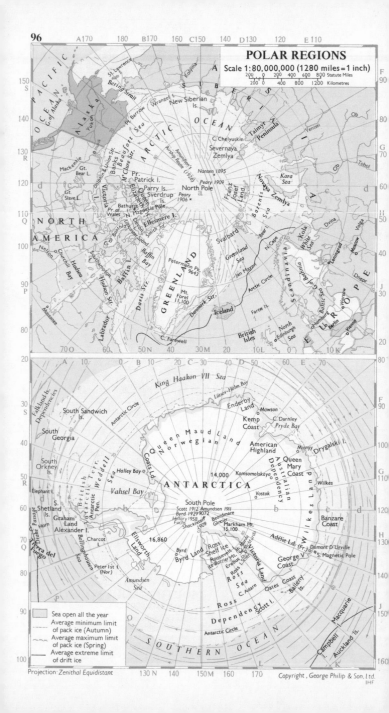

# POLAR REGIONS

Scale 1:80,000,000 (1280 miles = 1 inch)

200   0   200   400   600   800 Statute Miles
200   0   400   800   1200 Kilometres

A170   180   B170   160   C150   140   D130   120   E110

PACIFIC OCEAN

G. of Alaska

St. Lawrence I.

Bering Strait

Wrangel I.

New Siberian Is.

S I B E R I A

Pt. Barrow

Alaska

Yukon

Mackenzie

ARCTIC OCEAN

C. Chelyuskin

Taimyr Peninsula

Severnaya Zemlya

Ob

Yenisei

Tobol

Amundsen's Airship Route (1926)

Nansen 1895

Peary 1909

NORTH POLE

Peary 1906

Gt. Bear L.

Victoria I.

Banks I.

M'Clure Str.

Prince Patrick I.

Parry Is.

Sverdrup Is.

Bathurst I.

Pr. of Wales I.

Magnetic Pole

Franz Josef Land

Novaya Zemlya

Kara Sea

Gt. Slave L.

Dolphin & Union Str.

Beaufort Sea

NORTH AMERICA

Boothia Pen.

Queen Elizabeth Is.

Ellesmere I.

Smith Sd.

Barents Sea

Bear I.

N. Cape

Kola Pen.

White Sea

Dvina

Volga

Moscow

Leningrad

E U R O P E

Nelson

Churchill

Hudson Bay

Labrador

Coppermine

Fury & Hecla Str.

Foxe Chan.

Baffin I.

Baffin Bay

GREENLAND

Petermann Pk. 9643

Mt. Forel 11,100

Greenland Sea

Jan Mayen

Svalbard

Scandinavia

Gulf of Bothnia

Baltic Sea

Dnepr

Warsaw

Berlin

Vienna

ARCTIC CIRCLE

Nares Strait

Davis Str.

Denmark Str.

Iceland

Faroe Is.

North Sea

British Isles

C. Farewell

Edinburgh

N O R T H   A M E R I C A

70   60   50   40   30   20   10
O   N   M   L   K

150   140   130   120   110   100   90   80

F90   G70   d60   H50   J30   K20

---

20   A   10   B   20   C   30   D   40   50   E   60   70   80

King Haakon VII Sea

Lützow-Holm Bay

Falkland Is. Dependencies

Antarctic Circle

South Sandwich Is.

South Georgia

Enderby Land

Mawson

Kemp Coast

C. Darnley

Prydz Bay

Queen Maud Land

Norwegian

American Highland

South Orkney Is.

Coats Ld.

British Antarctic Terr.

Weddell Sea

Halley Bay

14,000

Komsomolskaya

Mirny

Drygalski I.

Queen Mary Coast

Elephant I.

S. Shetland Is.

Graham Land

Alexander I.

Vahsel Bay

ANTARCTICA

SOUTH POLE

Vostok

Wilkes

Banzare Coast

Drake Passage

Horn

Tierra del Fuego

Bellingshausen Sea

Charcot

Ellsworth Land

16,860

Scott 1912 Amundsen 1911

Byrd 1929 90°72'

Hillary 1958

Fuchs 1958

Shackleton 1909

Beardmore Glacier

Markham Mt. 15,100

Peter I st I. (Nor)

Amundsen Sea

Byrd

Byrd Land

Ross Shelf Ice

Roosevelt I.

de Barrier Mt.

Ross I.

Erebus

Victoria Land

Adélie Ld. (Fr.)

S. Magnetic Pole

Dumont D'Urville

George V Coast

Wilkes Land

Ross Sea

C. Adare

Oates Coast

Bailey I.

Scott I.

Macquarie I.

Campbell I.

Auckland Is.

Ross Dependency

Antarctic Circle

S O U T H E R N   O C E A N

Projection: Zenithal Equidistant

130   N   140   150   N   160   170

Copyright, George Philip & Son, Ltd.

IHF

30   40   50   60   70   80   90   100
S   R   Q   P

80   90   100   110   120   130   140   150   160
F   G   d   H   J

## Legend

Sea open all the year

Average minimum limit of pack ice (Autumn)

Average maximum limit of pack ice (Spring)

Average extreme limit of drift ice

# INDEX

## ABBREVIATIONS

* Renamed Nzeto

61 Bainsdale Cc
84 Baitadi Hd
30 Baja Bb
90 Baja, Pta., Ab
72 Bakala Cf
13 Bakel Cf
84 Baker Cc
78 Baker, L. Hb
85 Bakersfield Cd
30 Bakony Forest Ab
73 Bakourma Df
35 Baku Jg
49 Balabac, I. Cc
49 Balaghat Hh
60 Balaklava, South
   Australia Ab
33 Balaklava,
   U.S.S.R. Fg
71 Balama Cf
49 Balambangan,
   I. Cc
47 Blangir Jh
73 Balashov He
47 Balasore Lh
31 Balaton, L. Ab
9 Balbriggan Ec
31 Balchik Gd
67 Balclutha Bg
13 Baldegger See Ca
26 Balearic Is. Cb
48 Bali, I. Cd
27 Balikesir Cb
49 Balikpapan Cd
95 Balisa Ec
31 Balkan Mts. Ed
34 Balkhash, & L. Ke
9 Ballaghadereen Cc
61 Ballarat Bc
61 Ballina,
   Australia Da
9 Ballina, Mayo Bb
9 Ballina,
   Tipperary Cd
9 Ballinasloe Cc
9 Ballinluig Ed
9 Ballinrobe Bc
9 Ballinascarthy Ce
9 Ballyholon Bd
9 Ballycastle,
   Antrim Ea
9 Ballycastle,
   Mayo Bb
9 Ballyclare Fb
9 Ballymena Eb
9 Ballymoney Ea
9 Ballymote Cb
9 Ballyshannon Cb
48 Balmoral Je
47 Balrampur Je
60 Balranald Bb
90 Balsas, R. Dd
13 Balsthal Ba
33 Baltaa Ef
11 Baltic Sea Cd
9 Baltimore, Ire. Be
89 Baltimore,
   U.S.A. Ge
18 Baltrum I. Ga
44 Baluchistan,
   Dist. Bc
43 Bam Hd
70 Bamako Df
71 Bamba Ee
17 Bamberg Bd
43 Bampur Hd
72 Banalia Dc
95 Bananal I. Eb
9 Banbridge Eb
7 Banbury Fe
73 Banda Atjeh Ac
47 Banda, Mad. P. Gf
47 Banda, Ut. P. Hf
49 Banda Sea Dd
49 Banda Is. Dd
13 Bandalsam, mt. Dc
43 Bandar Abbas Hd
43 Bandar-
   Charak Gd
43 Bandar-e-
   Lengeh Gd
* 43 Bandar-e-
   Pahlavi Fb
43 Bandar-e-Rig Gd
** 43 Bandar-e-Shah Hc
† 43 Bandar-
   Shahpur Fc
48 Bandar Seri Bega-
   wan Cc
94 Bandera Cd
27 Banderma Ca
44 Bandjarmasin Cd
9 Bandon & R. Ce
75 Banduka Ea
13 Bandundu Bd
48 Bandung Bd
80 Banff, Canada Cb
8 Banff & Co.,
   Scotland Ec
44 Bangalore Df
49 Bangalow Da
72 Bangassou Cc
49 Banggai Is. Dd
49 Banggi, I. Cc
48 Banka, I. Bd

48 Bangkok Bb
45 Bangladesh, st. Gd
9 Bangor, Ire. Fb
72 Bangui Bc
9 Bangweulu, L. Ef
91 Bani Dc
40 Baniyas Bb
28 Banjaluka Fb
71 Banjul Bd
48 Banjuwangi Cd
91 Bankipore Kf
78 Banks I. Ea
33 Bankura Lg
22 Bantu Cb
22 Banská Ed
22 Banska Bystrica Ed
9 Bantry & B. Be
71 Banyo Hg
96 Banzare Coast Hc
31 Bar Eb
19 Bar le Duc Ef
91 Baracoa Db
91 Barahona Dc
26 Baran Ff
82a Baranof I. Ec
93 Baranovichi Ee
94 Barao
   de Melgaço Eb
95 Barbacena Gd
91 Barbados, I. Fd
70 Barbas, C. Bd
95 Barberton,
   South Africa Ec
88 Barberton,
   U.S.A. Ed
91 Barbuda, I. Fc
62 Barcaldine Cc
29 Barcelona, Italy Ce
16 Barcelona, Sp. Ca
92 Barcelona, Ven. Cb
92 Barcelos Cb
62 Barcoo R. Bc
68 Bardei Dc
23 Bardejov Ed
13 Bardu Db
45 Bareilly Gd
34 Barents Sea Fb
14 Barfleur Cc
5 Barga Je
91 Bargal Ed
29 Bari Ff
73 Baringo, L. Fc
47 Baripada Lh
47 Barisal Ng
48 Barisan Mts. Bd
48 Barito R. Cd
50 Barkha Cc
64 Barkly
   Tableland Fb
95 Barkly West Cc
50 Barköl Db
65 Barlee L. Bc
29 Barletta Ed
46 Barmer Cf
7 Yarmouth Ge
34 Barnaul Ld
18 Barneveld Eb
72 Barnsley Fd
71 Baro Gg
63 Baroren Dc
47 Barpeta Ne
52 Barquisimeto Ca
95 Barra Ad
8 Barra, I. Ad
72 Barra Hd. Ad
75 Barra Pt. Fb
61 Barraba Db
47 Barrackpore Mg
94 Barranco Dd
92 Barranquilla Ba
89 Barre Jb
95 Barreiras Fd
95 Barretos Fd
85 Barrie Fb
82a Barrow, Alaska Ca
6 Barrow, Eng. Dc
64 Barrow Creek Ec
72 Barry Df
87 Bartlesville Ad
23 Bartoszyce Fa
8 Barvas Bb
61 Barwon R. Ca
13 Basel (Basle) &
   cant. Ba
49 Basilan I. Dc
29 Basilicata
   (Lucania) reg. Fd
13 Basle, see Basel
16 Basongo Cc
12 Basongo Provs. Ba
43 Basra Fc
59 Bass Strait Hf
80 Bassano, Can. Cb
29 Bassano, Italy Cb
43 Bassein Ge

91 Basseterre Fc
20 Bassigny,
   district Da
47 Basti Je
15 Bastia Bg
14 Basturtäsh Ec
69 Bata Dc
49 Bataan I. Db
91 Batabano & Gulf
   of Bb
49 Batan Is. Da
49 Batangas Db
30 Bataszek Bb
29 Batavia Fc
13 Batchelor Ea
87 Batesville Bd
7 Bath Ef
61 Bathurst,
   Australia Cb
81 Bathurst, Can. Cb
78 Bathurst, C. Ea
64 Bathurst I.,
   Australia Ea
75 Bathurst I.,
   Canada Ha
49 Batjan I. Dd
91 Baton Rouge Be
48 Battambang Bb
7 Battle Hg
88 Battle Creek Cc
79 Battle Harbour Mc
73 Batu, mt. Fb
48 Batu Is. Ad
33 Batumi Hg
92 Baturité Fc
49 Baucau (Vila
   Salazar) Dd
71 Bauchi Gf
70 Baugie Fa
94 Baures Cb
95 Baus Ec
16 Bautzen Fc
90 Bavispe Ca
48 Bawean, I. Cd
71 Bawku Ef
88 Bay City Cc
76 Bay of Whales Lb
89 Bay Shore Jd
66 Bay View Fc
91 Bayamo Cb
14 Bayeux Cc
51 Bayinhot Ec
15 Bayonne Cf
17 Bayreuth Dd
40 Bayrut Bc
40 Bayt ad Din Bc
40 Bayt Lahm
   (Bethlehem) Bd
9 Beachy Head Hg
7 Bear I. Hb
96 Beardmore
   Glacier Na
53 Beata C. Dc
84 Beatrice Gc
20 Beaucaire Cf
61 Beaudesert Da
89 Beaufort Ec
78 Beaufort Sea Da
74 Beaufort West Cd
20 Beaujolais, dist. Cd
9 Beauly & R. Dc
87 Beaumont Be
20 Beaume Cb
14 Beauvais Ec
20 Beauval Db
70 Beaverdam Cc
66 Beawar Ec
70 Béchar Eb
74 Bechuanaland Cc
88 Beckley Ef
7 Bedford &
   Co., England Ge
88 Bedford, U.S.A. Ge
10 Beersheba Bd
61 Bega Cc
75 Beira Ea
38 Beirut Cb
75 Beitbridge Eb
70 Beja, Port. Ab
70 Béja, Tunisia Ga
95 Bela Cc
95 Bela Crkva Cc
95 Bela Vista,
   Brazil Ec
94 Bela Vista, Par. Dd
70 Belaya Ff
73 Belaya R. Le
9 Belcher Is. Jc
92 Belém Fc
9 Belfast Fb
26 Belfort, & Terr. Ee
14 Belgaum Ce
7 Belgium,
   Kingdom Fe
33 Belgorod
   Dnestrovsk Ef
33 Belgrade Cc
46 Belitung, I. Bd
90 Belize Gd
79 Bell I., Lab. Mc
79 Bell I., Newf. Db

80 Bella Coola Bb
75 Bella Vista Dc
88 Bellaire Ed
44 Bellary Df
15 Beile I. Ec
79 Belle Isle, Str.
   of Mc
20 Belledonne, Chaine
   de, mts. Dd
88 Bellefontaine Dd
20 Bellegarde Dc
61 Bellerive Cd
61 Belleville, Can. Bb
86 Belleville,
   U.S.A. Cd
61 Beilingen Db
84 Bellingham Bb
96 Bellingshausen
   Sea Qc
13 Bellinzona Cb
28 Belluno Da
64 Belly R. Da
95 Belo Horizonte Gc
35 Belogorsk Pd
32 Belomorsk Fd
33 Beloye, L. Gc
32 Belozersk Gd
33 Belozerskaya Jf
60 Beitana Ab
85 Belton Ge
7 Belturbet Db
34 Belukha, Mt. Le
62 Belyando R. Cc
86 Bemidji Bb
61 Ben Lomond, mt.,
   N.S.W. Db
61 Ben Lomond, mt.,
   Tas. Cd
8 Ben Nevis, mt. Dd
8 Ben Wyvis, mt. Dc
60 Benalla Cc
47 Benares, see
   Varanasi
65 Bencubbin Be
34 Bend Bc
39 Bender Belia Ee
39 Bender Cassim Dd
13 Bendery Ef
60 Bendigo Bc
20 Benevento Ed
45 Bengal, B. of Fe
45 Bengal, W., st. Fd
62 Benghazi Eb
72 Benguela Af
70 Beni Abbés Eb
31 Beni Suef Cc
68 Benin Cc
7 Benin,
   Bight of Fh
71 Benin City Gg
82 Bennett Ab
19 Bensheim He
73 Bentiu Db
88 Benton Harb. Bc
71 Benue, R. Gg
35 Beppu Bd
7 Berat Bc
32 Berber Cd
39 Berbera Dd
33 Berdichev Ef
39 Bereda Ed
32 Berdyansk
   (Osipenko) Bf
33 Berezina R. Ee
32 Berezniki Ld
72 Bergama Cb
13 Bergamo Hd
18 Bergen, Neth. Db
11 Bergen, Nor. Bc
18 Bergen-op-
   Zoom Dc
18 Bergisch
   Gladbach Gc
47 Berhampore Mf
47 Berhampur Kj
3 Bering Sea Eb
82a Bering Str. Ab
84 Berkeley Bd
7 Berkshire, Co. Ff
16 Berlin Eb
77 Bermuda, I. Me
13 Bern, & cant. Bb
16 Bernay Dc
16 Bernburg Dc
13 Berner Alpen,
   mts. Bb
22 Beroun Cd
20 Besançon Ee
45 Betaré-Oya Ab
75 Bethal Dc
74 Bethanien Bc
40 Bethlehem (Bayt
   Lahm), Israel &
   Jordan Bd

75 Bethlehem, South
   Africa Dc
89 Bethlehem,
   U.S.A. Hd
75 Bethulie Dd
19 Bethune Bd
81 Betsiamites Cb
47 Bettiah Ke
65 Beverley Be
73 Beverwijk Db
7 Bexhill Hg
27 Beypazari Db
27 Beysehir, L. Db
35 Bezhitza Fe
15 Béziers Ef
46 Bhachau Cg
75 Bhagalpur Lf
45 Bhamo Hd
47 Bhamragarh Hh
46 Bhandara Gh
47 Bharatpur, Raj. Fe
47 Bharatpur,
   Mad. P. Hg
24 Bharuch Dh
46 Bhatinda Ec
47 Bhatpara Mg
46 Bhaunagar Dh
46 Bhilwara Ef
74 Bhima R. De
46 Bhiwandi Dj
46 Bhiwani Fd
74 Bhopal Fg
46 Bhubaneswar Kh
46 Bhuj Bg
46 Bhusawal Eh
45 Bhutan, st. Gc
12 Biala, Kraków Ed
53 Biala
   (Podlaska) Gb
22 Bialograd Gb
23 Bialowieza Gb
23 Bialystok Gb
15 Biarritz Cf
54 Bibai Db
21 Biberach Ha
51 Bibiani Eg
7 Bicester Ff
13 Bida Gg
46 Bidar Fk
89 Biddford Kc
72 Bié Bf
72 Bié Plateau Bf
13 Biel Ba
17 Bielefeld Hb
21 Biella Gd
13 Bielsk Gb
58 Bien Hoa Bb
65 Big Bell Bd
83 Big Rapids Cd
85 Big Spring Fe
32 Biggar Db
7 Biggleswade Ge
28 Bihac Eb
47 Bihar, & st. Kf
34 Bisk Ld
54 Bijapur De
30 Bijeljina Bc
43 Bijar Fb
83 Bikaner Dd
51 Bikin Hb
72 Bikoro Bd
54 Bikura De
7 Bilaspur Jg
48 Bilauk Taung Ra.,
   mts. Ab
26 Bilbao Ba
27 Bilecik Da
34 Bilek Ld
84 Billings Db
27 Biloxi Ce
74 Bimbéreké Ff
9 Bindura Ea
39 Binghamton Hc
48 Binh Dinh Bb
43 Bir Hd
63 Birdum & R. Ec
65 Birdsville Ad
85 Biren Natrum Ed
43 Birjand Hc
24 Birkenhead Dd
30 Bîrlad Fb
7 Birmingham,
   England Fe
87 Birmingham,
   U.S.A. Ce
35 Birnin-Kebbi Ff
35 Birobidzhan Ge
9 Birr Dc
32 Birsk Ld
4 Biscay, Bay of Ef
28 Biscegie Ed
67 Bischofshofen Ed
7 Bishop's
   Stortford Hf
70 Biskra Fb
64 Bismarck Fb
62 Bismarck Arch. Gg
84 Bismarck Sea Gg
30 Bistrita Eb
34 Bitlis Eb
31 Bitola Ce
29 Bitonto Fd

* Renamed Anzali
** Renamed Bandar Törkman
† Renamed Bandar Khomeyni

74 Bitterfontein Bd
29 Bivona Df
5 Biwa, L. Cc
70 Bizerte Fa
28 Bjelovar Fb
10 Bjørnfjell Db
30 Black Crisul, R. Db
4 Black Sea Md
71 Black Volta, R. Eg
62 Blackall Cc
62 Blackball Cc
6 Blackburn Ed
6 Blackpool Dd
9 Blackrock Dd
8 Blackwater, R. Ec
65 Blackwood R. Sad
5 Blagoveshchensk Pd
62 Blair Athol Cc
8 Blair Atholl Ed
8 Blairgowrie Ed
80 Blairmore Cc
20 Blanc, Mont, mt. Ed
60 Blanche L. Aa
84 Bianco, C., U.S.A. Bc
7 Blandford Eg
18 Blankenberge Cc
91 Blanquilla, I. Fd
69 Blantyre Fg
28 Bled Ea
67 Blenheim Ed
70 Blida Fa
8 Blind River Da
23 Blöckenstein Cd
75 Bloemfontein Dc
14 Blois Dd
5 Bloody Foreland Ca
86 Bloomington,Ill. Cc
86 Bloomington, Ind. Be
61 Blue Mountains, see Katoomba Db
62 Blue Mud. B. Aa
39 Blue Nile, Bahr el Azraq, R. Cd
8 Blue Ridge Ef
88 Bluefield Cf
91 Bluefields Bd
7 Bluff Bg
95 Blumenau Ef
6 Blyth Fb
11 Bo Bc
92 Boa Vista Cb
47 Bobbili Jj
71 Bobo-Dioulasso Ef
33 Bobruisk Ee
18 Bocholt Fc
18 Bochum Gc
25 Bodaibo Od
8 Boddam Gc
46 Boden Eb
1 Bodensee, L. Da
46 Bodha Fj
8 Bodjonegoro Cd
7 Bodmin Cg
10 Bodo Bb
27 Bodrum Cb
72 Boende Cd
55 Bofu Bd
74 Bogenfels Bc
12 Bogense Dd
7 Boggeragh Mts. Cd
70 Boghari Fa
7 Bognor Regis Gg
84 Bogo Bd
92 Bogota Bb
92 Bogra Mf
7 Bohemian Forest
82 Bohol, I. Dc
39 Bohotleh De
44 Boise Cc
70 Bojador, C. Cc
11 Boknafjord Bd
28 Bokote Cd
28 Bokungu Cd
44 Bolan Pass Bc
14 Bolbec Dc
61 Boleroo Centre Ab
22 Boleslawiec Cc
22 Boliden Ec
92 Bolivia, rep. Cd
28 Bolobo Bd
28 Bologna Cb
22 Bologne Da
32 Bologoye Fd
35 Bolshevik I. Nb
6 Bolton Ed
27 Bolu Da
28 Bolzano Cb
95 Bom Despacho Fc
28 Boma Ae
14 Bombala Cc
28 Bombay Dj
50 Bomda Dc
72 Bomili Dc
72 Bomongo Bc
70 Bon, C. Ha
91 Bonaire, I. Ed
81 Bonavista Db
72 Bondo Cc

49 Bone, G. of Dd
8 Boness Ed
72 Bongandanga Cc
15 Bonifacio & Str.Bh
56 Bonin Is. Cb
8 Bonn Gd
65 Bonnie Rock Be
71 Bonny, B. of Gh
71 Bonthe Cg
18 Boom Dc
61 Boonah Da
79 Boothia, G. of Ja
78 Boothia Pen. Ha
6 Bootle Dd
8 Bor Eb
73 Borama Ga
43 Borazjan Gd
15 Bordeaux Ce
15 Borders, Co. Fe
60 Bordertown Bc
10 Bordeyri Aa
11 Borgholm Dd
28 Borgo S. Lorenzo Cc
21 Borgo Val di Taro He
21 Borgosesia Gd
32 Borisoglebsk He
33 Borisov Ee
72 Borja Bc
18 Borkum Fa
48 Borneo, I. Cc
12 Bornholm, I. Fa
32 Borovichi Fd
64 Borroloola Fb
72 Boru Branco Fb
43 Borujerd Fc
28 Bosa Bd
28 Bosanska Gradiška Fb
28 Bosnia & Hercegovina, prov.Fb
27 Bosporus, str. Ca
6 Boston, Eng. Hd
86 Boston,U.S.A. Kc
11 Bothnia, G. of Dc
30 Botosani Fb
30 Botou Ff
74 Botswana, st. Cb
18 Bottrop Fc
95 Botucatú Fd
72 Bouaké Dg
20 Bouches du Rhone, dept. Cf
26 Bougainville Hh
64 Bougainville C. Da
65 Boulder Cc
62 Boulia Ac
14 Boulogne Db
56 Bounty Is. Df
20 Bourbonnais, dist. Bc
20 Bourbonne Db
71 Bourem Ee
20 Bourg de Péage Dd
20 Bourg en Bresse Dc
20 Bourg St. Maurice Ed
15 Bourges Ed
20 Bourgogne, dist. Cc
80 Bourke Cb
7 Bournemouth Fg
71 Bourtitimit Ce
2 Bouvet Is. Hh
20 Bovino Ed
62 Bowen Cb
62 Bowling Green Bf
18 Boxtel Ec
7 Boyle Cf
9 Boyne, R. Ec
88 Boyne City Cb
84 Bozeman Db
72 Bozoum Bb
28 Bozüyük Dd
21 Bra Fe
28 Brac, I. Fe
8 Bracadale, & L. Bc
18 Bracebridge Fb
17 Brackley Fe
62 Bradenton Df
6 Bradford, Eng. Fd
89 Bradford,U.S.A.Fd
7 Bradford on Avon Ef
85 Brady Ef
8 Braemar Ec
8 Braes of Angus Dd
28 Braga Aa
28 Bragança, Braz. Ec
28 Bragança, Port. aa
47 Brahmanbaria Ng
47 Brahmani, R. Kh
45 Brahmaputra, R. Mf
61 Braidwood Cc
72 Braila Fc
86 Brainerd Bb
88 Brampton Fc
18 Branch Cb
16 Brandenburg Eb
17 Brandon, Eng. He
80 Brandon, Can. Dc
23 Braniewo Ea
23 Bransk Gb

81 Brantford Ab
64 Brasília Fc
30 Brașov Ec
18 Brasschaat Dc
22 Bratislava Dd
16 Braunschweig (Brunswick)
39 Brava De
9 Bray Ec
92 Brazil, rep. Dc
89 Brazilian Highlands Fc
72 Brazzaville Bd
7 Brecon Df
18 Breda Dc
74 Bredasdorp Cd
21 Bregenz Hb
10 Breiðafjörður Aa
16 Bremen Cb
16 Bremerhaven Cb
13 Bremgarten Ca
21 Bremer P. Kb
21 Bréscia Df
   (Wrocław)
28 Bressanone Ca
8 Bressay, Plaine de, dist. Dc
33 Brest, France Ac
33 Brest, U.S.S.R. De
72 Brestak Fd
72 Breu Branco Ec
61 Brewarrina Ca
23 Brezno Fd
72 Bria Cb
20 Briançon Ed
20 Briare Ab
20 Bricon Ca
21 Bridgeport Jd
89 Bridgeton He
65 Bridgetown, Australia Be
91 Bridgetown, West Indies Fd
13 Bridgewater Cb
7 Bridgwater Ef
20 Brie, Plaine de Cf
84 Brigham Dc
60 Brighton, Eng. Hg
60 Brighton, South Australia Ac
26 Brihuega Ba
29 Brindisi Fd
61 Brisbane Da
7 Bristol, Eng. Ef
89 Bristol, U.S.A. Kd
7 Bristol Channel Df
96 British Antarctic Territory Kc
78 British Columbia, prov. Bc
4 British Isles Ee
7 Brittany, reg. Bc
7 Brixham Dg
22 Brno Dd
8 Broad Law Ee
62 Broad Sound Cc
8 Broadford Bc
72 Brochet Db
62 Brockman Mt. Bc
89 Brockton Kc
89 Brockville Hb
28 Brod Cb
12 Brodersley Cb
79 Brodeur Pen. Ja
23 Brodnica Eb
69 Broken Hill, Australia, Bb
69 Broken Hill, (Kabwe) Zambia Eg
22 Bromberg (Bydgoszcz) Eb
87 Brookhaven De
87 Brookhaven Be
82aBrooks Range Bc
7 Broome Cb
8 Broughty Ferry Fd
75 Brownsville Gf
59 Brownwood Ge
7 Bruay Bd
54 Bruce Mt. Bc
17 Bruck Fe
18 Bruges (Brugge) Cc
16 Brühl Fd
18 Bruxelles, see Brussels
72 Brunette Downs Fb
13 Brunig Pass Cb
67 Brunner Ce
16 Brunswick, see Braunschweig
11 Brunswick B. Cb
95 Brusque Ef
18 Brussels (Brussel, Bruxelles) Dd
16 Bruthen Cc
18 Bruxelles, see Brussels
88 Bryan, Ohio Cd
87 Bryan, Tex. Ae

33 Bryansk Fe
92 Bucaramanga Bb
64 Buccaneer Arch. Cb
71 Buchanan Cg
30 Bucharest Fc
13 Buchs Da
8 Buckhaven Ed
8 Buckie Fc
89 Buckingham, Canada Hb
7 Buckingham &Co., England Ge
7 Buckinghamshire Ge
40 Budapest Bb
46 Budaun Gd
7 Bude Cg
22 Budejovice Cd
33 Budennovsk Hg
10 Budir Ab
28 Budrio Cb
69 Buea Ce
92 Buenaventura Bb
93 Buenos Aires Df
93 Buenos Aires, prov. Cf
89 Buffalo, N.Y. Fc
84 Buffalo, Wyo. Ec
29 Buffaloria Fe
74 Buffels Bc
23 Bug, R., Pol. Fb
33 Bug R., U.S.S.R. Ff
49 Bugsuk, I. Cc
52 Buguma Ke
33 Buguruslan Ke
41 Buheirat-Murrat-el Kubra (Great Bitter Lake) Ce
41 Buheirat-Murrat-el Sughra (Little Bitter Lake) De
73 Bujumbura Dd
62 Buka I. Hh
72 Bukama De
73 Bukavu Dd
72 Bukene Ed
34 Bukhara Jf
48 Bukittingi Bd
73 Bukoba Ed
50 Bulak Cb
49 Bulan Db
46 Bulandshahr Fd
75 Bulawayo Db
5 Bulgaria, rep. Kg
48 Bulloo Downs & L.
63 Bulloo R. Bd
46 Bulls Ed
46 Bulsar Dh
35 Bulun Ph
62 Buna Gh
65 Bunbury Be
72 Buncrana Da
63 Bundaberg Dc
9 Bundoran Cb
8 Bunessan Bd
48 Bungaran Is. Bc
7 Bûr Sa'îd (Port Said) Ca
90 Bûr Taufiq Cf
42 Buraida Ed
43 Buraimi He
70 Buram Cb
39 Buran Dd
85 Burbank Cc
30 Burchun Cb
62 Burdekin R. Cb
27 Burdur Db
47 Burdwan Lg
7 Burg Ab
31 Burgas Fd
75 Burgersdorp Dd
28 Burghead Bc
26 Bûrgos Ba
11 Burgsvik Dd
15 Burgundy, reg. Fd
27 Burhaniye Cb
46 Burhanpur Fh
62 Burketown Ab
84 Burley Dc
88 Burlington, Iowa Bc
88 Burlington, N.C. Ff
88 Burlington, Vt. Jb
37 Burma, Union of, rep. Ng
45 Burma Road Nd
11 Burnett R. Dc
61 Burnie Cd
6 Burnley Fd
40 Burra Ab
61 Burren Junc. Cb
7 Burry Port Cf
27 Bursa Ca
8 Burton-on-Trent Fd
49 Buru, I. Dd
73 Burundi, st. Cd
6 Bury, Lancs. Ed
7 Bury, Suffolk He
7 Bury St. Edmunds He
43 Bushehr Gd

43 Bushire Gd
9 Bushmills Ea
42 Busra Dc
65 Busselton Be
18 Bussum Eb
31 Busto Arsizio Gd
72 Busu-Djanoa Cc
72 Buta Cc
73 Butare Dd
8 Butte Db
48 Butterworth Bc
49 Butung, I. Dd
33 Buturlinovka He
6 Buxton Fd
33 Buynaksk Jg
27 Büyük, R. Cb
30 Buzău Fc
13 Buzuluk Ke
30 Byala Dd
22 Bydgoszcz (Bromberg) Eb
13 Byelgorod Gd
11 Byglandsfjord Bd
79 Bylot I. Ka
96 Byrd Dd
96 Byrd Land Nb
60 Byrock Cb
61 Byron Bay, &C.Da
35 Byrrang Mts. Mb
12 Bytom Ec

94 Caazapa De
49 Cabanatuan Db
54 Cabezas Cc
69 Cabinda Df
81 Cabonga Res. Bb
8 Cabot Str. Cb
26 Cabrera, I. Cb
29 Caccamo Df
29 Cacequi Ee
95 Cachoeira Fd
72 Caconda Bd
28 Cadillac Cb
26 Cadiz & G. Ab
24 Caen Cc
5 Caernannau Mor (Kells) Ec
6 Caernarfon,& B. Cd
7 Caerphilly Df
95 Caetité Gb
49 Cagayan Dc
29 Cagli Dc
29 Cagliari Bc
21 Cagnes-sur-Mer Ff
91 Caguas Ec
15 Cahors Ec
21 Cahnarien Cb
31 Caicos I. Db
8 Cairn Gorm Ec
8 Cairn Toul, mt. Ec
62 Cairns Cb
38 Cairo Cb
7 Cairo Montenotte Ge
71 Calabar Gh
21 Calabria, reg. Fe
14 Calais Db
94 Calama Bd
79 Calamian Group, Is. Cb
30 Calarasi Fc
49 Calbayog Db
47 Calcutta Mg
13 Caldoro Fc
84 Caldwell Cc
74 Caledon Bd
8 Caledonian Canal Dc
94 Caleta Coloso Ad
80 Calgary Cb
92 Cali Bb
90 Californian, Gulf of Bb
82 California, st. Bc
74 Calitzdorp Cd
75 Callabo Gb
9 Callan Dd
92 Callao Bd
29 Caltagirone Ef
29 Caltanissetta Ef
20 Caluire et Cuire Cd
74 Calvinia Bd
91 Camaguey Cb
90 Camargo Cb
20 Camargue, dist. Cf
48 Camau, & pt. Bd
54 Cambay Dg
46 Cambay, G. of Ch
14 Cambodia, rep. Bh
7 Camborne Bg
14 Cambrai Eb
7 Cambridge, Co. He
7 Cambridge,Eng.He
7 Cambridge,Md.He
89 Cambridge, Mass. Kc
66 Cambridge,N.Z.Eb
88 Cambridge, Ohio Ed
64 Cambridge G. Db
61 Camden, Australia Db

89 Camden, U.S.A. He
72 Cameia Cf
28 Camerino De
71 Cameroon Pk. Gh
68 Cameroon, rep. De
92 Cameta Ac
94 Camiri Cd
92 Camocim Ed
62 Camooweal Ab
28 Campagna Ed
29 Campania, reg. Ed
56 Campbell I. Ed
61 Campbell Town, Tas. Cd
44 Campbellpore Cb
81 Campeilton Cb
61 Campbelltown Db
8 Campbeltown Ce
90 Campeche, & G. of Fd
91 Campechuela Cb
60 Camperdown Ec
30 Campina Ec
95 Campinas Fb
71 Campo Gh
94 Campo Gallo Ce
94 Campo Grande Ed
29 Campobasso Ed
95 Campos Gd
95 Campos Belos Fb
95 Campos, mts. Ed
30 Campulung Eb
90 Campulung, Pitesti Ec
80 Camrose Cd
48 Can Tho Bc
76 Canada Hc
7 Canada Ca
92 Canal Zone, Panama Bb
90 Cananea Ba
68 Canary Is. Ac
47 Canaveral, C. Df
7 Canberra Hf
95 Cangussu Fb
75 Canicado Eb
27 Cankiri Da
8 Canna I. Bc
44 Cannahore Df
15 Cannes Gf
8 Cannich Dc
7 Cannstatt Cd
85 Canon City Ed
80 Canora Db
74 Canowindra Cb
61 Canso, C. Cb
7 Cantabrian Mts. Aa
7 Canterbury, England HJ
67 Canterbury, dist., N.Z. Ce
67 Canterbury B. Df
67 Canterbury Plains Ce
87 Canton, Miss. Ce
88 Canton, Ohio Ed
51 Canton, China Fd
56 Canton I. Ed
21 Cantù Hd
91 Cap Haitien Dc
72 Capaia Ce
96 Cape Adare Lb
81 Cape Breton, I. Cb
71 Cape Coast Eg
74 Cape Province Cd
74 Cape Town Bd
2 Cape Verde Is. Fe
62 Cape York Pen. Ba
28 Capraja, I. Be
23 Capri, I. Ed
92 Capricorn Chan. Dc
29 Capua Ed
45 Car Nicobar, I. Hd
30 Caracal Ec
92 Caracas Ca
29 Caransebes Dc
91 Caratasca Lagoon Bc
95 Caratinga Gc
81 Carbonear Db
89 Carbondale Hd
28 Carbonia Bc
15 Carcassonne Ef
84 Carcross Db
91 Cardenas Bb
7 Cardiff Df
7 Cardigan Ce
7 Cardigan B. Ce
82 Cardston Ec
62 Cardwell Cb
30 Carei Db
91 Caribbean Sea Dd
95 Carinhanha Gb
29 Carini De
28 Carioforte Be
9 Carlingford Ec
7 Carlisle, Eng. Ec
85 Carlisle, U.S.A. Gd
7 Carlow & co. Ed
8 Carloway Bb
85 Carlsbad Fe
81 Carmacks Db
11 Carmagnola Fe
80 Carman Ec

7 Carmarthen Cf
40 Carmel, mt. Bc
72 Carmona Be
74 Carnarvon, South Africa Cd
65 Carnarvon, W. Austral. Ac
9 Carndonagh Da
9 Carnoustie Fd
9 Carnsore Pt. Ed
9 Carolina Fb
8 Caroline Is. Cc
30 Carpathians Mts. Eb
6 Carpentaria, Gulf of Aa
20 Carpentras De
9 Carpi Je
9 Carrantuohill, mt. Bc
28 Carrara Cb
9 Carren, L. Cc
9 Carrick-on-Suir Dd
9 Carrickfergus Fb
9 Carrickmacross Ec
71 Carrion Ab
63 Chad, rep. Dd
84 Carson City Cd
8 Carstairs Ee
26 Cartagena, Col. Ba
26 Cartagena, Sp. Bb
91 Cartago Be
67 Carterton Ed
87 Carthage Bd
92 Carúpano Ca
70 Casablanca Db
21 Casale Monferrato Gd
21 Casalpusterlengo Hd
28 Caserta Eb
14 Cashel Dd
61 Casino Da
84 Casper Ec
21 Caspian Sea Kc
88 Cass City Dc
29 Cassino Ed
28 Castel di Sangio Ed
21 Castellammare, Campania Gf
21 Castellammare, Sicily Df
28 Castellón de la Plana Bb
14 Castelo Branco Ab
8 Castlebay Ab
9 Castlebar Bc
9 Castleblaney Eb
9 Castleisland Bd
60 Castlemaine Bc
9 Castlerea Cc
64 Castlereagh B. Fa
9 Castletown Dd
9 Castres Ef
91 Castries Fd
26 Castro Overde Aa
30 Castropol Aa
91 Cat I. Cb
95 Catalão Fc
27 Catalca Ca
28 Catalonia, prov. Ca
94 Catamarca Ce
9 Catanduanes, I. Db
29 Catania Ef
29 Catanzaro Ff
91 Catoche, C. Gd
90 Catorce Dc
89 Catskill Mts. Hd
35 Caucasus Mts. Hg
44 Cauvery, R. Df
91 Cauto, R. Cb
29 Cavaillon Df
95 Caxambú Gd
92 Caxias Ec
95 Caxias do Sul Ee
92 Cayenne Db
28 Cazin Eb
92 Ceara, st. Ec
9 Cebu, & I. Db
9 Cedar City Dd
14 Cedar Falls Bc
86 Cedar Rapids Bc
65 Ceduna Ec
29 Cefalu Ec
29 Cegléd Bb
90 Celaya De
49 Celebes, I. Dc
49 Celebes S. Dc
28 Celje Ea
9 Celle Db
7 Cemaes Hd. Cd
17 Central America Jg
74 Central Makran Ra, mts. Ac
58 Centralia, Ill. Cd
88 Centralia, Wash. Bb
29 Ceram, I. & S. Dd
59 Ceram S. Df

21 Cerea Kd
94 Ceres, Arg. Ce
74 Ceres, C. Prov. Bd
24 Cerignola Ed
27 Cerkeş Eb
28 Cerknica Eb
28 Cervera Ca
29 Cerreto Eb
28 Cesena Db
27 Çeşme Cb
61 Cessnock Db
31 Cetinje Bd
70 Ceuta Da
20 Cevennes, mts. Be
27 Ceyhan Eb
36 Ceylon, see Sri Lanka Mj
52 Chachapoyas Bc
54 Chacharan Cd
74 Chaco Austral Ce
94 Chaco Boreal Cd
49 Chaco Central Cd
6 Chad, I. Dd
63 Chad, rep. Dd
84 Chadron Fc
92 Chagada Gd
3 Chagos Arch. Lf
47 Chakradharpur Kg
56 Chakwal Db
75 Chalantun Gb
46 Chalgaon Eh
20 Chalon-sur-Saône Cc
14 Chalons Dc
51 Chaman Bb
21 Chambéry Cd
75 Chambezi, R. Ef
20 Chamonix Ed
19 Champagne, Plaine de Df
14 Champagne, reg. Fc
48 Chiang Mai Ab
90 Chapa Fd
28 Chiari Bb
21 Chiavenna Hc
51 Chiayi Gd
52 Chiba & pref. Dc
88 Chicago Bd
86 Chicago Heights Bd
82a Chicagof I. Ec
7 Chichester Gf
55 Chichibu Cc
85 Chickasha Gd
84 Chico Bd
91 Chicoa Ed
89 Chicopee Jc
81 Chicoutimi Hb
79 Chidley, C. Lb
73 Chiengi De
21 Chieri Fd
28 Chieti Ec
94 Chiguana Bd
90 Chihuahua Cb
44 Chikmagalur Df
90 Chilapa Ed
63 Childers Dd
85 Childress Fc
93 Chile, rep. Bf
62 Chillagoe Bb
51 Chillan Bf
86 Chillecothe Bd
88 Chillicothe De
13 Chillon Ab
93 Chiloe I. Bg
90 Chilpancingo Ed
7 Chiltern Hills Gf
50 Chimai Ec
34 Chimkent Je
70 Chimo Kc
37 China Nf
91 Chinandega Ad
75 Chinavane Ec
24 Chinchilla Bb
44 Chinchou Gb
50 Chindwin Hb
75 Chinde Fa
45 Chindwin, R. Gd
47 Chinese Rep. Nf
72 Chingola Dd
72 Chinguar Bf
46 Chiniot Dd
20 Chinon Dd
54 Chinsura Ab
45 Chins Division Gd
51 Chinwangtao Fc
28 Chioggia Db
73 Chipata (Fort Jameson) Ef
86 Chippenham Ef
86 Chippewa Falls Bc
92 Chiquimula Ad
72 Chiquiquira Bb
51 Chiriqui, vol. Be
32 Chishmy Lc
21 Chisone, R. Fd
74 Chita Gd
74 Chitado Aa
44 Chitaldrug Df
44 Chitral & dist. Ca
45 Chittagong Gd
44 Chittoor Df
28 Chiusi Cc

21 Chivasso Fd
75 Chobe Swamp Ca
22 Chodziez Db
51 Choibalsan Fb
23 Chojnice Db
19 Choisy Bf
22 Chorzow Ec
94 Chosica Ac
52 Chongjin Ba
52 Chomutov Bc
52 Chongju Bb
55 Chonju Bb
93 Chonos Arch. Bg
55 Choshi Dc
22 Choszczno Cb
50 Chowkow Fc
46 Chotila Cg
67 Christchurch De
* 97 Christmas, I. Bd
51 Christiansted Fc
19 Christiansted Dc
31 Christiansten Fc
7 Christmas, I. Fc
51 Chuanchow Fd
55 Chūbu, dist. Cc
93 Chubut R. & prov. Cg
51 Chuchow Fd
32 Chudskoye, L. Ed
55 Chūgoku, dist. Bc
51 Chuhsien Fd
33 Chukot Ra. Uc
35 Chukot S. Vc
51 Chumatien Fc
52 Chunchon Bb
52 Chungju Bb
51 Chungking Ed
22 Chuquicamata Bd
11 Chur Db
80 Churchill Eb
80 Churchill, C. Eb
80 Churchill Pk. Bb
80 Churchill, R. Eb
35 Chusovoi Ld
32 Chusovoi Ld
21 Cicero Bd
27 Cide Da
23 Ciechanów Fb
51 Ciego de Avila Cb
92 Cienaga Ba
91 Cienfuegos Bb
21 Cilian Gates Db
7 Cinderford Ef
14 Cinto, mt. Ag
7 Cirencester Ff
90 Citlaltepetl, mt. Ed
28 Citta della Pieve Cc
29 Cittanova Fe
92 Ciudad Bolivar Cb
90 Ciudad del Carmen Fd
90 Ciudad Garcia Salinas Dc
90 Ciudad Juarez Ca
90 Ciudad Madero Ec
90 Ciudad Mante Ec
90 Ciudad Obregon Cb
26 Ciudad Real Bb
26 Ciudad Rodrigo Aa
90 Ciudad Victoria Ec
28 Cividale Da
28 Civitanova Dc
29 Civitavecchia Cc
47 Civril Cb
7 Clacton-on-Sea Jf
20 Clairvaux De
20 Clamecy Bb
7 Clanwilliam Bd
9 Clara Dc
14 Claraville Dc
60 Clare Ab
9 Clare, co. Bd
9 Clare I. Ic
89 Claremont Jc
9 Claremorris Cc
88 Clarksburg Ee
87 Clarksdale Be
88 Clarksville Bf
16 Claustal Zellerfeld
85 Clayton Fd
9 Clear, I. Be
12 Clermont Cc
20 Clermont Ferrand
88 Cleveland Ed
62 Cleveland C. Cb
9 Clifden, fne. Ad
9 Clifden, N.Z. Ag
80 Clinton, Can. Bb
67 Clinton, N.Z. Bg
89 Clinton, U.S.A. Gd
57 Clipperton I. Hc
9 Clona Kilty Bc
92 Cloncurry Bc
9 Cloncurry R. Bb
9 Clones Db
29 Clonmel Dd
9 Clontarf Ec
18 Cloppenburg Hb
86 Cloquet Bb
85 Clovis Fe
14 Cluj Dd
20 Cluses Ec
67 Clyde Bf
67 Clyde, R. Ee

* Renamed Kiritimati

8 Clydebank De
94 Coast Ra., Chile Be
84 Coast Ra., U.S.A.
8 Coatbridge De
79 Coat's I. Jb
94 Coats Coast Ab
90 Coatzacoalcos Fd
81 Cobalt Bd
60 Cobar Cb
9 Cobh Ce
81 Cobourg Bb
17 Coburg Dc
44 Cocanada Ee
44 Cochabamba Bc
44 Cochin Dg
81 Cochrane Ab
60 Cockburn Bb
3 Cocos (Keeling) Is. Mf
89 Cod, C. Kd
61 Coff's Harbour Db
89 Cognac Ce
89 Cohoes Jc
60 Cohuna Bc
44 Coimbatore Df
26 Coimbra Aa
32 Col du Pt. St. Bernard Ed
60 Colac Bc
7 Colchester Hf
80 Coleman Cc
9 Coleraine, Australia Be
9 Coleraine, Ire. Ea
90 Colima & mt. Dd
8 Coll, I. Bd
94 Collahuasi Bd
85 Collie Be
64 Collier B. Cb
8 Collingwood, Canada Eb
66 Collingwood, N.Z. Dd
62 Colmar Dd
18 Cologne (Köln) Gd
91 Colombia Fd
84 Colombia, rep. Bb
24 Colombo Dg
88 Columbus De
62 Colon, Panama Ce
91 Colon, W. Ind. Bb
8 Colonsay, I. Bd
85 Colorado Desert Ce
85 Colorado Plat. Dd
85 Colorado, R. Cd
82 Colorado, st. Cc
84 Colorado Springs Fd
87 Columbia, S.C. De
87 Columbia, Tenn.Bg
83 Columbia, Dist. of Fc
84 Columbia, R. Bb
72 Columbus Ae
87 Columbus, Ga. De
88 Columbus, Ind. Ce
87 Columbus, Miss.Ce
28 Comacchio Db
94 Comayagua Ad
45 Comilla Gd
34 Commentry Ac
34 Communism Pk. Kf
21 Como Hd
21 Como, L. di Hd
93 Comodoro Rivadavia Cg
93 Comodoro Rivadavia, prov. Cg
44 Comorin, C. Dg
44 Comoro, is. Gd
90 Comox Bc
19 Compiegne Bc
71 Conakry Cg
93 Concepción,Arg.Df
94 Concepción, Bol.Cc
94 Concepción, Paraguay Da
85 Concepción, C. Be
90 Concepción del Oro Dc
94 Concepción, L. Cc
93 Conception Bf
90 Conchos, R. Cb
87 Concord, N.C. Dd
89 Concord, N.H. Kc
94 Concordia, Arg. Df
83 Concordia, U.S.A. Gd
93 Condamine R. Cd
95 Condeuba Gd
91 Condobolin Cb
48 Condore Is. Bc
14 Confolens Dd
92 Congo, rep. De
9 Congo (ex. Belg.) Rep. see Zaire
Ef
37 Congo, R. Dd
9 Connacht, prov. Bc
88 Conneaut Ed
83 Connecticut, st. Fb

8 Connel Cd
9 Connemara Bc
88 Connersville Ce
30 Constanta Gd
70 Constantine Ga
11 Contookoo Fg
87 Conway Bd
8 Conwy Dd
9 Conwy, R. Dd
64 Cooch Behar Me
57 Cook Is. Me
67 Cook, Mt. Ce
67 Cook Str. Ed
62 Cooktown Cb
9 Cookstown Eb
61 Coolangatta Ce
65 Coolgardie Ce
61 Cooma Cc
66 Coonamble Cb
60 Coongoola Ca
63 Cooper Cr. Ad
44 Coorg, St. Df
61 Cootamundra Cb
61 Cootehill Db
12 Copenhagen Rd
94 Copiapo Ae
87 Copley Ab
81 Coppercliff Ab
78 Coppermine Fb
30 Corabia Ed
56 Coral Sea Cd
29 Corato Fd
19 Corbeil Essonnes Bf
28 Corbin Cf
94 Córdoba, Arg. Cf
26 Córdoba, Sp. Bb
93 Córdoba, prov. Cf
82 Cordova Db
27 Corfu, see Kérkira Ab
27 Corinth Cb
9 Cork & co. Ce
9 Cork Harbour Ce
81 Corner Brook Db
81 Cornwall Ab
7 Cornwall, co. Cg
94 Corocoro Bc
94 Coroico Bc
95 Coromandel Eb
64 Coromandel Coast Ef
23 Coronation G. Fb
93 Coronel Pringles Cf
60 Corowa Cc
60 Corozal Gd
85 Corpus Christi Gf
94 Corque Bc
94 Corrientes Cc
94 Corrientes, C. Cc
15 Corse-du-Sud, dept.Bh
15 Corsica (Corse) I.
87 Corsicana Ae
28 Cortina Da
89 Cortland Gc
21 Cortona Cc
27 Corum Da
95 Corumba, Fed. Dist., Braz. Fc
94 Corumba Goias, Brazil Dc
94 Corvallis Bd
90 Cosamaloapan Ed
20 Cosenza Fe
20 Cosne Ab
64 Cossack Bc
93 Costa Rica, rep. Bd
49 Cotabato Dc
94 Cotagaita Bd
20 Côte d'Or, ridge & dept. Cb
7 Cotswold Hills Ef
20 Cottiennes, Alpes, mts. Bc
16 Cottbus Fc
86 Council Bluffs Ac
20 Cours Cc
14 Coutances Cc
7 Coventry Fe
26 Covilha Aa
88 Covington Ce
65 Cowan L. Ce
8 Cowdenbeath Ed
7 Cowes Fg
61 Cowra Cb
95 Coxim Ec
95 Cozumel, I. Gd
15 Cracow Dd
61 Cradle Mt. Dd
30 Craiova Dc
13 Crail Bb
80 Cranbrook Dd
92 Crateus Ec
88 Crawfordsville Bd
14 Crécy Dc
19 Creil Be
21 Crema Hd
21 Cremona Jd
28 Cres, I. Eb

86 Creston Bc
27 Crete (Kriti) L. Bb
27 Crete, Sea of Cb
62 Crewe Kd
6 Crewe Eg
95 Criciuma Fe
8 Crieff Ed
33 Crimea Ff
9 Croagh Patrick, mt. Bc
28 Croatia, prov. Eb
87 Crockett Ae
75 Crocodile, R. Db
8 Cromarty Dc
6 Cromer Je
67 Cromwell Bf
86 Crookston Ab
74 Cross, C. Ab
62 Crotone Fe
62 Croydon, Australia Bb
7 Croydon, Eng. Gf
3 Crozet, Is. Kh
95 Cruz Aita Ee
95 Cruzeiro Gd
92 Cruzeiro do Sul Bc
69 Cuando, R. Bd
74 Cuangar Ab
91 Cuba, I. & rep. Cb
27 Cubuk Da
91 Cúcuta Bb
44 Cuddalore Df
44 Cuddapah Df
65 Cue Bd
94 Cuenca Bc
26 Cuenca Bb
90 Cuernavaca Ed
26 Cuevas de Vera Bb
94 Cuevo Cd
90 Cuiabá Dc
55 Cuillin Hills Bc
90 Culiacan Cc
90 Culoz Dd
67 Culverden De
60 Cumberland, Canada Bc
89 Cumberland, U.S.A. Fc
79 Cumberland Pen. Lb
79 Cumberland Sd. Lb
6 Cumbria, Co. Ec
8 Cumnock De
27 Cumra Db
69 Cunene, R. Aa
9 Cunnamulla Ca
60 Curaçao Ca
91 Curaçao, I. Ed
91 Curaçao I. Ca
93 Curico Bf
62 Curitiba Fe
87 Curtis I. Dc
7 Cushing Ad
77 Cusset Bc
47 Cuttack Ke
16 Cuxhaven Cb
92 Cuyo Is. Db
92 Cuzco Bd
27 Cyclades, see Kikladhes Bb
27 Cyprus, I. Db
47 Czechoslovakia Jf
23 Czeremcha Gb
22 Czestochowa Ec

74 Damaraland, dist. Bb
40 Damascus (Esh Sham) Cc
73 Dambacha Fa
43 Damghan Gb
38 Damietta Cb
64 Dampier Bc
64 Dampier Arch. Bc
64 Dampier Land Cb
49 Dampier Str. Ef
71 Dan Gora Gf
89 Danbury Jd
47 Dandeldhura Hd
60 Danenong Cc
11 Dannemora Dc
66 Dannevirke Fd
30 Danube Ee
88 Danville, Ill. Bd
88 Danville, Ky. Cf
88 Danville, Va. Ff
22 Danzig (Gdansk) Ea
43 Dar'a Cc
73 Dar-es-Salaam Fe
47 Darbhanga Ke
43 Darcan Jd.
47 Dardanelles, str. Ca
64 Dargaville Da
47 Darjeeling Me
63 Darling Downs Dd
63 Darling Ra. Be
60 Darling R. Bb
6 Darlington Fc
22 Darlowo Da
19 Darmstadt He
60 Darnick Bb
96 Darnley, Cape Ec
7 Dartmoor Cg
81 Dartmouth, Canada Cb
7 Dartmouth, England Dg
62 Daru Fi
94 Darwin Ea
43 Daryacheh-y-Namak L. Gc
43 Daryacheh-ye-Sistan, L. Jc
43 Dasht-i-Kavir, reg. Gb
43 Dasht-e-Lut, reg. Hc
46 Datia Gf
32 Daugavpils Ed
39 Daulis Ee
80 Dauphin Eb
20 Dauphine, dist. Dd
94 Davao, & G. Dc
86 Davenport Bc
92 David Ab
79 Davis Str. Ma
13 Davos Db
43 Dawiatabad Hd
7 Dawlish Dg
72 Dawson Db
80 Dawson Creek Bb
62 Dawson R. Cc
65 Day Dawn Bd
94 Dayton, Can. Cb
83 Dayton, U.S.A. Ce
77 Daytona Beach Df
74 De Aar Cd
72 De Behagle Bb
35 De Long Is. Sb
28 De Pere Ab
87 De Soto Bd
40 Dead Sea Bd
65 Deakin De
7 Deal Hj
88 Dearborn Dc
85 Death Valley Cd
73 Debe Habe Hf
73 Debica Fc
39 Debra Tabor Cd
73 Debre Markos Fa
30 Debrecen Cb
87 Decatur, Ala. Ce
47 Decatur, Ga. De
88 Decatur, Ill. Cd
88 Decatur, Ind. Dd
44 Deccan, plat. Df
2 Deception Bc
6 Dee, R. Ed
48 Defiance Cd
6 Dehra Dun Gc
72 Dem Zubeir Db
70 Dej Db
77 Dekese Cd
86 Del Rio Ff
8 Delagoa B. Ec
83 Delaware Ec
8 Delaware, st. Fc
33 Delemont Ba
15 Delft Db
44 Deitziji La
73 Delgado ,L.F. Gf
38 Deigo Cc

46 Delhi Fd
27 Deice R. Fb
90 Delicias Cb
20 Delle Fb
18 Delmenhorst Ha
61 Deloraine Cd
43 Delvada mt. Cb
72 Demba Ce
92 Demerara Db
85 Deming Ee
64 Demonstre Ca
87 Demopolis Ce
18 Den Helder Db
6 Denbigh Dd
62 Denham Ra. Cc
26 Denia Cb
60 Deniliquin Bc
27 Denizli Cb
85 Denmark, Australia Be
4 Denmark, King.Gd
8 Denny Ed
62 D'Entrecasteaux Is. Hh
65 D'Entrecasteaux Pt.
84 Denver Ed
46 Deolali Dj
47 Deoria Je
46 Dera Ghazi Khan Cf
46 Dera Ismail Khan Cg
33 Derbent Jg
85 Derby, Austral. Cb
6 Derby, co., Eng. Fd
9 Derg, L. Cd
18 Derna Eb
39 Derudeb Cd
28 Derwenta Fb
6 Derwent, R., Gd
86 Des Moines Bc
73 Dese Fa
31 Desenzano del Garda Jd
43 Desna R. Ee
71 Dessa Ff
18 Dessau Ec
18 Detmold Hc
18 Detroit Dc
13 Deurne, Belg. Dc
18 Deurne, Neth. Dc
30 Deva Dc
18 Deventer Fb
6 Deveron Fc
7 Devon, co. Dg
79 Devon, I. Ja
7 Devonport, Eng.Cg
66 Devonport, N.Z. Eb
61 Devonport, Tas. Cd
46 Dewas Fg
32 Dhaba Dd
43 Dhahran Gd
47 Dhamtari Hh
47 Dhangarbi Hd
43 Dhank He
47 Dharwar Le
47 Dhaulagiri, mt. Jd
47 Dhekelia Ab
27 Dhidhimótikhon Ca
30 Dholpur Fe
14 Dhrol Cg
47 Dhubri Me
46 Dhulia Eh
95 Diamantina Gc
28 Diamantina R. Bc
72 Dibaya Ce
72 Dibaya-Lubue Bd
73 Dibbi Gc
45 Dibrugarh Gc
34 Dickinson Fb
73 Dick's Hd. Gd
34 Dickson I. Kb
7 Didcot Ff
* 69 Diego Suarez Gg
48 Dien Bien Phu Ba
14 Dieppe Dc
19 Differdange Ee
81 Digby Cb
20 Digne Ee
20 Digoin Bc
20 Dijon Db
33 Dikhtau Hg
27 Dikili Cb
68 Dikwa Bd
43 Dilam Fe
19 Dili Gd
72 Dilolo Df
11 Dimbokro Eg
60 Dimboola Bc
31 Dimitrovgrad Db
31 Dimitrovo Dd
49 Dinagat L. Db
47 Dinajpur Mf
14 Dinan Bc
14 Dinard Bc
73 Dincha Fb
9 Dingle Bay Ad
73 Dinguiraye Cf
8 Dingwall Dc
71 Diorbet Bf
28 Dir, dist. Fb

* Renamed Kaga Bandoro

* Renamed Antsiranana

73 Dire Dawa Gb
65 Dirk Hartog I. Ad
64 Disappointment
L. Gc
79 Disko, I. Mb
46 Diu Ch
95 Divinopotis Gd
86 Dixon Cc
42 Diyarbakir Eb
43 Dizak Jd
49 Djajapura
(Sukarnapura) Gf
48 Djakarta Bd
70 Djanet
(Ft. Charlet) Gd
71 Djang Hg
48 Djatinegara Bd
48 Djember Cd
70 Djerba I. Hb
73 Djerid, Chott Gb
73 Djibouti, st. Ga
73 Djidjelli Ga
·2 Djolu Cc
10 Djupivogur Cb
32 Dmitrov Gd
33 Dnepr (Dnieper),
R. Fe
33 Dneprodzer-
hinsk Ff
33 Dnepropetrovsk Ff
33 Dnestr (Dniester),
R. Ef
28 Doboj Gb
30 Dobrogea, dist. Gc
22 Dobrzyn Bb
23 Dobšiná Fd
7 Dodecaanese, Is. Cb
5 Dodge City Fd
7 Dodman Pt. Cg
73 Dodoma Fe
18 Doetinchem Fb
46 Dohad Eg
18 Doi Luang, mts. Bb
81 Dolbeau Bb
20 Dôle Db
7 Dolgellau De
72 Dolisie Ad
93 Dolores Df
11 Dombas Bc
72 Dombe Grande Af
20 Dombes, dist. Cc
32 Domesnes Dd
91 Dominica, I. Fc
71 Dominican Rep. Dc
21 Domodossola Gc
7 Don R. Ge
33 Don R. Hf
7 Doncaster Fd
7 Dondo Ae
44 Dondra Head Dg
7 Donegal, & co. Cb
7 Donegal B. Cb
33 Donetsk Gf
83 Dongara Ad
34 Dongola Cd
73 Dongou Be
6 Donnelly's
Crossing Da
20 Donzère Ce
40 Dor (Tantura) Bc
21 Dora Baltea, R. Fd
20 Dora Riparia,
R. Ed
7 Dorchester Eg
15 Dordogne, R. De
18 Dordrecht Dc
10 Dore, R. Bd
8 Dores Dc
74 Doring R. Bd
71 Dornbirn Hb
8 Dornoch Dc
30 Dorohoi Fb
10 Dorotea Dc
7 Dorset, co. Eg
18 Dorsten Fc
71 Dortmund Gc
71 Dosso Ff
7 Dothan Ce
19 Douai Denain Bd
71 Douala Gh
7 Doubs, R. &
dept.
6 Doubtful I. B. Be
81 Doucet Bb
6 Douglas, Eng. Cc
85 Douglas, U.S.A. Ae
72 Doumé Gh
7 Dover, Eng. Hf
89 Dover, U.S.A. Kc
7 Dover, Str. of Jg
11 Doverfjell Bc
73 Dowa Ef
74 Dowagiac Bc
9 Down, Co. Fb
9 Downpatrick Fb
70 Dra, R. Dc
20 Drac, R. De
33 Dragobych Df
15 Draguignan Gf
96 Drake Passage Qd
33 Drakensberg,
mts. Dc
27 Dráma

11 Drammen Cd
19 Dravell Bf
22 Drawsko Cf
16 Dresden Ec
30 Drina, R. Bc
9 Drogheda Ec
9 Droichead Dc
9 Dromahair Cb
20 Drôme, R. &
dept.
47 Drug Hh
80 Drumheller Cb
20 Drummond I. Db
62 Drummond Ra. Cc
89 Drummondville Jb
96 Drygalski I. Fc
19 Du Bois Ed
30 Dubawnt, L. Da
80 Dubawnt, R. Da
61 Dubbo Cb
9 Dublin, Ire. Ec
9 Dublin, U.S.A. De
9 Dublin, Co. Ec
33 Dubovka Hf
71 Dubréka Cg
28 Dubrovnik Ac
62 Duchess Ac
34 Dudinka Lc
7 Dudley Ee
26 Duero, R. Aa
28 Dugiotok, I. Eb
62 Duifken Pt. Ba
18 Duisburg Fb
53 Duk Fadiat Ed
71 Duku Hf
9 Dulawan Dc
86 Duluth Bb
9 Duma Cc
49 Dumaran, I. Cb
9 Dumbarton De
8 Dumfries Ee
8 Dumfries &
Galloway,Co. De
20 Dümmer See Hb
30 Dun Laoghaire Ec
30 Duna, R. Bb
30 Dunafoldvár Bb
30 Dunaujvaros Bb
67 Dunback Cf
8 Dunbar Fd
3 Dunbarton Dd
25 Duncan Ge
9 Dundalk Eb
8 Dundee, Nat. Ec
3 Dundee, Scot. Fd
*72 Dundo Cf
20 Dunedin Cf
8 Dunfermline Ed
9 Dungannon Eb
92 Dungarpur Dg
19 Dungarvan, B. Dd
7 Dungeness Hg
19 Dungloe Cb
23 Dunkeld Ed
7 Dunkery Beacon Df
14 Dunkirk, Fr. Eb
88 Dunkirk, U.S.A. Fc
9 Dunnaway Bae
8 Duns Fe
7 Dunstable Gf
61 Dunwich Da
20 Durance, R. De
90 Durango, Mex. Dc
85 Durango,
U.S.A. Ed
87 Durant Ae
75 Durant Ad
18 Düren Ed
6 Durham, Eng. Fc
89 Durham, U.S.A. Ff
8 Durham, Co. Fc
8 Durness Db
31 Durres Bd
27 Dursunbey Cf
34 Dushanbe Jf
18 Düsseldorf Fc
83c Dutch Harbor Ea
81 Duverge Dc
27 Düzce Db
3 Dvina Eb
46 Dwarka Bg
8 Dyceon Fc
7 Dyfed, Co. Cf
51 Dzamyn Ude Fb
13 Dzaudzhikau, see
Ordzhonikidze
32 Dzerzhinsk Hd
34 Dzhambul Ke
33 Dzhankoi Ff
73 Dzhugdzhur Ra.,
18 Dzialdow, R. Ba
23 Dzialdowo Fb
51 Dzun-Mod Eb
23 Dzungaria, reg. Cb

89 Eackawana Fc
23 East Bedskids,
mts.
45 East Bengal Gd
88 East Chicago Bd
18 East Frisian Is. Ga

7 East Grinstead Gf
8 East Linton Fe
88 East Liverpool Ed
75 East London Ed
8 E. Lothian, Co. Fe
18 East Schelde, R. Cc
35 East Siberian S. Tb
7 East Sussex,
Co. Fg
7 Eastbourne,
England Hg
67 Eastbourne,
N.Z. Ed
57 Easter I. He
44 Eastern Ghats,
mts. Df
52 Eastleigh Fg
81 Eastmain Ba
89 Easton Hd
30 Eau Claire Bc
7 Ebbw Vale Df
12 Ebeltoft Dc
19 Eberbach Je
16 Eberswalde Eb
21 Ebingen Ha
71 Ebolowa Hh
26 Ebro, R. Ca
78 Echo Bay Fb
8 Eccleshan Ee
92 Ecuador, rep. Bc
39 Ed Damer Cd
39 Ed Debba Cd
38 Ed Dirr Cc
39 Ed Dueim Cd
18 Edam Eb
18 Ede Eb
71 Edéa Hh
65 Edel Land Ad
75 Edenburg Dc
9 Edenderry Ec
18 Eder See Hd
82 Edessa Ba
60 Edhuca Bc
67 Edievale Bf
8 Edinburgh Ed
27 Edirne Ca
50 Edmonton Cb
81 Edmundston Cb
75 Edremit Cb
80 Edson Cb
18 Eekloo Cc
29 Egadi Is. Df
30 Eger Cb
11 Egersund, see
Eigersund Bd
23 Eglisau Ca
10 Egridir Db
27 Egridir, L. Db
92 Egua Cb
68 Egypt, rep. Fc
55 Ehime, pref. Bd
11 Eigersund
(Egersund) Bd
8 Eigg I. Bd
44 Eight Degree
Chan. Cg
64 Eighty Mile
Beach Cb
39 Eil De
62 Einasleigh &
R. Bb
73 Eindhoven Ec
13 Einsiedeln Ca
37 Eisenach Dc
16 Eisenhütten-
stadt Fb
7 Eisleben Db
76 Eketahuna Ed
71 El Aaiun Cc
73 El Agowa Da
38 El Arish Cc
85 El Centro Cd
94 El Cerro Cc
94 El Chorro Cd
90 El Cuyo Gd
90 El Diaz Gd
70 El Djouf Dd
67 El Dorad Ec
18 El Faiyûm Cc
61 El Fasher Kd
61 El Fuerte Cb
91 El Gallo Ad
68 El Geneina Kd
70 El Goléa Fb
70 El Jadida Db
67 El Jauf Dc
73 El Jebelein Ea
81 El Juwara Bd
38 El Kamlin Cd
34 El Khandaq Cd
38 El Khârga Cc
39 El Muglad Bd
36 El Obeid Cd
83 El Odaiya Ed
70 El Oued Gb
71 El Oulig Fe
41 El Qantara Cc
41 El Suweis
(Suez) Cc
94 El Zappallar Dg
42 Elazig Db
28 Elba. I. Cc
23 Elbag Ea

31 Elbasan Ce
16 Elbe, R. Cb
33 Elbrus, mt. Hg
43 Elburz, mts. Gb
73 Eldoret Fc
85 Electra Ge
29 Elena Dc
74 Elephant, R. Bb
85 Elephant Butte
Reservoir Ee
91 Eleuthera I. Ca
8 Elgin Ec
73 Elgon, mt. Fc
39 Elhur De
8 Elie Fd
72 Elila, R. Dd
60 Elizabeth,
Australia Ab
89 Elizabeth,
U.S.A. Hd
89 Elizabeth City Gf
88 Elizabethton Df
88 Elkhart Cd
31 Elkhovo Fd
8 Elkins Fe
84 Elko Cc
84 Ellensburg Bb
79 Ellesmere I. Ja
75 Elliot Dd
45 Ellon Fc
44 Ellore Ec
76 Ellsworth Land Pb
27 Elmali Cb
89 Elmira Gc
18 Elmshorn Ja
90 Elota, R. Cc
46 Eltham Bc
88 Elwood Cd
7 Ely, Eng. He
89 Ely, U.S.A. Bb
88 Elyria Dd
94 Embarcacion Cd
73 Embu Fd
18 Emden Ga
22 Emerald Cc
80 Emerson Ec
61 Emmaville Da
18 Emmen Fb
73 Emmerich Fc
13 Emmental dist. Bb
18 Emmerich Fc
75 Empangeni Ec
18 Empedrado De
18 Empoli Cc
86 Emporia, Kan. Ad
89 Emporia, Va. Gf
62 Emu Park Dc
39 En Nahud Bd
94 Encarnación De
60 Encounter B. Ac
27 Emmali Cb
78 Emmerhch Fc
95 Encruzilhada Ef
49 Ende Dd
82 Endeavour Str. Ba
12 Endelave I. Dd
56 Enderbury I. Ed
65 Enderby Land Dc
89 Enderby Land Dc
89 Endicott Gf
62 Enes Fg
13 Engadin Eb
13 Engelberg Cb
33 Engels Je
6-7 England, King.
81 Englehart Ab
47 English Bazar Mf
85 Enid Gd
*75 Enkeldoorn Db
18 Enkhuizen Eb
29 Enna Ef
9 Ennis Bd
9 Enniscorthy Ed
9 Enniskillen Db
9 Enschede Fb
73 Entebbe Fc
94 Entre Rios Df
71 Enugu Gg
71 Enugu Ezike Gg
62 Epa Gb
7 Epernay Ec
73 Epinal Gc
27 Epirus, dist. Bb
7 Epping Hf
71 Equatorial Guinea,
st. Gh
73 Er Rahad Cd
91 Erba Hd
27 Erciyas, mts. Eb
27 Ereğli, Turkey Da
27 Ereğli, Turkey Db
16 Erfurt Dc
70 Erg Chech Ed
73 Erg Edehan Hc
18 Erhlein Fb
88 Erie Dc
88 Erie, L. Dc
88 Erie, L. Dc
36 Erimo, C. Db
27 Erlangen Dd
65 Eridunda Ed
75 Ermelo Ec
46 Ernakulam Dg
9 Erne, L. Db
44 Erode Df

74 Erundu Bb
22 Erz Gebirge (Ore)
Mts. Bc
42 Erzincan Db
42 Erzurum Eb
74 Esan, C. Db
27 Esbjerg Bd
88 Escanaba Bb
19 Esch Ee
18 Eschweiler Fd
26 Escorial Ba
90 Escuinapa de
Hidalgo Dc
43 Esfahan Gc
40 Esh Sham
(Damascus) Dc
76 Eshowe Ec
10 Eskifjördur Ca
11 Eskilstuna Dd
27 Eskişehir Db
65 Esperance Ce
26 Espichet, C. Ab
22 Espinho Aa
92 Espirito Santo,
prov. Ed
80 Esquimalt Bd
70 Essaouira Db
33 Essau Db
18 Essen Fc
7 Essex, co. Hf
19 Esslingen Jf
14 Essonne, dept. Ec
93 Estados, I. de los
(Staten I.) Ch
75 Estcourt Dc
30 Estergom Bb
80 Estevan Dc
32 Estonia, S.S.R. Ed
76 Estrela, Sa. da Aa
24 Estremadura,
prov. Bb
26 Estremoz Bb
19 Etaples Ad
46 Etawah De
68 Ethiopia, st. Fe
8 Etive, L. Cd
29 Etna, Mt. Ef
8 Eton Cc
74 Etosha Pan Ba
88 Ettrick Ee
94 Eucalyptus Bc
95 Eucla De
88 Euclid Ed
60 Eudunda Ab
84 Eugene Bc
60 Eulo Ba
43 Euphrates, R. Fc
84 Eureka Bc
12 Euroa Cc
2 Europe, cont. Hc
18 Euroopoort Dc
17 Euston Eb
88 Evanston Bc
88 Evansville Bf
65 Everard L. Ab
47 Everest, Mt. Le
87 Everglades Df
88 Everett Bb
7 Evesham Fe
20 Evian Eb
26 Évora Ab
14 Evreux Dc
27 Evrykhou Db
27 Evvoia, I. Bb
88 Ewab Is. Ed
94 Exaltación Bb
7 Exeter Dg
7 Exmoor Dd
7 Exmouth Dg
64 Exmouth G. Ac
73 Eyasi, L. Ed
8 Eyemouth Fe
10 Eyrabakki Ab
60 Eyre De
8 Eyre L. Ad
65 Eyre Peninsula Ab
7 Ezine Cb

28 Fabriano Dc
54 Fachi He
68 Fada Ad
28 Faenza Cb
50 Fagaras Ec
83 Fair I. Ga
28 Fairbanks Db
67 Fairlie Cf
22 Faizabad,
Afghanistan Gb
47 Faizabad, India Je
47 Fakfak Ef
90 Falcon Dam Eb
94 Falkland Is. Dh
93 Falkland Is.
Dependencies Ea
89 Fall River Kd
7 Falmouth Bg
74 False Ts. Bd
12 Falster, I. Ee
11 Falun Dd
27 Famagusta Db
79 Famaka Ed
43 Famaka Cd
43 Fannan Is. Ba
28 Fano Dc

* Renamed Luachimo

* Renamed Chivhu

12 Fanö, I. Bd
43 Fanuch, Hd
69 Farafangana Gh
38 Farafra Oasis Bc
44 Farah Ab
39 Farasan, Is. Dd
7 Fareham Fg
78 Farewell, C. Nc
84 Fargo Fd
86 Fairbault Bc
71 Farim Bf
80 Farina Aa
7 Farnborough Gf
7 Farnham Gf
26 Faro, Portugal Ab
11 Farö, Sweden Dd
27 Fársala Bb
43 Farsund Bd
43 Fasa Gd
9 Fastnet I. Be
46 Fatehgarh (Far-rukhabad) Ge
46 Fatehpur, Raj. Ee
47 Fatehpur, Ut. P. Hf
51 Patshan Fd
27 Favara Df
10 Faxaflói Ab
47 Fayetteville Cd
46 Fazilka Dc
70 F'Dérik (Fort Gouraud) Cd
67 Featherston Ed
66 Feilding Ed
61 Feldkirch Hb
90 Felipe Carillo Puerto Gd
7 Felixstowe Jf
28 Feltre Ca
51 Fengkieh Ec
57 Fenyang Ec
33 Feodosiya Gf
9 Fermanagh, Co. Db
28 Fermo Dc
46 Ferozepore Ec
28 Ferrara Cb
20 Ferrières Aa
26 Ferrol Aa
70 Fès Db
90 Fesmilo Dc
8 Fetlar Inset
69 Fianarantsoa Gh
25 Ficksburg Dc
21 Fidenza Je
3 Fife, co. Ed
26 Figueras Ca
74 Figuig Eb
66 Fiji Is. Gk
71 Filyas Da
27 Filyos, R. Da
21 Finale Ligure Ec
8 Findhorn Ec
66 Findlay Dd
56 Finisterre, C. Aa
7 Finland, Rep. Lc
11 Finland, G. of Ed
80 Finlay Forks Bb
11 Finnmark, dist. Eb
10 Finnsnes Db
62 Finschhafen Gh
73 Finsteraarhorn, mt. Bb
9 Fintona Db
21 Florenzuola d'Arda He
71 Firat (Euphrates), R. Db
28 Firenze see Florence
70 Firminy Cd
46 Firozabad Ge
7 Fishguard Cf
73 Fitchburg Kc
46 FitzroyCrossing Db
21 Fivizzano Je
28 Flagstaff Dd
Flandre Orientale, prov.
18 Flandres, Plaines des Cc
13 Flateyr Aa
62 Flattery C. Cb
6 Fleetwood Dd
11 Flekkefjord Bd
74 Flensburg Ca
80 Flin Flon Db
65 Flinders Is. Be
63 Flinders I. Cc
65 Flinders Ras. Ab
62 Flinders R. Bb
88 Flint Dc
28 Florence Ala. Cc
46 Florence, S.C. Ee
28 Florence (Firenze) Cb
94 Florencia Cd
49 Flores, I. Dd
45 Flores S. Cd
95 Florianópolis Fe
87 Florida, Ib. Df
83 Florida, st. Ed
70 Florida Keys Df

91 Florida Str. Bb
27 Florina Ba
11 Florö Bd
13 Fluela P. Db
18 Flushing (Vlissingen) Cc
62 Fly R. Fh
30 Focşani Fc
62 Fofo Fofo Gh
28 Foggia Ed
9 Foix Df
11 Folda Cc
28 Foligno Dc
7 Folkestone Hj
28 Follonica Cc
80 Fond du Lac, Canada Db
86 Fond du Lac, U.S.A. Cc
9 Fonseca, G. of Ad
19 Fontainebleau Bf
51 Foochow Fd
19 Forbach Fe
81 Forbes Cb
87 Fordyce Be
71 Forécariah Cg
79 Forel, Mt. Ob
20 Forez, Monts du Bd
8 Forfar Fd
8 Forii Db
26 Formentera, I. Cb
Formosa I., see Taiwan
94 Formosa, Argentina De
95 Formosa, Braz. Fc
8 Forres Ed
20 Forsyth Bb
12 Forst Fc
81 Fort Albany Aa
87 Fort Augustus Dc
54 Fort Ayacucho Dc
75 Fort Beaufort Dd
70 Fort Charlet, see Djanet Gd
84 Fort Collins Ec
80 Fort Corrales Cd
* 69 Fort Dauphin Gh
91 Fort de France Fd
84 Fort Dodge Dc
8 Fort D'Orbigny Cd
81 Fort Erie Fc
70 Fort Flatters (Bordj Omar Driss) Gc
86 Fort Frances Bb
80 Fort Fraser Bb
20 Fort George Bb
80 Fort Gouraud (F'Dérik) Cd
80 Fort Grahame Bb
80 Fort Guachalla Cd
73 Fort Jameson (see Chipata) Ef
80 Fort Lamy Dd
70 Fort Lapertine (Tamanrasset)Gd
87 Fort Lauderdale Df
80 Fort Liard Bc
81 Fort Mackay Cb
80 Fort McMurray Cb
78 Fort McPherson Bb
84 Fort Morgan Fd
46 Fort Munro Bd
87 Fort Myers Df
87 Fort Nelson Eb
78 Fort Norman Eb
84 Fort Peck, Res. Eb
80 Fort Providence Cc
80 Fort Reliance Da
80 Fort Resolution Cb
87 Fort Sandeman Bc
81 Fort Severn Aa
80 Fort Simpson Bc
94 Fort Siracusas Cd
87 Fort Smith, Can. Cb
87 Fort Smith U.S.A. Bd
80 Fort Vermilion Cb
† 75 Fort Victoria Eb
88 Fort Wayne Eb
8 Fort William, Scot. Cd
85 Fort Worth Cd
80 Fort Yukon Db
94 Forte Coimbra Db
8 Forte Rocades Ba
64 Fortescue & R. Bc
8 Forth, Firth of Fd
21 Fossano Fe
74 Fougeres Cc
20 Fourchambault Bb
74 Fourmies Dd
71 Fouta Djaion, mt. Cd
39 Foveaux Str. Bg
51 Fowey Cd
65 Fowlers B. Ae
83x Fox Is. Kf
79 Foxe Basin Kb
79 Foxe Channel Jb
78 Foxe Pen. Kb

9 Foxford Cb
66 Foxton Ed
9 Foyle De
9 Foynes Bd
95 Foz de Iguaçú De
75 Franca Fd
79 Francavilla Fd
4 France, Rep. Ff
73 Franceville Ad
20 Franchecomte, dist. Dc
75 Francistown Db
88 Frankfort, Ind. Bd
88 Frankfort, Ky. Ce
74 Frankfurt a.O. Fb
19 Frankfurt a.M. Hd
88 Franklin Fd
78 Franklin, terr. Ha
60 Frankston Cc
74 Fransfontein Ab
81 Franz Ab
74 Franz Josef Ld., Is. Ga
13 Fraser I. Dd
9 Fraserburg Cd
9 Fraserburgh Fc
22 Frasne Ec
23 Frauenfeld Ca
93 Fray Bentos Df
28 Frederica Cd
7 Frederick Ge
89 Fredericksburg Fd
81 Fredericton Cb
12 Fredericksberg, & Co. Fd
75 Frederikshaab Nb
12 Frederikshavn Db
12 Frederikvaerk Ed
11 Fredrikstad Cd
7 Freetown Cg
11 Freiburg Fb
17 Freising Dd
85 Fremantle Be
88 Fremont, Mich. Bc
88 Fremont, Ohio Dd
92 French Guiana Db
90 Fresnillo Dc
85 Fresno Cd
19 Freudenstadt Hf
65 Freycinet Estuary Ad
13 Fribourg, & cant. Bb
19 Friedberg Hd
21 Friedrichshafen Hb
66 Friendly Is., see Tonga Is.
18 Friesland, prov. Ea
8 Frockheim Fd
26 Fruili Venezia Giulia, reg. Db
90 Frobisher, L. Db
79 Frobisher B. Lb
79 Frobisher Bay Lb
10 Frohavet Bc
33 Prolovo Hf
7 Frome Ef
90 Frome L. Ab
29 Frosinone Ed
88 Frostburg Fe
10 Fröya, I. Bc
34 Frunze Ke
95 Frutal Fd
51 Fuchow Fd
90 Fuerte, R. Cd
19 Fuerteventura Bc
53 Fuji-san, mt. Cc
53 Fujisawa Cc
53 Fujiyama, mt., see Fuji-san Cb
51 Fukien, prov. Fd
54 Fukuchiyama Cc
53 Fukui Cc
55 Fukui & pref. Cc
54 Fukuoka: & pref. Dc
54 Fukushima, & pref. Dc
53 Fukuyama Bd
51 Fulton Cc
55 Funabashi Cc
19 Funchal Bb
11 Fundy, B. of Cb
13 Furka P. Cb
90 Fürth Fd
17 Fürth Dd
75 Fuse Cd
21 Füssen Jb
51 Fushun Gb
51 Fuyang Hb
51 Fuyu Gb
70 Gabès Cb
74 Gabès, G. of Hb
74 Gabon, rep. Df
75 Gaborone Db
39 Gabredarre De
31 Gacko hd
64 Gadhada Ch
71 Gadsden Cd
26 Gaeta Dd
12 Gafsa Gb
33 Gagry Hg
87 Gainesville, Ga. De

87 Gainesville, Fla. Df
65 Gairdner L. Fe
92 Galapagos Is. Ad
8 Galashiels Ee
32 Galati Fc
79 Galatina Gd
11 Gaidhöpiggen, mt. Bc
24 George Cd
86 Galesburg Bc
32 Galich Hd
26 Galicia, prov. Aa
40 Galilee, S. of Bc
62 Galilee L. Cc
39 Galiabat Cd
21 Gallarate Gd
44 Galle Dg
29 Gallipoli, Italy Fd
27 Gallipoli, Turkey, see Gelibolu Ca
10 Gällivare Eb
42 Galloway Df
85 Gallup Ed
87 Galveston Bf
9 Galway & co. Bc
9 Galway B. Bc
71 Gambaga Ef
68 Gambia, st. Ad
71 Gambia, R. Cf
72 Gambeama Bd
73 Ganale Dorya, R. Gb
73 Gandar Fa
81 Gander Db
26 Gandia Bb
47 Ganga, Mouths of the Mh
47 Ganga (Ganges), R. Lf
46 Ganga Nagar Ec
51 Gangtok Me
20 Gannat Bc
65 Gantheaume B. Ad
71 Gao Ee
20 Gap Ee
79 Garad De
61 Garam Ca
19 Gard, dept. Be
47 Garda, L. di Jd
73 Gardala Fb
85 Garden City Fd
19 Garmisch-Partenkirchen Fa
14 Garonne, R. Ce
72 Garoua Ab
71 Garraway Dh
84 Garrison Res. Fb
52 Gartok Cc
84 Garua Bc
48 Garut Bd
88 Gray Bd
13 Gascony Cf
13 Gascony, reg. Cf
65 Gasgoyne R. Ac
72 Gashaka Ab
62 Gasmata Hh
81 Gaspé Cd
81 Gaspé Pen. Cb
26 Gata, C. de Bb
6 Gateshead Fc
20 Gatinais, dist. Aa
* 79 Gatooma Da
47 Gauhati Ne
31 Gávdhos, I. Bf
11 Gävle Dc
64 Gawler Ab
65 Gawler Ranges Fe
71 Gaya, Dahomey Ef
47 Gaya India Kf
24 Gaylord Cb
12 Gaydak Dd
19 Gaza Bd
12 Gaza (Danzig) Ea
39 Gedaref Cd
22 Gediz, R. Cb
74 Geelong Bc
74 Geeraards-bergen Dd
61 Geeveston Cd
71 Geidam Hf
73 Geita Ed
8 Gek Ab
9 Gela Ef
18 Geldrop Ec
84 Geleen Ed
27 Gelibolu (Gallipoli) Ca
19 Gelsenkirchen Gc
27 Gemlik Ca
18 Gendringen Fc
72 General Carneiro Bc
72 General Machado Bc
89 Geneva, O.F.S. Gc
13 Geneva, L. of, see Léman, L. Ab
13 Genève (Geneva), Switz. Db
20 Genissi Amaat Gc
32 Genk Ed

20 Genlis Db
21 Genoa, see Genova
21 Genova (Genoa) Ge
21 Genova, G. di Gf
33 Geogievsk Hg
65 Geographe B. Be
65 Geographe Chan. Ac
74 George Cd
96 George V. Coast Jb
13 George, L. Ed
79 George, R. Lc
48 George Town, Malaya Bc
62 Georgetown, Australia Bb
88 Georgetown, Canada Fc
71 Georgetown, Gambia Cf
92 Georgetown, Guyana Db
33 Georgia Hg
83 Georgia, st. Ec
86 Georgian B. Ec
62 Georgina R. Ad
17 Gera Ec
65 Geraldton Ad
23 Gerlachovka, mt. Fd
75 Germiston Dc
75 Germany, st. He
75 Germiston Dc
28 Gerona Ca
27 Gerze Ea
20 Gevaudan, dist. He
39 Gezira Cd
49 Geelvink B. Ff
29 Gerbogufd De
47 Ghaghra (Gogra) R. Je
68 Ghana, st. Be
74 Ghanzi Cd
70 Ghardaia Fb
70 Ghazaouet Ea
46 Ghaziabad Fd
46 Ghazni Bb
28 Ghent Cc
50 Gheorgherli Eb
73 Gbudamis Cb
51 Giant (Krkonose) Mts. Cc
9 Giant's Causeway Ec
74 Gibeon Bc
26 Gibraltar Ab
26 Gibraltar, Str. of Da
64 Gibson Desert Cc
20 Gien Ab
19 Giessen Hd
55 Gifu & pref. Cc
8 Gigha, I. Be
26 Gijon Aa
62 Gilau Gh
* 56 Gilbert Is. Dc
62 Gilbert R. Bb
21 Gilgandra Cb
44 Gilgit, & Dist. Ca
7 Gillingham Hj
41 Gineifa Cf
65 Gingin Be
64 Giralia Ac
6 Girdle Ness Fc
47 Giridih Lf
21 Girishk Ab
15 Gironde, R. Ce
8 Girvan De
66 Gisborne Gc
28 Giulianova Dc
30 Giurgiu Ed
35 Gizhiga Tc
53 Gizycho Fa
12 Giżycko Fa
12 Glace Bay Cb
62 Gladstone, Queensland Dc
65 Gladstone, South Australia Ab
88 Gladstone, U.S.A. Bb
13 Glarus Da
8 Glasgow De
7 Glastonbury Ef
27 Glauchau Ec
32 Glazov Kd
61 Glen Innes Da
8 Glenbarr Be
71 Glencoe Cd
85 Glendale Ce
9 Glenealy Ed
60 Glenelg Ab
79 Glengarriff Be
61 Glenmorgan Cd
19 Glenrothes Ed
61 Glenreagh Db
8 Glens Falls Jc
52 Gliwice Ec
85 Globe De
26 Glogów Dc
32 Glotovo Jc
11 Gloucester, Australia Db
7 Gloucester, & co., England. Ef

* Renamed Faradofay
† Renamed Masvingo
‡ Renamed Xangongo
* Renamed Kadoma
* Renamed Kiribati

89 Gloucester, U.S.A. Kc
16 Glückstadt Cb
33 Glushitsa Ke
17 Gmunden Dh
22 Gniezno Db
44 Goa Ce
74 Gobabis Bb
94 Gobernador Gordillo Bf
50-51 Gobi or Shamo, des. Eb
74 Gochas Bb
48 Gŏcŏng Bb
7 Godalming Gf
47 Godavari, R. Hh
68 Goderich Ec
78 Godhaab Mb
83 Godhavn Mb
46 Godhra Dc
44 Godwin Austen, Mt., see K2
18 Goeree, I. Cc
18 Goes Cc
95 Goiania Fc
95 Goias Ec
62 Goias, st. Ec
46 Gojra Dc
27 Gök, R. Db
27 Gökceada Ca
84 Golden Gate Hd
67 Goldsboro Ec
22 Goleniow Cb
50 Golma Dc
8 Golspie Dc
33 Goma Dd
33 Gomel Fe
61 Gomera, I. Bc
90 Gomez Palacio Db
43 Gonabad Hc
47 Gonda He
91 Gonaives Dc
39 Gonder Cd
47 Gonda Hh
75 Gonye Rapids Ca
8 Good Hope Eb
74 Good Hope, C. of Bd
61 Goondiwindi Da
61 Goodna Da
63 Goomalling Be
60 Goombalie Ca
8 Goose Lc
46 Gop Bg
47 Gorakhpur Je
72 Gore, N.Z. Bg
72 Goré, Cent. Afr. Rb
9 Gorey Ed
43 Gorgan Gb
28 Gorinchen Dc
33 Goris Jh
28 Gorizia Db
32 Gorki Hd
13 Gorlice Fc
16 Görlitz Fc
33 Gorlouka Gf
9 Gormanston Ec
31 Gorna Oryakhovitsa Ed
62 Goroka Db
75 Gorongoza Mts. Ad
49 Gorontalo Dc
9 Gort Cc
22 Gorzów Cb
47 Gosainthan, mt. Kd
13 Goschenen Cb
61 Gosford Db
88 Goshen Cd
28 Gospic Eb
33 Gostyn Dc
11 Göteborg Cd
17 Gotha Dc
11 Gotland I. Dd
55 Goto, Is. Id
11 Gotska Dd
16 Göttingen Cc
16 Gottwaldov (Zlin) Dd
18 Gouda Db
81 Gouin Res. Bb
61 Goulburn Cb
15 Gould Mt. Bb
15 Gourdon De
74 Gourits, R. Cd
71 Gourma-Rarous Ee
64 Gove Fa
94 Goya Bb
65 Goyders Lagoon Ad
72 Goz Beida Ca
39 Goz Regeb Cc
75 Graaff Reinet Cd
82 Gracac Eb
91 Gracias á Dios, C. Bd
28 Gradisca Db
61 Grafton, Australia Da
84 Grafton, U.S.A. Gb
22 Grafton C. Cb
82a Graham I. Ec
94 Graham Land Qc
75 Grahamstown Dd
23 Grajewo Gb

8 Grampian, Co. Fc
8 Grampians mts. Dd
70 Gran Canaria, I. Bc
94 Gran Chaco, reg. Cd
21 Gran Paradiso, mt. Fd
91 Granada, Nic. Ad
26 Granada, Spain Bb
9 Granard Dc
81 Granby Bb
87 Grand Bahama I. Ef
71 Grand Bassam, I. Ef
85 Grand Canyon Dd
91 Grand Cayman, I. Bc
81 Grand Falls Db
84 Grand Forks Gb
84 Grand Haven Cc
84 Grand Island Gc
84 Grand Junction Ed
71 Grand Lahou Dh
80 Grand Rapids, Canada Eb
80 Grand Rapids, U.S.A. Cc
73 Grande Comore, I. Gf
90 Grande de Santiago, R. Dc
21 Grande Prairie Cb
80 Grandfords Cc
84 Grangeville Cb
86 Granite City Cd
62 Granity Cd
8 Grantown Ec
15 Grasse Gf
13 Graubünden (Grisons) cant. Db
8 Gravelines Bb
18 's Gravenhage (The Hague) Db
17 Graz Fe
66 Great Abaco, I. Ca
8 Great Australian Bight. De
66 Great Barrier I. Eb
84 Great Barrier Reef Cb
84 Great Basin Cd
78 Great Bear L. Eb
12 Great Belt Dd
84 Great Berg, R. Bd
7 Great Divide, mts. Cc
7 Great Dunmow Hf
84 Great Falls Db
78 Great Fish R., Canada Cd
75 Great Fish, R., South Africa Dd
47 Great Himalaya Ra. Hd
11 Great Inagua I. Db
46 Great Indian Des. (Thar Des.) Ce
74 Great Karasberge, mts. Bc
74 Great Karoo, reg. Cd
51 Great Khingan Mts. Gb
74 Great Namaqualand Bb
45 Great Nicobar I. Gg
21 Great Ruaha, R. Fe
8 Great St. Bernard, Col du, P. Bc
84 Great Salt Lake Dc
80 Great Slave L. Ec
63 Great Victoria Des. Dd
79 Great Whale, R. Ec
11 Great Winterberg, mt. Dd
74 Great Winterhoek, mt. Bd
7 Great Yarmouth Je
82 Great Zab R. Eb
81 Greater Antilles Cc
6 Greater Manchester, Co. Ed
48 Greater Sunda Is. Cd
27 Greco, C. Dc
63 Greece, st. Kh
84 Greeley Fc
88 Green B. Bb
88 Green Bay Bb
15 Green Is. Hg
67 Green Island Cf
65 Greenbushes Be
88 Greencastle Be
9 Greenfield Jc
7 Greenland Ed
8 Greenock Df
70 Greensboro Ff
20 Greensburg Cd
71 Greenville, Lib. Dg
81 Greenville, Mich. Cd

87 Greenville, Miss. Be
89 Greenville, N.C. Gg
71 Greenville, S.C. De
7 Greenwich Hf
63 Gregory L. Ad
62 Gregory Ra. Bb
16 Greifswald Ea
12 Greina Dc
26 Grenada Db
91 Grenada, I. Fd
87 Grenade Ce
11 Grenadines, Is. Fd
61 Grenfell Cb
15 Grenoble Ge
62 Grenville C. Ba
61 Greta Db
49 Grey Ra. Bd
77 Greymouth Cc
75 Greytown, Nat. Ec
71 Greytown, N.Z. Ed
60 Grimith Cb
90 Grijalva R. Fd
7 Grimsby Gd
81 Grimstad Bd
13 Grindelwald Cb
62 Griqualand West, dist. Cc
3 Gris Nez, pt. Db
13 Grisons, cant., see Graubünden
33 Grodek Gb
33 Grodno De
23 Grodzisk Fb
23 Grójec Fc
81 Gronau Gb
10 Grong Cc
18 Groningen, Netherlands Fa
92 Groningen, Surinam Db
10 Grónöy Cb
70 Grootfontein Ba
62 Groote Eyland I. Aa
20 Grosne, R. Cc
16 Grossenhain Ec
26 Grosseto Cc
80 Grouard Db
33 Groznyy Jg
13 Gstaad Bb
23 Grudziadz Eb
13 Gruyères Bb
33 Gryazi He
33 Gryazovets Hd
23 Grybów Fd
95 Guaçu Gd
90 Guadalajara, Mexico Dc
26 Guadalajara, Spain Ba
26 Guadalaviar, R. Bb
26 Guadalcanal Dc
26 Guadalquivir, R. Ab
26 Guadarrama, Sa. de Ba
91 Guadeloupe, I. Fc
26 Guadiana, R. Ab
95 Guaíra Ed
91 Guajará-Mirim Bb
11 Guajira, G. of Cc
90 Guamúchil Cb
90 Guanajuato Dc
91 Guantanamo Cc
94 Guaqui Bc
90 Guapuava Ee
39 Guardafui, C. Ee
12 Guastalla Je
7 Guatemala Jg
90 Guatemala, rep. Cd
71 Guayabal Cb
61 Guayama Ec
92 Guayaquil Bc
90 Guaymas Bb
32 Gubakha Lc
28 Gubbio Dc
21 Guebwiller Fb
9 Guelma Ga
20 Guelph Ab
20 Guerches d'Aubois Ad
15 Guéret Dd
14 Guernsey, I. Cc
7 Guildford Gf
63 Guinea, G. of Be
61 Guinea, rep. Ad
89 Guinea-Bissau Ad
46 Gujarat, st. Cc
61 Gujranwala Eb
46 Gujrat Eb
18 Gulbarga De
43 Gulf of Gulfport Ce
73 Gulu Ec
95 Guma Bc
16 Gumma, pref. Cc
18 Gummersbach Gc
74 Guna Ff
79 Gunnbjorn Fd. Pb
21 Gunnedah Db
44 Guntakal Db
44 Guntur Ee

72 Gunza Af
46 Gurdaspur Eb
47 Gurkha Kd
34 Guryev He
71 Gusau Gf
16 Güstrow Eb
18 Gütersloh Hc
90 Gutierrez Fd
92 Guyana, st. Db
15 Guyenne De
81 Guyra Db
44 Gwadar Ac
46 Gwalior Ge
75 Gwanda Db
*75 Gwelo Db
7 Gwent, Co. Ef
7 Gwynedd, Co. Cd
63 Gympie Dd
55 Gyoda Cc
30 Gyöngyös Cb
30 Györ Ab
80 Gypsumville Eb
30 Gyula Cb

44 Haapamaki Ec
32 Haapsala Dd
18 Haarlem Db
18 Habaswein, wadi Bd
54 Hachijo Shima, I. Cd
54 Hachinohe Db
8 Haddington Fe
12 Haderslev Cd
50 Hadnal Da
39 Hadhramaut, dist. Dd
52 Haeju Bb
43 Hafar al Batin Fd
40 Haffah Cb
46 Hafizabad Db
10 Hafnarfjördur Ab
16 Hagen Hc
89 Hagerstown Ge
55 Hagi Bd
19 Haguenau Gf
40 Haifa Bc
42 Hail Ed
31 Hailar Fb
84 Hailey Dc
81 Haileybury Bb
7 Hailsham Hg
51 Hailun Fb
10 Hailuoto Eb
48 Haiphong Ba
91 Haiti, rep. Dc
54 Haiya Cd
42 Haiyaniya Ed
30 Hajdúnós-
23 Hajnówka Gb
54 Hakodate Db
46 Hala Bd
42 Halab (Aleppo) Db
40 Halaib Cc
40 Halba Cb
76 Halberstadt Dc
8 Halcombe Ed
11 Halden Cd
84 Haldwanim Gd
84 Hale Mt. Bd
81 Halifax, Can. Cb
7 Halifax, Eng. Fd
62 Halifax B. Cb
7 Hall De
28 Halle, Belg. Cd
16 Halle, Ger. Dc
96 Halley Bay Ab
10 Hällnäs Dc
64 Hall's Creek Db
49 Halmahera, I. Dc
11 Halmstad Cd
7 Hals De
10 Haltiatunturi, mt. Eb
12 Halundborg Ed
46 Halvad Cg
55 Hamada Bd
40 Hamadan Cb
40 Hamah (Hama) Cb
16 Hamamatsu Cd
65 Hamelin Pool Ad
54 Hamhung Ba
50 Hami Cb
60 Hamilton, Australia Bc
81 Hamilton, Can. Ab
71 Hamilton, N.Z. Eb
8 Hamilton, Scot. De
88 Hamiltown Ce
18 Hamlin Jb
18 Hamm Ec
43 Hamman Fe
60 Hammerfest Ea
64 Hammersley Range Bc
88 Hammond Bd
7 Hampden Cf
7 Hampshire, co. Ff
89 Hampton Gf
44 Hamun-i-Mashkel, L.
42 Hanak Dc
54 Hanamaki Dc

19 Hanau Hd
57 Hanchung Ec
55 Handa Cd
85 Hanford Cd
51 Hangchow Fc
11 Hanko Ed
11 Hanko Fc
67 Hanmer Dd
6 Hann, mt. Db
30 Hanna Cb
16 Hanover Cb
48 Hanoi Ba
52 Hanoi Db
48 Hanover Ge
30 Hansand Bb
46 Hansi Ed
51 Hantan Fc
10 Haparanda Eb
46 Hapur Fd
51 Haql Dd
43 Haradh Fe
73 Harer Gb
51 Harbin Gb
88 Harbor Beach Dc
88 Harbour Grace Db
16 Harburg Cb
21 Hardanger Fd. Bc
18 Harderwijk Eb
46 Hardwar Gd
39 Hargeisa De
48 Hari R. Bd
7 Harlech Ce
18 Harlingen, Neth. Ea
85 Harlingen, U.S.A. Gf
10 Härnosänd Dc
8 Harris, dist. Bc
63 Harrisburg Gd
75 Harrismith Dc
81 Harrison Bd
6 Harrogate Fd
10 Harstad Db
12 Harsyssel dist. Bc
7 Hart Bc
74 Hartebeest Jd
7 Hartland Pt. Cf
Fc Hartlepool Fc
*75 Hartley Ea
7 Harwich Jf
46 Haryana, st. Fd
43 Hasa, reg. Fd
27 Hasan, mt. Db
18 Hasselt Ed
70 Hassi Messaoud Gb
8 Hastings, Eng. Hg
88 Hastings, Mich. Bc
84 Hastings, Neb. Gc
66 Hastings, N.Z. Fc
7 Hatfield Gf
80 Hatteras, C. Ed
30 Hatvan Bb
11 Haugesund Bd
66 Hauraki G. Eb
21 Haut Rhin, dept. Fb
15 Haute-Corse, dept. Bg
20 Haute Loire, dept. Bg
20 Haute Marne, dept. Da
20 Haute Saône, dept. Db
20 Haute Savoie, dept. De
20 Hautes-Alpes, dept. De
70 Hautes Plateaux Fa
70 Hauts Plateaux, reg. Fb
67 Havelock Dd
67 Havana Bb
67 Havelock Dd
89 Haverhill Kc
84 Havre Ea
27 Havza Ea
71 Hawaii, I. Fc
72 Hawaiian Is. Fc
79 Hawash, R. Dd
66 Hawera Ec
8 Hawick Fe
66 Hawke's Bay, dist.
61 Hay Bb
80 Hay River Ca
76 Hayange Fe
86 Haywards Heath
88 Hazard Df
17 Hazaribagh Dg
18 Hazebrouck Bb
80 Hazelton Bb
16 Hazelton Hd
54 Healesville Cb
3 Heard I. Lh
31 Hearst Ec
14 Hearts Ab
16 Hebron, Can. Lc
40 Hebron (Al Khalil), Jordan Bd
57 Hedgehope Bg
18 Heemstede Db
18 Heerde Fb
18 Heerenveen Eb
18 Heerlen Ed
Ab Hegyeshalom Ab

* Renamed Gweru
* Renamed Chegutu

74 Heideberg Cd
19 Heidelberg, Ger. He
75 Heidelberg,
  Transvaal Dc
75 Heilbron Dc
19 Heilbronn Je
75 Heilungkiang,
  prov. Gb
11 Heinola Fc
42 Hejez, reg. Dd
10 Hekla, mt. Bb
22 Hel Ea
84 Helena Db
8 Helensburgh Dd
66 Helensville Eb
44 Helmand, R. Ab
18 Helmond Ec
11 Heisingborg Cd
12 Helsingör Fc
11 Helsinki Ec
7 Helston Bg
26 Henares, R. Ba
11 Hendaye Cf
19 Henderson Ff
18 Hengelo Fb
19 Hengyang Fd
19 Hénin-Beau-
  mont Bd
11 Henty Cc
45 Henzada He
44 Herat Ab
20 Hérault, R. &
  dept. Bf
62 Herberton Cb
28 Herceg Novi Gc
7 Hereford & Wor-
  cester, Co. Ee
18 Herentals Dc
18 Herford Hb
43 Heri Rud Jb
13 Herisau Da
64 Hermannsburg Ec
74 Hermanus Bd
7 Hermitage Ce
90 Hermosillo Bb
18 Herne Gc
7 Herne Bay Jf
81 Heron Bay Ab
87 Herrin Cd
18 Hersfeld Jd
18 Herstal Ed
7 Hertford & co. Of
63 Hervey B. Dc
40 Herzliya Bc
12 Hesselö, I. c
62 Heywood Bc
56 Hibbing Bb
88 Hickory Eg
30 Hidalgo del
  Parral Cb
70 Hierro, I. Bc
79 High Atlas, mts.Eb
88 High Point Fg
80 High River Cb
23 High Tatra, mt.Ed
7 High Wycombe Gf
70 Highland, Co. Cc
18 Highland Parks Bc
32 Hiiumaa, I. Cd
34 Hikone Cc
66 Hikurangi Ea
16 Hildersheim Cb
42 Hilla Ec
12 Hillerö Fd
56 Hillston Cb
83b Hilo Db
18 Hilversum Eb
46 Himachal Pradesh,
  St. Fc
46 Himatnagar Dg
55 Himeji Bd
41 Himmelbjerget Cc
12 Himmerland Cc
40 Hims (Homs) Cb
52 Hinchinbrook I, Cb
72 Hinde Rapids De
44 Hindu Kush,
  mts. Ba
80 Hines Creek Cb
44 Hingol R. Bc
11 Hinnoy, I. Db
55 Hino, C. Bc
13 Hinterrhein, R. Db
55 Hiroshima &
  pref. Bd
7 Hirson De
91 Hispaniola, I. Dc
44 Hissar Da
55 Hitachi Dc
7 Hitchin Gf
10 Hitra, I. Bc
12 Hjaelm, I. Cc
11 Hjälmaren Dd
12 Hjorring Cb
48 Hoa Binh Ba
73 Hobart Cd
12 Hobro Cc
48 Ho Chi Minh
  City Bb
13 Hochdorf Ca
19 Höchst Hd
19 Hochwan Ec
19 Hockenheim He

39 Hodeida Dd
80 Hodgson Eb
30 Hódmező
  Vasarhely Cb
70 Hodna, Chott de Fa
22 Hodonin Dd
17 Hof, Ger. Dc
10 Hof, Iceland Cb
51 Hofei Fc
10 Hofsos Ba
43 Hofuf Fd
18 Hohenlimburg Gc
70 Hoggar, mts. Cd
51 Hoihow Fd
51 Hokang Hb
67 Hokitika Ce
54 Hokkaido I.,
  pref. & dist. Db
51 Holbaek Ed
51 Holbrook Cc
84 Holdredge Gc
51 Holguin Cb
61 Holland Dd
85 Hollywood Ce
40 Holon Bc
12 Holstebro Bc
10 Holt Bb
6 Holy I. Cd
2 Holyhead Cd
88 Holyoke Jc
9 Holywood Fb
18 Holzminden Jc
71 Hombori Ee
39 Homburg Ge
82a Homer Cc
51 Homs, Libya Db
40 Homs, Syria, see
  Hims
51 Honan, prov. Fc
90 Honduras Fg
71 Honduras, Gulf Ac
91 Honduras, rep. Ad
11 Hönefoss Cc
14 Honfleur Dc
48 Hong-Ha, R. Ba
51 Hong Kong, Br.
  CrownColony Fd
57 Honolulu Fb
51 Honshu, I. Cc
18 Hoogeveen Fb
7 Hook of Hol-
  land Db
18 Hoorn Eb
87 Hope He
70 Hopedale Lc
51 Hopei, prov. Fc
65 Hopetoun Ce
51 Hopetown Cc
9 Horal Hammar,
  L. Fc
16 Hordenberg Fb
39 Hordio Ed
93 Horn, C. Ch
10 Hornavan Cb
89 Hornell Gc
51 Hornsby Db
11 Hornslandet Dc
18 Hornum Cb
52 Horsens Cd
9 Horsham,
  Australia Bc
7 Horsham, Eng. Gf
11 Hortent Cc
40 Hoshiarpur Cc
87 Hot Springs Be
18 Hou R. Bd
20 Houhora Da
57 Houma Be
18 Houston Af
59 Hovd Db
61 Howe C. Dc
51 Howe C., West, Bf
10 Howrah Mg
9 Howth Ec
8 Hoy, I. Eb
11 Hoyanger Bc
27 Hoyran, L. Db
22 Hradec Králové Cc
51 Hsinchu Gd
45 Hsipaw Hd
51 Huallen Gd
72 Huambo Bf
51 Hsuchang Fc
92 Huancayo Bd
94 Haunchaca Cb
84 Huddersfield Fd
79 Hudson B. Jb
80 Hudson Bay
  Junc.
80 Hudson Hope Bb
79 Hudson Str. Kb
48 Hué Bb
26 Huelva Ab
26 Huesca Ba
62 Hughenden Bc
87 Hugo Be
70 Huhehot Fb
90 Huixtla Fd
51 Hulan Fb
51 Huldo Ec
51 Hull, Can. Bb

6 Hull, England Gd
94 Humahuaca Bd
92 Humaita Cb
75 Humansdorp Dd
6 Humber, R. Gd
6 Humberside,
  Co. Gd
80 Humboldt Db
84 Humboldt B. Bc
84 Humboldt R. Cc
23 Humenné Fd
10 Hunafloi Aa
4 Hunan, prov. Fd
12 Hundested Ed
52 Hungary, rep. Jf
60 Hungerford Ba
52 Hungnam Bb
7 Hungshui Ho,
  R. Ed
7 Hunstanton He
18 Hunte, R. Hb
61 Hunter Db
66 Hunterville Ec
7 Huntington,
  England Ge
88 Huntington,Ind.Cd
88 Huntington,
  West Virginia De
60 Huntly, Scot. Ec
66 Huntly, N.Z. Eb
87 Huntsville, Ala. Ce
88 Huntsville, Can. Fb
63 Huntsville, Tex. Ae
51 Hupei, prov. Fc
58 Hurghada Cc
88 Huron, C. Db
9 Husi Gb
55 Hutchison Gd
18 Huttwil Bc
51 Hwainan Fc
11 Hwang Ho, R. Fc
51 Hwangshih Fc
50 Hweitseh Ed
45 Hyden Be
7 Hyderabad,
  India De
46 Hyderabad,Pak.Bf
52 Hyères & Iles.d' Gf
55 Hyogo, pref. Bc
7 Hythe HJ

32 Iasi Ef
71 Ibadan Ef
92 Ibaqué Bb
51 Ibaraki, pref. Dc
18 Ibbenduren Gb
26 Ibiza & I. Cb
7 Ibo Gf
10 Iceland, I., st. Bc
51 Ichang Fc
55 Ichikawa Cc
54 Ichinomiya Cc
54 Ichinoseki Dc
51 Ichun Gb
82 Idaho, st. Bb
84 Idaho Falls Dc
19 Idar Oberstein Ge
72 Idd el Ghanam Ca
27 Idhi, mt. Cb
* 73 Idi Amin Dada,
  L. Dd
27 Ierapetra Cb
28 Iesi Bc
71 Ife Eg
7 Ifni Cc
33 Iganie Gb
94 Igarka Lc
21 Iglesias Bc
95 Iguazu & Falls Ee
92 Iguala Bd
32 Iguatu Fc
10 Iisalmi Fc
18 IJmuiden Db
11 IJsselmeer Eb
27 Ikaria, I. Cb
55 Iki, I. Ad
28 Il'men, L. Fd
51 Ilebo (Port
  Francqui) Cd
14 Ile de France,
  prov. Ec
14 Ile et Vilaine,
  dept. Ce
23 Ilek, & R. Ke
62 Ilfracombe,
  Australia Bc
7 Ilfracombe, Eng.Cf
27 Ilgin Db
21 Ill, R. Fa
39 Illig De
51 Illinois, st. Eb
54 Illizi (Fort de
  Polignac) Bc
32 Ilmen, L. Fd
49 Iloilo Db
51 Imabari Bd
52 Imandra L. Fb
26 Imola Cb
21 Imperia Gf
45 Impfondo Bc
45 Imphal Gd

24 In Salah De
67 Inangahua Dd
10 Inari & L. Fb
20 Inca Cb
27 Incesu Eb
52 Inchon Bb
45 Indaw Hd
3 Indian Ocean Lf
36 Indian Union,
  rep. Lg
88 Indiana Fd
83 Indiana, st. Ec
88 Indianapolis Be
32 Indiga Jb
48 Indo China, reg.Bb
77 Indonesia, rep. Fb
61 Indooroopilly Da
46 Indus, R. Bc
46 Indus, Mouths of
  the Af
48 Indramaju Id
27 Ineboiu Da
72 Ingende Bd
62 Ingham Cb
66 Inglewood,N.Z. Ec
61 Inglewood,
  Queensland Da
60 Inglewood,
  Victoria Bc
17 Ingolstadt Dd
75 Inhambane Ea
25 Inharrime Ef
9 Inishmore I. Bc
55 Inland Sea Bd
27 Inn, R. Jb
8 Inner Hebrides Bc
51 Inner Mongolia,
  Aut. Reg. Fb
62 Innisfail Cb
21 Innsbruck Kb
51 Inowroclaw Bb
44 Inquisivi Bd
13 Interlaken Bb
28 Inuvik Db
67 Invercargill Bg
51 Inverell Da
51 Inverkeithing Ed
63 Inverness & co. Dc
8 Inverurie Fc
75 Inyanga Mts. Ea
75 Inyati Da
23 Inza Je
27 Ioannina Bb
28 Iolanda Cb
51 Iona, I. Bd
27 Ionian Is. Bb
27 Ionian S. Cb
27 Ios, I. Cb
83 Iowa, st. Db
51 Ipin Ed
48 Ipoh Bc
51 Ipswich,
  Australia Da
7 Ipswich, Eng. Je
92 Ipu Cb
44 Iquique Ad
92 Iquitos Bc
27 Iráklion Cb
36 Iran, King. Jf
90 Irapuato Dc
36 Iraq, rep. Hf
91 Irazú, vol. Bd
40 Irbid Bc
71 Irbit Jd
9 Ireland De
33 Irgiz Je
6 Irish S. Cg
35 Irkutsk Nd
7 Irmak Db
88 Iron Mt. Ab
88 Iron River Cb
88 Ironton De
86 Ironwood Cb
45 Irrawaddy,R. Hd
34 Irtysh R. Kd
73 Irumu Dc
10 Irvine De
8 Irwin De
60 Irymple Bb
55 Isahaya Bd
72 Isangi Cc
29 Ischia Bd
27 Ischl Ee
55 Ise, R. Cd
14 Iserfjord Ed
26 Isère,R.& dept.Dd
28 Iserlohn Ed
29 Isernia Bd
41 Iseo, & L. di Cd
54 Ishikari B. Db
55 Ishikawa, pref. Cc
14 Isigny Dc
73 Isiro Dc
27 Iskenderun Eb
27 Iskilip Da
80 Island L. Eb
8 Islay, I. Bc
6 Isle of Man Cc
7 Isle of Wight,
  & Co. Fg
41 Ismā'īliya Cc
27 Isparta Cb

40 Israel, st. Bc
27 Istanbul Ca
27 Istiaia Bb
28 Istra, reg. Db
27 Istranca Mts. Ca
95 Itaporá Hd
92 Itatuna Fd
42 Itaete Dd
95 Itapi Fe
4 Italy, rep. Hg
95 Itamte, mt. Gc
93 Itapura Bd
89 Ithaca Gc
27 Itnaki Bb
55 Ito Cd
60 Ivanhoe Bb
33 Ivano-Frankovsk
32 Ivanovo Hd
68 Ivory Coast,rep.Be
41 Ivrea Fd
51 Iwakuni Bd
54 Iwamizawa Db
54 Iwanuma Dc
51 Iwata Cc
42 Iwate, pref. Dc
7 Iwo Fg
94 Ixiamas Bb
18 Izegem Cd
53 Iznevsk Kd
33 Izmail Ef
27 Izmir (Smyrna) Cb
27 Izmit Da
27 Iznik Da
42 Izra Cc
55 Izumo Bc

40 Jabal an
  Nusayriyah
  mts. Cb
40 Jabal ash Sharqi
  (Anti-Lebanon)
  mts. Cb
43 Jabal at Tuwaiq,
  mts. Ee
42 Jabal Ibrahim,
  mt. Ee
42 Jabal Shammar,
  mts. Dd
47 Jabalpur Gg
40 Jabean Bb
43 Jabrin Gg
95 Jacareznho Fd
88 Jackson, Mich. Cc
87 Jackson, Miss. Be
88 Jackson, Ohio De
87 Jackson, Tenn. Cd
65 Jackson Mt. Bc
87 Jacksonville,
  Fla. De
86 Jacksonville,Ill.Bd
67 Jacksons Ce
10 Jackvik Db
51 Jacmel Dc
46 Jacobabad Bd
18 Jade & B. Ha
26 Jaén Bb
42 Jaffna Dg
47 Jagdalpur Hj
33 Jagersfontein Dc
46 Jagraon Ec
46 Jagtial Gj
43 Jahrom Gd
40 Jaipur Ed
10 Jakobshavn Mb
23 Jalalabad Cb
90 Jalapa Enri-
  quez Ed
46 Jalgaon Eh
14 Jalna Ej
23 Jalo Hd
46 Jalor Df
47 Jalpaiguri Me
91 Jamaica, I. Cc
47 Jamalur, East
  Pakistan Md
47 Jamalpur, India Lf
49 Jamdena Bd
81 James B. Aa
61 Jamestown,
  Australia Ab
84 Jamestown,
  N.D. Gb
88 Jamestown,
  N.Y. Fc
35 Jammer, B. Db
46 Jammu Eb
46 Jammu & Kashmir,
  St. Db
46 Jamnagar Cg
46 Jampur Cd
47 Jamshedpur Lg
34 Jan Mayen I. Bb
24 Jand Db
36 Janesville Db
9 Janin Bc
75 Janseville Cd
95 Januária Cc
37 Japan, king. Rf
3 Japan, S. of Cd
49 Japen I. & str. Ff
40 Jarash Bc
23 Jaroslaw Gc

8 Kintore Fc
8 Kintyre, dist. Ce
27 Kiparissia Bb
72 Kipushi Dd
51 Kir, prov. Gb
35 Kirensk Nd
34 Kirigizia Ke
51 Kirin Gb
62 Kiriwini Is. Hh
8 Kirkcaldy Ed
46 Kirklee Dj
10 Kirkenes Fb
27 Kirklareli Ca
8 Kirkmichael Ed
42 Kirkuk Eb
8 Kirkwall Fb
32 Kirov Jd
33 Kirovabad Jg
32 Kirovograd Ff
32 Kirovsk Fb
8 Kirriemuir Ed
33 Kirsanov He
17 Kirpehir Db
10 Kiruna Eb
72 Kirundu Dd
51 Kiryu Cc
72 Kisangani Dc
55 Kisarazu Cc
46 Kishangarh Ce
23 Kishinev Ef
55 Kishiwada Cd
46 Kishtwar Eb
51 Kisi Hb
73 Kisiju Fe
30 Kisköros Bb
30 Kiskunfelegy-haza Bb
30 Kiskunhalas Bb
73 Kismayu Gd
55 Kiso, R. Cd
70 Kisujszállás Cb
54 Kitakami, R. Dc
55 Kitakyūshū Bd
73 Kitale Fc
54 Kitami Db
81 Kitchener Ab
27 Kithira, I. Bb
27 Kithnos, I. Bb
80 Kitimat Bb
73 Kitwe Df
17 Kitzingen Dd
53 Kiukiang Fd
73 Kivu, L. Ec
32 Kizel Ld
27 Kizil, R. Da
72 Kladno Cc
17 Klagenfurt Fe
52 Klaipeda Bd
74 Klamath Falls Bc
51 Klaohsien C
11 Klausen P. Cb
74 Kiawer Bd
75 Klerksdorp Dc
35 Kletskaya Hf
8 Kleve Fc
51 Klin Gd
22 Klobuck Ec
22 Klodzko Dc
78 Klondike Db
17 Klosterneuburg Gd
13 Klosters Db
35 Klyuchevsk Vol.Td
7 Knighton Ee
17 Knittelfeld Fe
18 Knokke Cc
88 Knoxville Df
74 Knysna Cd
55 Kobaric Da
55 Kobayashi Bd
55 Kobe Cd
12 KöbenhavnsCo. Fd
19 Koblenz Gd
28 Kocevje Eb
55 Kochi & pref. Bd
82aKodiak & I. Cc
72 Koforidua Eg
55 Kofu Cc
71 Köge Fd
44 Kogota Dc
44 Kohat Cb
65 Kohima Ge
55 Kojima Bd
65 Kojonup Bd
34 Kokand Ke
34 Kokchetav Jd
50 Kokiu Ed
10 Kokkola Ec
88 Kokomo Bd
55 Kokura Bd
32 Kola Fb
32 Kola Pen. Gb
32 Kolar Fd
52 Kolarovgrad Fd
46 Kolayat (Srikolayabji) Dp
71 Kolkla Cd
12 Kolding Cd
11 Kolepom I. Fg
32 Kolguyev Jb
34 Kolguyev I. Gc
44 Kolhapur Ce
22 Kolin Cd

18 Köln, see Cologne Gd
22 Kolo Eb
22 Kolobrzeg Ca
51 Kolokani Df
32 Kolomna Gd
22 Kolomyya
22 Koiwezi
55 Kolyma R. & Ra. Sc
42 Kôm Ombo Cd
35 Komandorskiye Is. Td
22 Komárno Ee
75 Komatipoort Ec
53 Komatsushima Bd
27 Komotini Ca
48 KompongCham Bb
22 Kompong Som Bb
35 Komsomolets I. Ma
96 Komsomolska-ya Fb
35 Komsomolsk Qd
32 Kondopoga Fc
33 Konevo Gc
51 Kongmoon Fd
72 Kongolo Dc
11 Kongsberg Bd
22 Konin Ec
28 Konjic Fc
32 Konosha Hc
33 Konotop Fd
55 Konskie Fc
32 Konstantin-ovski Hf
13 Konstanz Da
47 Kontar Hk
27 Konya Db
73 Konza Fd
22 Koper Db
72 Kopervik Bd
28 Koprinvica Fa
34 Korat, see Nakhon Ratchasima
18 Korbach Hd
27 Korce Ba
28 Korcula, I. Fc
57 Korea, N. & S. Reps. Qf
52 Korea Str. Bb
27 Kórinthos Bb
55 Koriyama Dc
27 Korkuteli Db
51 Kornat, I. Ec
46 Koro S. Hk
60 Koroit Bc
33 Korosten Ee
55 Korsakov Re
11 Korsör Ed
33 Korsun Ff
18 Kortrijk Cd
60 Korumburra Cc
27 Kos, I. Cb
22 Koscian Db
61 Kosciusko, mt. Cc
23 Kosice Fd
39 Kosti Cd
33 Kostroma Hd
22 Kostrzyn Cb
22 Kosvenski Kamen Ld
22 Koszalin Da
22 Koszeg Ab
46 Kota Ef
48 Kota Bharu Ec
22 Kotabaru Sebuku Cd
49 Kota Kinabalu Cc
52 Kote Cd
52 Kotelnich Jd
22 Kotelnikovski Hf
51 Kotka Fc
52 Kotlas Jc
55 Kotli Db
51 Kotoor Bd
55 Kotri Bf
55 Kotuy R. Nb
72 Kouango Cb
70 Koudougou Ef
51 Kouroussa Df
13 Kovel Ee
72 Kovik Kb
22 Kovzhd Gc
51 Kowloon Fd
27 Kozani Bd
44 Kozhikode Df
52 Kozhva Lb
23 Kozienice Fc
33 Koziatoc Fc
31 Kpandu Fg
48 Kra, Isthmus of Bc
11 Kragero Bd
33 Kragujevac Cd
48 Krakatau I. Bd
23 Kraków (Cracow) Ec
22 Králicky Sneznik, mt. Dc
33 Kraljevo Cd
23 Kramatorsk Gf
51 Kranskop Ec
23 Krasnik Fc
33 Krasnoarmeisk Je
33 Krasnodar Gf
32 Krasnokamsk Ld

32 Krasnoufimsk Ld
34 Krasnovodsk He
33 Krasnoyarsk Md
33 Krasny He
33 Krasny Kut Je
23 Krasnytaw Gc
48 Kratie Bb
18 Krefeld Fb
33 Kremenchug Ff
17 Krems Fe
69 Kribi De
44 Krishna R. De
47 Krishnanagar Mg
11 Kristiansand Bd
10 Kristiansund Bc
11 Kristinehamn Cd
27 Kriti, see Crete Bb
33 Krivoy Rog Ff
28 Krk, I. Eb
22 Krkonose (Giant) Mts. Cc
22 Kromeriz Dd
22 Kromfors Dc
32 Kronshtadt Fd
75 Kroonstad Dc
33 Kropotkin Hf
51 Krosno Fd
22 Krotoszyn Dc
28 Krško Eb
75 Krugersdorp Dc
52 Krumlov Cd
50 Krusevac Cd
52 Krzepice Ec
70 Ksar el Kebir Db
48 Kuala Lipis Bc
26 Kuala Lumpur Bc
93 Kuala Selangor Bc
48 Kuala Trengganu Bc
33 Kuba Jg
33 Kuban Gf
50 Kucha Cb
28 Kuching Cc
46 Kuda Cg
48 Kudus Cd
32 Kudymkar Kd
94 Kuh-e-Hazaran, mt. Hd
15 Kuhmo Fc
91 Kuivaniemi Fb
91 Kuji Db
92 Kuldja Cb
81 Kulwin Bc
26 Kuma Hf
71 Kuma R. Jg
89 Kumamoto & pref. Bc
27 Kumara Ce
27 Kumasi Eg
44 Kumbakonam Df
46 Kunch Cd
32 Kungho Ec
32 Kungur Ld
50 Kunlun Shan, mts. Cc
50 Kunming Ed
52 Kunsan Bb
10 Kuopio Fc
49 Kupang De
33 Kupyansk Gf
33 Kura R. Jg
55 Kurashiki Bd
42 Kurdistan, reg. Db
55 Kure Bd
34 Kurgan Jd
50 Kuria Muria, Is. Ed
33 Kuril Is. Re
52 Kurland Bd
44 Kurnool De
52 Kurow Cf
51 Kurrikurri Db
33 Kursk Ge
51 Kursumlija Cd
33 Kuruman & R. Cc
55 Kurume Bd
32 Kurya Lc
50 Kushiro Db
26 Kushka Je
33 Kushtia Mg
13 Kussnacht Ca
27 Kütahya Cb
33 Kutaisi Hg
65 Kutch, Gulf of Bg
23 Kutno Eb
72 Kutu Bd
58 Kutum Ed
32 Kuvandyk Lf
45 Kuwait, st. Fd
54 Kuwana Cc
33 Kuybyshev Ke
33 Kuze, Isthmus of Db
11 Kragero Bd
51 Kwangchow Fd
51 Kwangju Bb
33 Kwangsi-Chuang Aut. Dist.
50 Kwangtung Fd
51 Kwangtung, prov. Fd
51 Kweichow, prov. Ed
51 Kweilin Fd
51 Kweiyang Ed
23 Kwidzyn Db

72 Kyabe Bb
33 Kyakhta Nd
45 Kyaukse Hd
8 Kyle of Lochalsh Cc
60 Kyneton Bc
54 Kyo, C. Bc
73 Kyoga, L. Ec
61 Kyogle Da
52 Kyongju Bb
54 Kyoto & pref. Cc
32 Kytlym Ld
55 Kyushu, I. & dist. Bd
31 Kyustendil Dd
34 Kzyl Kum Des. Je
34 Kzyl Orda Je

21 La Bochetta P. Ge
91 La Ceiba Ac
13 La Chaux de Fonds Aa
92 La Chorrera Bc
16 La Coruña Aa
84 La Crosse Bc
16 La Esperanza Cb
26 La Estrada Aa
88 La Fayette Bd
88 La Folette Cf
70 La Goulette Ha
64 La Grange Cb
20 la Grand Combe Ce
92 La Guaira Ca
26 La Linea Ab
26 La Louvère Dd
26 La Mancha, dist. Bb
93 La Pampa, prov. Cf
92 La Paraqua Cb
94 La Paz, Bolivia Bc
94 La Paz, Par. Df
90 La Paz, & is. Bb
84 La Plata, R. de Df
88 La Porte Bd
94 La Rioja Be
15 La Roche sur Yon Cd
15 La Rochelle Cd
91 La Romana Ec
91 La Serena Ae
92 La Tagua Bb
81 La Tuque Bb
81 La Union Bc
26 La Union Bb
94 La Vega Dc
71 Labe Cf
22 Labe (Elbe) R. Cb
79 Labrador Lc
49 Labuan, I. Cc
49 Labuha Dd
8 Labuk R. Cc
80 Lac la Biche Cb
80 Lac Jeannine Ca
92 La Paz, Mts. de Af
44 Laccadive Is. Cf
13 Lachen Ca
81 Lachine Bb
60 Lachlan R. Bb
81 Lacombe Cb
89 Laconia Kc
43 Ladis Jd
72 Ladismith Cd
52 Ladoga, L. Fc
56 Ladrone Is, see Mariana Is.
75 Ladybrand Dc
75 Ladysmith, Canada Bc
75 Ladysmith, Natal Dc
62 Lae Db
12 Laesö, I. Eb
87 Lafayette Be
55 Lages Ee
95 Lagöa dos Patos, L. Ef
71 Lagos, Nig. Fg
26 Lagos, Port. Ab
77 Lagrange De
55 Laguna Fe
85 Laguna Madre Gf
46 Lahore Eb
11 Lahti Fc
68 Lai De
61 Laidley Da
43 Laila Fe
74 Laingsburg Cd
87 Lake Charles Be
87 Lake City De
85 Lake Grace Be
79 Lake Harbour Ld
87 Lakeland Df
81 Lakes Entrance Cc
88 Lakewood Ed
47 Lakhimpur He
46 Lakhpat Bg
83 Lakselv Ea
44 Lakshadweep Is. Cf
47 Lalitpur Gf
9 Lambay I. Ec
26 Lamego, R. Aa
27 Lámia Bb
64 Limmen Bight Fa

7 Lampeter Ce
73 Lamu Gd
83bLanai, I. Cb
8 Lanark Ed
6 Lancashire, co. Ed
6 Lancaster Ec
79 Lancaster Sd. Ja
51 Lanchow Ec
72 Landana Ae
17 Landeck De
15 Landes, dept. Ce
21 Landsberg Ja
7 Land's End Bg
17 Landshut Ed
10 Langanes Ca
74 Langeberge, mt. Cc
12 Langeland Ee
13 Langenthal Ba
1 Lageoog, I. Ga
12 Langsele Dc
20 Languedoc, dist. Hf
88 Lansing Cc
12 Lanusei Bc
70 Lanzarote, I. Cc
49 Laoag Db
14 Laon Ec
48 Laos, st. Bb
88 Lapeer Dc
70 Lapland, region Fb
5 Laptev Sea Ob
16 Lapua Ec
23 Lapy Gb
43 Lar Gd
70 Larache Da
84 Laramie Ec
85 Laredo Gf
28 Larino Ed
27 Larisa Bb
27 Larkana Be
27 Larnaka Dc
9 Larne Fb
11 Larvik Bd
20 Larzac, Causse du, mts. Bf
85 Las Cruces Ef
64 Las Khoreh Dd
86 Las Palmas Ac
95 Las Piumas Cg
90 Las Tres Marias, Is. Cc
85 Las Vegas, Nev. Cd
85 Las Vegas, New Mexico Fd
45 Lashio Hd
22 Lask Ec
83 Latakia (Al Ladhiqiyah) Bb
29 Latina Dd
8 Latheron Eb
61 Latrobe Cd
32 Latvia Bd
6 Lau or Eastern Group, Is. Hk
8 Lauder Ee
13 Lauben Ba
7 Launceston, England Cg
61 Launceston,Tas.Cd
95 Laura Eb
87 Laurel Ce
86 Laurium Cb
55 Lauro Müller Fe
13 Lausanne Ab
49 Laut I. Cd
14 Laval Cc
85 Laverton Cd
13 Lavis Bc
95 Lavras Gd
65 Lawlers Cd
71 Lawra Ef
86 Lawrence, Kan. Ad
89 Lawrence,Mass.Kc
67 Lawrence, N.Z. Bf
85 Lawton Ge
11 Laxa Cd
36 Laysan I. Eb
29 Lazio, prov. Dd
16 le Chambon-Feugerolles Cd
15 Le Creusot Ce
14 Le Havre Dc
70 Le Kef Ga
14 Le Mans Dd
54 Le Marinel Df
16 Le Puy Bd
12 Le Touquet Db
14 Le Tréport De
86 Leadville Ed
69 Leali Eg
88 Leamington, Canada Dc
7 Leamington, England Fe
86 Learmonth Ac
86 Leavenworth Ad

88 Lebanon, Ind. Bd
87 Lebanon, Mo. Bd
89 Lebanon, Pa. Gd
40 Lebanon, st. Bc
75 Lebombo Mts. Ec
7 Lecce Gd
21 Lecco, & L. di Fd
17 Lechtaler Alpen, mts. Jb
22 Leczyca Eb
7 Ledbury Ee
80 Leduc Cb
9 Leeds Fd
60 Leeton Cb
18 Leeuwarden Ea
65 Leeuwin C. Be
91 Leeward Is. Fc
49 Legaspi Db
7 Leghorn (Livorno) Cc
28 Legnago Cc
21 Legnano Gd
22 Legnica Dc
44 Len Db
16 Lene Cb
74 Lehututu Cd
7 Leicester & co. Fe
21 Leinhardt Ra. Cc
62 Leicnharut R. Ab
18 Leiden Db
60 Leigh Creek Ab
9 Leinster, prov. Ec
16 Leipzig Ed
26 Leiria Ab
11 Leirvik Bd
80 Leismer Cb
8 Leitn Ke
9 Leitrim, co. Cb
9 Leixlip Ec
9 Léman, L. (L. of Geneva) Ab
12 Lemvig Bc
35 Lena, R. Pc
34 Leninabad Je
33 Leninakan Hg
34 Leningrad Fd
34 Leninogorsk Ld
34 Leninsk Kuznetski Ld
21 Leno Jd
14 Lens Eb
29 Lentini Ef
13 Lenzburg Ca
15 Leoben Fa
17 Leobe Dc
9 Leogane Dc
7 Leominster, England Ee
89 Leominster, U.S.A. Bd
91 Leon, Nicaragua Ad
90 Leon, Mexico Dc
26 León & prov. Aa
62 Leongatha Cd
25 Leonora Cd
62 Leopold II, L. Bd
90 Lerdo Db
26 Lérida Fa
20 Léros, I. Cc
31 Lerwick Inset
9 Les Cayes Dc
31 Leskovac Dd
8 Leslie Ed
75 Lesotho, st. Ec
91 Lesser Antilles Fd
49 Lesser Sunda Is. Ce
18 Lessines Cd
27 Lésvos, I. Cb
22 Leszno Dc
20 Lethbridge Cc
45 Letpadan He
9 Letterkenny Db
80 Leukerbad Bb
18 Leuven Dd
17 Levádhia Bd
18 Levanto Bb
8 Leven Fd
8 Leven, L. Ed
64 Levêque C. Cb
66 Leverkusen Fc
66 Levier Ab
66 Levin Ab
23 Levis Bb
26 Levoca Fd
27 Levtas, I. Bb
16 Levuka, I. Gk
7 Lewes Hg
8 Lewis, dist. Bb
31 Lewisporte Db
84 Lewiston Cb
84 Lewistown Eb
66 Lexington Ce
49 Leyte, I. Db
23 Lezajsk Gc
50 Lhasa Dd
35 Liaoning, prov. Gb
57 Liaoyang Gb
57 Liaoyuan Gb
74 Liebe, see Andara Ca
85 Liberal Fd
22 Liberec Cc
68 Liberia, rep. Afr. Be
9 Libreville De

68 Libya, king. Dc
38 Libyan Des. Bc
29 Licata Df
13 Lichfield Fe
72 Lichtenburg Dc
23 Liezbark Fa
21 Liechtenstein, st. Hb
21 Liège Ee
17 Lienz Ee
52 Liepaja Dd
18 Lier Dc
21 Liestal Ba
19 Lietard Bd
19 Lievin Bd
21 Liguria, prov. Ge
28 Ligurian S. Dc
72 Likasi Df
72 Likati Cc
52 Likholavi Gd
15 Lile Kb
11 Lillehammer Cc
80 Lilliesand Bd
80 Lillooet Cb
92 Lima, Peru Gd
88 Lima, U.S.A. Cd
25 Limanowa Fd
27 Limassol Ce
9 Limavady Ea
17 Limburg Cc
95 Limeira Fd
9 Limerick & co. Cd
72 Limjorci Jd
27 Limnos, I. Cb
15 Limoges De
91 Limon De
15 Limousin Dc
16 Limpopo, R. Db
73 Limuru Fd
21 Lina Ed
93 Linares, Chile Hf
90 Linares, Mexico Ec
9 Linaskea Db
8 Lincoln & co., England Gd
67 Lincoln, N.Z. De
84 Lincoln, U.S.A. Gc
21 Lindau Hb
14 Lindesnes Bd
21 Lindi Fe
27 Lindos Cb
81 Lingayen & G. Db
18 Lingen Gb
48 Lingga Arch. Bc
21 Lingoe Bb
29 Linguaglossa Ef
70 Linguere Ae
7 Linney Hd. Cf
52 Linola Dc
11 Linz Fd
35 Lions, G. of Ff
25 Lipari, Is. Ef
23 Lipetsk Ge
21 Lipno Eb
18 Lippstadt Hc
23 Lira Ec
52 Lisala Cc
26 Lisbon Ab
9 Lisburn Eb
9 Lisianski I. Eb
13 Liski Ce
61 Lismore, Australia Da
9 Lismore, Ire. Cd
52 Lisnaskea Db
81 Listowel, Can. Bd
9 Listwel, Ire. Bd
20 Lithgow Db
72 Lithinon, C. Bc
52 Lithuania Dd
21 Litomerice Cc
87 Little Abaco, I. Ef
81 Little Barrier I. Eb
13 Little Belt Cd
88 Little Current Eb
89 Little Falls, Minn. Bb
89 Little Falls, N.Y. Hc
46 Little Rann Cc
81 Little River Dd
87 Little Rock Ed
21 Littlehampton Gg
51 Liuchow Ed
61 Liverpool, Australia Db
81 Liverpool, Can. Cb
9 Liverpool, Eng. Ed
72 Livingstone Db
73 Livingstone Ge
9 Livny Ge
67 Livramento Df
20 Livron Ce
7 Lizard Pt. Bg
23 Ljubljana Ea
11 Ljusdal Dc
6 Llandudno Dd
7 Llanelli Cf
7 Llanfyllin De
85 Llano Estacado Fe
69 Loango Df
69 Loangwa Fg

75 Lobatsi Dc
72 Lobito Af
13 Locarno Dc
8 Lochaber Cd
9 Lochmaddy Ac
89 Loch Haven Gd
61 Lockhart Cc
89 Lockport Fc
47 Lou (Lydda) Dc
46 Loahran Cd
7 Lockerbie Fd
72 Lodja Cd
21 Lodi Gd
22 Łódź Ec
10 Lofoten Is. Cb
88 Logan Dc
78 Logan, Mt. Db
88 Logansport Bd
26 Logrono Ba
19 Loir Jd
20 Loire, R. & dept. Cd
47 Loire-Atlantique, dept. Dc
20 Loiret, dept. Cc
18 Lokeren Cc
72 Lokoiama Bd
12 Lolland, I. Ee
30 Lom, Bulgaria Dd
11 Lom, Norway Bc
72 Lomami, R. Cd
21 Lombardia, prov. Hd
49 Lombok, I. Cd
71 Lome Fg
22 Lombela & R. Cd
72 Lomie Ac
8 Lomond, L. Dd
23 Lomza Gb
18 London, Can. Ab
7 London, Eng. Hf
9 Londonderry & co. Db
85 Long Beach Ce
9 Long Eaton Fe
7 Long I., Bahamas Cc
89 Long I., U.S.A. Jd
48 Long Xuyen Bb
20 Longford, Ireland Dc
9 Longford & co., Ireland Dc
81 Longlac Ab
72 Longreach Bc
20 Longview Bd
18 Longwy Ee
18 Loningen Gb
20 Lons le Saunier Dc
10 Lonsdal De
7 Looe Cg
65 Loongana De
9 Loop Hd. Bd
51 Lopphavet Ea
68 Loralai Bd
72 Lorca Bb
56 Lord Howe I. Ce
85 Lordsburg Ee
95 Lorena Fd
18 Loreto Bd
19 Lorient Bd
14 Lorraine, reg. Gc
85 Los Alamos Ed
90 Los Angeles Ed
90 Los Mochis Cc
90 Loshkar Ola Jd
21 Lošinj, I. Eb
8 Lossiemouth Ec
20 Lot, R. Ae
87 Lotagipi Swamp Eb
8 Lothian, Co. Ed
72 Loto Cd
13 Lobschberg Tunnel Bb
71 Louga Be
7 Loughborough Fe
9 Loughrea Cc
85 Louis Trichardt Eb
90 Louisiade Arch. Cd
86 Louisiana, st. Dc
66 Louisville Ce
15 Lourdes Cf
9 Louth, co. Ec
32 Lovat Fd
23 Low Tatra, mt. Ed
72 Lowa Cd
89 Lowell Kc
90 Lower California Bb
67 Lower Hutt Bb
35 Lower Tunguska, R. Mc
7 Lowestoft Je
23 Loyev Fe
56 Loyalty Is. De
72 Loyang Fc
72 Lozere, dept. De
72 Luanda Ae
48 Luang Prabang Bb
73 Luangwa, R. Ef
73 Luanshya Df

73 Luapula. R. Df
23 Lubaczów Gc
23 Luban Cc
69 Lubango Dg
23 Lubartów Gc
23 Lubawa Eb
85 Lubbock Ec
16 Lübeck Db
22 Lublin Gc
15 Lubny Fe
72 Lubudi Df
72 Lubumbashi Df
23 Lubutu Dd
21 Lucca Cc
26 Lucena Bb
23 Lucenec Ed
23 Lucera Ed
51 Luchow Ed
16 Luckenwalde Db
47 Lucknow He
18 Lüdenscheid Gc
74 Lüderitz (Angra Pequena) Bc
46 Ludhiana Ec
88 Ludington Bb
7 Ludlow Ee
21 Ludvika Bc
16 Ludwigsburg Jf
15 Ludwigshafen Ce
72 Luebo Ce
72 Lufira, R. De
72 Lufkin Bd
21 Luga Ed
15 Lugano Cb
72 Lugansk, see Voroshilovgrad Gf
73 Lugenda, R. Ff
73 Lugh Ferrandi Gc
26 Lugo, Spain Aa
28 Lugo, Italy Cc
51 Lugoj Cc
72 Luhaiya Dd
21 Luino Gd
72 Luisa Cf
72 Lukenie, R. Bd
72 Lukolela Bd
72 Luków Gc
72 Lukea Eb
27 Lüleburgaz Ca
72 Lulonga, R. Bc
72 Lulua, R. Ce
72 Luluabourg, see Kananga
45 Lumding Gc
67 Lumsden Bf
11 Lund Cd
7 Lundy I. Cf
72 Lüneburg Db
72 Lüneburg Heath Cb
16 Lünen Gc
19 Lunéville Ff
33 Luni Df
33 Luninets Ee
73 Luofo Bc
8 Lurgan Eb
69 Lusaka Bd
72 Lusambo Cd
73 Lushoto Fd
73 Lüt-ta (Port Arthur-Dairen)
7 Luton Gc
23 Lutsk Ee
4 Luxembourg, st. Gf
38 Luxor Cb
23 Luzern Ca
95 Luziania Ff
23 Luzicke Hory Cc
49 Luzon, I. Db
33 Lvov Dr
55 Lyakhov Is. Rb
*46 Lyallpur Dc
10 Lycksele Dc
7 Lydd Hg
40 Lydda (Lod) Bd
75 Lydenburg Ed
67 Lyell Bd
7 Lyme Regis Eg
7 Lymington Fg
84 Lynchburg Ff
8 Lyndhurst Ab
9 Lynn Kc
80 Lynn Lake Db
20 Lyon (Lyons) Ce
20 Lyonnais, dist. Cd
11 Lysekil Cd
73 Lyttelton Be
73 Lyudinovo Fe

42 Ma'an Dc
51 Maanshan Fc
11 Maarianhamina Dc
40 Ma'arrat an Nu'man Da
27 Maas, R. Ed
18 Maaseik Ed
18 Maastricht Ed
75 Mabrouk Bd
85 McAllen Cd
51 Macao Fd
92 Macapá Db
7 Macclesfield Ed
49 McCluer G. Ef
87 McComb Be
84 McCook Fc
64 Macdonald L. Dc
64 McDonnell Ranges Ec
8 Macduff Fc
27 Macedonia, prov. Ba
92 Maceió Fc
71 Macenta Dg
28 Macerata Ed
44 Machilipatnam Ee
7 Machydlwy Dd
*71 Macias Nguema Biyoga, I. Gh
62 Mackay Cc
44 Mackay L. Dc
88 Mackesport Ed
78 Mackenzie B. Da
78 Mackenzie Mts. Db
62 Mackenzie R., Australia Cc
78 Mackenzie, R., Canada Eb
78 Mackenzie, terr. Fb
78 Mackinaw City Cb
82 McKinley, mt. Cb
15 Macksville Db
61 Maclean Da
75 Maclear Dd
66 McLennan Cb
16 Macleod Cc
96 McMurdo Sd. Kb
29 Macomer Bd
26 Mâcon, France Cc
84 Macon, U.S.A. De
72 Macondo Cf
3 Macquarie I. Ph
69 Madagascar, I. Gg
62 Madang Gh
7 Madaripur Ng
11 Madeira, I. Ab
68 Madeira, R. Dd
46 Madera Cc
4 Madhya Pradesh, st. Hg
22 Madimba Ad
39 Madinat al Shaab Dd
72 Madingou Ad
86 Madison, Ind. Ce
84 Madison, Wis. Cc
88 Madisonville Bf
49 Madiene Cd
44 Madras Df
93 Madre de Dios, I. Bh
9 Madrid Ba
46 Madura, I. Cd
46 Madurai Dg
55 Maebashi Cc
75 Mafeking, Can. Db
†75 Mafeking, Cape Province Dc
65 Mafra Cc
73 Mafia, I. Fd
35 Magadan Sd
92 Magadi Fd
75 Magato Hills Eb
71 Magburaka Cg
46 Magdala Cg
81 Magdalen Is. Hd
90 Magdalena Gc
16 Magdeburg Db
45 Magelang Cd
89 Magellan's str. Bh
2 Magenta Gd
21 Mageride, Monts de la, mts. Be
21 Maggiore, Lago Gd
96 Magnetic South Pole Jc
34 Magnitogorsk Hd
91 Magos Jd
52 Mahabaleshwar Dc
85 Mahakam R. Cc
46 Maharashtra, st. Ce
67 Mahé Df
67 Maheno Cf
26 Mahón Gb
7 Mai Ndombe, L. Bd
43 Maidan-i-Naftan Fc
7 Maidstone Hf
33 Maiduguri Hg
34 Maikop Gg
34 Maimana Hc
16 Maine, st. Gb
14 Maine-et-Loire, dept. Cd
46 Mainpuri Fd
16 Mainz Cd
21 Maira, R. Gd
70 Maison Carrée Fa
61 Maitland Db
55 Maizuru Cc
26 Majorca, see Mallorca, I. Cb
†69 Majunga Cg

* Renamed Shah Faisalabad
† Renamed Bioko
† Renamed Mafikeng
‡ Renamed Mahajanga

71 Maka-Koullbentane Cf
75 Makarikari Salt-pan Cb
49 Makasar Str. Cd
71 Makeni Cg
33 Makeyevka Gf
33 Makhachkala Jg
73 Makindu Fd
30 Mako Db
23 Maków Ed
44 Makran, prov. Hd
72 Makumbi Ce
55 Makurazaki Bd
44 Malabar Coast Df
48 Malacca Bc
48 Malacca, str. of Bc
84 Malad City Dc
26 Maladetta, Mt. Ca
26 Málaga Bb
73 Malakal Eb
48 Malang Cd
72 Malanje Be
11 Malaren, L. Dd
75 Malatele Dd
42 Malatya Db
69 Malawi Fg
•48 Malay Pen. Ac
37 Malaya, st. Oj
43 Malaysia, st. Bc
65 Malcolm Ed
18 Maldegem Cc
44 Maldive Is. Cg
7 Maldon Hf
27 Maléa, C. Bb
46 Malegaon Eh
11 Mali, st. Df
73 Malindi, Kenya Gd
75 Malindi, Rhod. Da
8 Mallaig Cd
26 Mallorca (Majorca), I. Cb
9 Mallow Cd
10 Malmberget Eb
19 Malmedy Fd
74 Malmesbury, Cape Province Bf
7 Malmesbury, England Ff
11 Malmö Cd
33 Maloshuika Gc
24 Malta, I. Ec
74 Maltahohe Bb
44 Malvan Ce
1 Malvern Ed
74 Mamou Cg
6 Man, I. of Ce
61 Manado Dc
64 Managua Ad
61 Manapouri Af
50 Manass Cb
52 Manaus Cc
6 Manchester Ed
89 Manchester, U.S.A. Jc
37 Manchuria, reg. Qe
11 Mandal Bd
45 Mandalay Hd
39 Mandeb, Bab el, Str. of Dd
47 Mandla Hg
46 Mandsaur Ef
46 Manfredi Bg
30 Manfredonia Ed
60 Mangalore, Austral. Cc
44 Mangalore, India Cf
66 Mangaweka Ec
69 Mangoche Fg
66 Mangonui Da
50 Mangyai Dc
43 Manicoré Cc
92 Manifa Af
47 Manikpur Hf
49 Manila Db
61 Manilla Db
45 Manipur Gd
27 Manisa Cb
88 Manistee Bb
88 Manistique Bb
80 Manitoba, L. Bb
78 Manitoba, prov. Hc
88 Manitoulin I. Bb
88 Manitowoc Bb
92 Manizales Bb
46 Manjhand Bf
46 Mankato Bc
61 Manly Db
46 Manmad Eh
44 Mannar, & G. Dg
19 Mannheim He
44 Manokwari Ef
79 Mansel I. Jb
88 Mansfield, Australia Cc
88 Mansfield, U.S.A. Dd
33 Mansura Cb
88 Manton Cb
73 Mantova Jd
32 Manturovo Hd
66 Manukau Eb

62 Manus I. Gg
63 Many Peaks Dc
73 Manyara, L. Fd
35 Manych Hf
33 Manyoni Ec
46 Manzai Cb
41 Manzala, L. Bb
91 Manzanillo, Cuba Cb
90 Manzanillo, Mexico Dd
62 Maprik Fg
75 Maputo Ec
39 Maqdala Cd
42 Maqna Dd
39 Maqualle Cd
93 Mar del Plata Df
92 Maracaibo & L. Ba
92 Maracay Ca
43 Maragheb Fb
92 Marajo L. Ec
65 Maralinga Ed
92 Maranhao, st. Ec
63 Maranoa R. Cd
92 Mareeba Cb
74 Mariental Bb
11 Mariestad Cd
87 Marietta, Ga. Dc
88 Marietta, W.Va. Ee
35 Mariinsk Ld
88 Marinette Bb
95 Maringa Ed
58 Marion, Ind. Cd
88 Marion, Mich. Cb
88 Marion, Ohio Dd
31 Maritsa, R. Ed
40 Marj U'yun Bc
7 Market Drayton Ee
7 Market Harborough Ge
6 Market Weighton Gd
89 Markham, Mt. Ja
23 Marlbork Ea
7 Marlborough Ff
67 Marlborough, dist. Dd
27 Marmara, S. of Ca
27 Marmaris Cb
19 Marne, R. Ce
60 Maroona Bc
57 Marquesas Is. Gd
86 Marquette Cb
70 Marrakech Db
60 Marree Aa
75 Marromeu Fa
34 Marsa Fatma Dd
29 Marsala Df
15 Marseilles Ff
71 Marshall, Lib. Cg
87 Marshall, U.S.A. Bc
56 Marshall Is. Dc
86 Marshalltown Bc
12 Marstal Dd
11 Marstrand Cd
45 Martaban, & G. Chan. Ga
47 Marti He
91 Marti Cb
67 Martinborough Ed
91 Martinique, I. Fd
88 Martins Fy Ed
89 Martinsburg Fe
88 Martinsville, Ind. Be
88 Martinsville, Va. Ff
66 Marton Ed
66 Marugame Bd
92 Marupa Fc
66 Marupara Fc
46 Marwar Ef
63 Maryborough, Queens. Dc
60 Maryborough, Vic. Bc
83 Maryland, st. Fc
84 Marysville Bd
68 Marzuq Dc
73 Masaka Ed
52 Masan Bb
91 Masaya Ad
49 Masbate, & I. Db
70 Mascara Fa

75 Maseru Dc
43 Mashhad Hb
75 Mashonaland, dist. Ea
73 Masindi Ec
38 Masira, G. of Ed
43 Masjed Soley-man Fc
43 Maskati, R. Jd
86 Mason City Bc
11 Mass Cd
28 Massa Cb
83 Massachusetts, st. Fb
75 Massangena Ed
89 Massena Hb
20 Massif Central, plat. Cc
67 Masterton Ed
44 Mastuj Ca
55 Masuda Bd
43 Masurian Lakes Fb
75 Matabeleland, dist. Da
51 Matad Fb
72 Matadi Ae
91 Matagalpa Ad
71 Matam Ce
90 Matamoros Ec
43 Matane Cb
82 Matanuska Db
91 Matanzas Bb
27 Matapan, see Tainaron Bb
92 Mataram Cd
26 Mataró Ad
92 Mataura Bg
30 Matehuala Dc
29 Matera Fd
30 Mateszalka Eb
46 Mathura Fe
74 Matjesfontein Cd
92 Mato Grosso st. Dd
75 Matobe Eb
91 Matopo Hills Db
34 Matruh Bb
50 Matsue Bc
54 Matsumae Dc
55 Matsumoto Cc
55 Matsuyama Bd
55 Matsuzaka Cd
13 Matterhorn, mt. Bc
66 Mau Ranipur Gf
71 Maubeuge Cd
45 Maubin He
53 Mauer L. Fa
57 Maui I. Fb
74 Maun Ca
83 Mauna Loa, vol. Dc
20 Maurienne, dist. Ed
68 Mauritania, rep. Bc
3 Mauritius, I. Kg
37 Maushij Dd
90 Mawson Ec
91 Mayaguana, I. Db
91 Mayaguez Ed
8 Maybole De
87 Mayfield Cd
9 Maynooth Ec
9 Mayo, co. Bc
38 Mazari-i-Sharif Fb
90 Mazatlan Cc
32 Mazelkia Dd
75 Mazoe Ea
29 Mazzard Df
75 Mbabane Ec
73 Mbale (Aber-corn) Ec
71 Mbalmayo Hh
72 Mbanza Congo Ae
72 Mbandaka Bc
72 M'Bomu, R. Cc
72 Mbuji-Mayi Ce
78 M'Clintock Chan. Ga
78 M'Clure Str. Ea
85 Mead, L. Dd
88 Meadville Ed
9 Meath, co. Ec
14 Meaux Ec
18 Mechelen Dc
11 Mécheria Eb
48 Medan Ac
91 Médéa Fa
92 Medellin Bb
71 Medenine Be
30 Medias Eb
80 Medicine Hat Cb
42 Medina, Saudi Arabia De
26 Medina, Spain Ba
18 Medinaceli Ba
4 Mediterranean S Jh
15 Medoc, dist. Ce
26 Meekatharra Bd
46 Meerut Fd
27 Megara Bb
45 Meghalaya, st. Gc
27 Megiste, I. Cb
46 Mehsana Dg
51 Meihsien Fd

45 Meiktila Hd
13 Meiringen Cb
16 Meissen Ec
72 Meiyanga Ab
20 Mejean, Causse, mts. Be
39 Mekele Cd
46 Mekhtar Bc
70 Meknès Db
48 Mekong R. Ba
49 Melalap Cc
60 Melbourne Bc
21 Melegnano Hd
29 Melfi Ed
80 Melfort Db
70 Melilla Ea
33 Melitopol Gf
95 Melo Ef
*75 Meisetter Ea
7 Melton Mowbray, Ge
80 Melville Db
8 Melville B. Aa
64 Melville C. Ba
64 Melville I., Australia Ea
78 Melville I., Can. Fa
79 Melville Pen. Jb
69 Memba Gg
21 Memmingen Jb
87 Memphis Cd
43 Menai Ahmadi Fd
88 Menasha Ad
27 Menderes, R. Cb
93 Mendoza, & prov. Cc
27 Menemen Cb
29 Meni Df
48 Menggala Bd
70 Melilla Ea
60 Menindee Bb
48 Menkong Hc
88 Menominee Bd
26 Menorca, I. Cb
41 Mentawal is. Ad
21 Menton Ff
70 Menzel Temime Ha
65 Menzies Cd
18 Meppen Gb
21 Merano Kc
49 Merauke Gg
39 Merca Be
44 Mercara Df
39 Mercedes De
66 Mercer Eb
45 Mergui & Arch. Hf
46 Merida, Mexico Gc
26 Merida, Spain Ab
92 Merida, Cord. de Bb
87 Meridan Cd
89 Meriden Jd
18 Merksem Dc
86 Merowe Cd
65 Merredin Be
86 Merrill Cb
7 Mersea, I. Jf
16 Merseburg Dc
6 Mersey, R. Ed
6 Merseyside, Co. Ed
27 Mersin Db
7 Merthyr Tydfil Df
19 Merzig Fe
85 Mesa De
39 Mesewa Cd
73 Meshra er Req Db
27 Mesolongion Bb
42 Mesopotamia, reg. Ec
29 Messina, Italy Ee
75 Messina, Trans. Db
27 Messini, G. of Bb
28 Mestre Db
73 Metemma Fa
8 Methil Ed
67 Methven Ce
28 Metlika Eb
14 Metz Gc
90 Mexicali Aa
90 Mexico Ed
77 Mexico, Rep. Hf
77 Mexico, G. of Kf
32 Mezen & R. Hb
19 Mézières De
30 Mezotur Cb
66 Mhow Eg
87 Miami Df
43 Mianeh Fb
46 Mianwali Cb
75 Miaoli Gd
88 Michigan, L. Bb
83 Michigan, st. Bb
88 Michigan City Bd
81 Michipicoten Harb. Cb
31 Michurin Fd
33 Michurinsk He
7 Mid Glamorgan Df
70 Middle Atlas, mts. Db
75 Middelburg, Cape Province Dd
18 Middelburg, Netherlands Cc

6 Middlesbrough Fc
90 Middlesex Gd
89 Middletown, Conn. Jd
89 Middletown, New York Hd
88 Middleton, Ohio Ce
7 Midhurst Gg
88 Midland, Can. Fa
88 Midland, Mich. Cc
85 Midland, Tex. Fe
65 Midland Junction Be
9 Midleton Ce
47 Midnapore Lg
56 Midway I. Eb
27 Midye Ca
55 Mie pref. Cd
22 Miedzychód Cb
23 Miedzyrzec Gc
30 Miercurea Cluc Eb
26 Mieres Aa
55 Mihara Bd
11 Mikkeli Fc
27 Mikonos Cb
21 Milano (Milan) Hd
27 Milas Cb
7 Mildenhall He
60 Mildura Bb
63 Miles Dd
84 Miles City Eb
89 Milford He
7 Milford Haven Bf
70 Miliana Fc
6 Miling Be
20 Millau Be
18 Millelland Canal Gb
81 Millertown Db
60 Millicent Bc
27 Milos Bb
9 Milton Malbay Bd
88 Milwaukee Bc
43 Minab Hd
55 Minamata Bd
26 Minas de Rio Tinto Ab
92 Minas Gerais, st. Ed
45 Minbu Ge
21 Mincio, R. Jd
49 Mindanao, I.& S. Dc
21 Minoel, R. Ja
18 Minden Hb
23 Minsk Fe
23 Minsk Mazowiecki Fb
53 Minusinsk Md
38 Minya Cc
50 Minya Konka, mt. Ed
41 Miraj Ce
46 Miram Shah Cb
94 Miranda, Braz. Dd
26 Miranda, Spain Ba
21 Mirandola Ke
20 Mirecourt Ea
43 Mirfa Ge
48 Miri Cc
75 Mirny Fc
46 Mirpur Khas Bf
47 Mirzapur Jf
43 Mishaab Fd
88 Mishan Hb
88 Mishawaka Bd
48 Miskolc Ca
40 Misōōl, I. Ed
55 Mississippi, R. Bd
83 Mississippi, st. Fc
84 Missouri, R. Ed
84 Missouri, st. Dc
11 Mistassini, L. Ba
29 Mistretta Df
63 Misurata Db
63 Mitchell, Australia Cd
84 Mitchell, U.S.A. Gc
62 Mitchell R. Bb
60 Mitchelstown Cd
47 Mitilini Cb
55 Mito Dc
30 Mitrovica Bc
54 Mitsugo, I. (Tori Shima) Cd
11 Mittagong Db
13 Mittenwald Be
72 Mitzick Ac

* Renamed Peninsular Malaysia

* Renamed Chimanimani

* Renamed Namibe

89 New Bedford Kd
85 New Braunfels Gf
87 New Brighton De
89 New Britain Jd
62 New Britain, I. Hh
79 New Brunswick,
   prov. Ld
56 New Caledonia Dc
88 New Castle, Ind. Cc
88 New Castle, Pa. Ed
26 New Castle,
   prov. Bb
8 New Cumnock Ee
81 New Glasgow Cb
62 New Guinea,
   Terr. of Gg
83 New Hampshire,
   st. Fb
62 New Hanover,
   I. Hg
89 New Haven Kd
* 56 New Hebrides Dd
87 New Iberia Be
62 New Ireland, I. Hg
89 New Jersey, st. Fc
88 New
   Kensington Jd
89 New London Jd
8 New Mexico, st. Cc
61 New Norfolk Cd
87 New Orleans Bf
88 New
   Philadelphia Ed
66 New Plymouth Ec
91 New Providence
   I. Ca
7 New Quay Ce
7 New Radnor De
9 New Ross Ed
35 New Siberian
   Is. Qb
59 New South Wales,
   st. He
86 New Ulm He
80 New
   Westminster Bc
89 New York Jd
83 New York, st. Fb
66 New Zealand,
   st. Dc
73 Newala Ff
79 Newark, N.J. Hd
89 Newark, N.Y. Gd
58 Newark, Ohio Dd
88 Newaygo Cc
89 Newburgh Hd
89 Newbury Ff
89 Newburyport Kc
61 Newcastle,
   Australia Db
81 Newcastle, Can. Cb
6 Newcastle,Eng. Fb
9 Newcastle, Ire. Bd
75 Newcastle, Nat. Dc
_9 Newcastle, N.
   Ire. Fb
64 Newcastle
   Waters Eb
85 Newchastleton Ee
65 Newdegate Be
79 Newfoundland,
   prov. Lc
7 Newhaven Hg
89 Newmarket Fe
87 Newport, Ark. Bd
87 Newport, Eng. Fg
8 Newport, Ire. Bc
89 Newport, R.I. Kd
7 Newport, Scot. Fd
7 Newport, Wales Ef
89 Newport News Gf
7 Newquay Bg
9 Newry Eb
87 Newton, Iowa Bc
88 Newton, Mass. Kc
7 Newton Abbot Eg
8 Newtown
   Forbes Dc
9 Newtown
   Stewart Db
6 Newtownards Fb
43 Neyriz Gd
33 Neyshabur Hb
33 Nezhin Fe
74 Ngami, Former
   L. Cb
68 Ngaoundere De
67 Ngapara Cf
75 Nguru Hf
60 Nhill Bc
32 Niagara Falls Fc
71 Niamey Ff
48 Nias, I. Ac
71 Nicaragua, rep. Kg
91 Nicaragua, L. Ad
29 Nicastre Fe
21 Nice Ff
45 Nicobar Is. Gg
29 Nicosia, Italy Ef
27 Nicosia, Cyprus Db
91 Nicoya Pen. Ad
31 Niedersachsen,
   prov. Hb
26 Nienburg Cb

92 Nieuw Nickerie Dh
18 Nieuwpoort Bc
20 Nievre, dept. Bb
27 Niğde Db
71 Niger Delta Gh
68 Niger, rep. Dd
71 Niger, R. Df
68 Nigeria, Fed. of Ce
8 Nigg Dc
67 Nigtchaps Bf
54 Niigata & pref. Lc
55 Niihama Bd
82bNiihau, I. Aa
54 Niitsu Cc
18 Nijmegen Ec
35 Nikolayevsk Rd
33 Nikolayevski Je
33 Nikolayew Ff
32 Nikolsk Jd
33 Nikopol Ff
31 Nikšić Bd
54 Nile, R. Cc
88 Niles Ed
44 Nilgiri Hills Df
20 Nimes Cf
44 Nimmitabel Cf
44 Nine Degree
   Chan. Cg
51 Ningpo Gd
51 Ningsia Hui, Aut.
   Reg. Ec
51 Ningteh Fd
51 Ninove Dc
80 Nipawin Db
81 Nipigon Ab
88 Nipissing, L. Fa
31 Nis Gd
31 Nisko Gc
54 Nissum Fd. Bc
93 Niteroi Gd
32 Nitra Ed
66 Niuafu, I. Hk
9 Niue I. Ed
19 Nivelles Dd
20 Nivernais, dist. Bc
48 Nizamabad Gj
35 Nizhne Kolymsk Sc
32 Nizhne Toyma Hc
33 Nizhneudinsk Md
34 Nizhniy Tagil Hd
69 Njole De
29 Nocera Ed
58 Noda Cc
20 Nogales Ba
55 Nogata Bd
33 Noginsk Mc
32 Noginsk Gd
22 Nolima Ea
82aNome Bb
48 Nong Khoi Bb
18 Noord Beveland,
   I. Cc
18 Noord Brabant,
   prov. Dc
18 Noord Holland,
   prov. Db
18 Noordoost
   Polder Eb
72 Noqui Ae
32 Nordby Bd
80 Nordegg Cb
18 Norden Ab
18 Nordenham Ha
54 Norderney, I. Ga
11 Nordfjordeid Bc
18 Nordhausen Dc
18 Nordhorn Gb
18 Nordkinn, C. Fa
18 Nordreisa Eb
35 Nordvik Ob
18 Norfolk, Neb. Cc
48 Norfolk, Va. Gf
7 Norfolk, co. He
56 Norfolk I. De
35 Norilsk Lc
62 Norman R. Bb
78 Norman Wells Eb
14 Normandy, reg. Cc
22 Normanby I. Hh
62 Normanton Bb
12 Nórresundby Cb
39 Norristown Hd
11 Norrköping Dd
11 Norrsundet Dc
11 Norrtalje Dd
65 Norseman Ce
2 North America Ec
92 North Atlantic
   Ocean Eb
80 North
   Battleford Db
81 North Bay Bb
84 North Bend Ab
8 North Berwick Fd
10 North C. Fa
83 North Carolina,
   st. Ec
88 North Chan., L.
   Huron Da
82 North Dakota,
   st. Cb

7 North Downs Hf
7 North Foreland Hf
16 North Frisian Is. Ca
66 North Island Ec
78 North Magnetic
   Pole Ha
8 North Minch Cb
85 North Pagai, I. Bd
84 North Platte Fc
96 North Pole Ca
8 North Ronaldsay
   I. Fa
4 North Sea Df
89 North
   Tonawanda Fc
8 North Uist, I. Ac
64 North West C. Ac
6 North YorkshireFc
65 Northam Be
65 Northampton,
   Australia Ad
34 Northampton &
   co., England Ge
89 Northampton,
   U.S.A. Jc
9 Northern
   Ireland Eq
58 Northern
   Territory Ec
6 Northumberland,
   co. Eb
81 Northumberland
   Str. Cb
78 Northwest
   Territories Hb
89 Norwalk Jd
4 Norway, King. Gc
12 Norwegian S. Gb
7 Norwich Je
22 Noshiro & I. Db
74 Nossob, R. Cc
29 Nota Ef
22 Notec, R. Cb
81 Notré Dame B. Db
6 Nottingham &
   co. Fe
75 Notwani Db
70 Nouadhibou,
   Ras Ac
71 Nouakchott Ce
* 72 Nova-Chaves Cf
44 Nova Goa Ce
91 Nova Granada Fd
75 Nova Lima Gd
75 Nova Mambone Ed
79 Nova Scotia,
   prov. Ld
75 Nova Sofala Db
75 Nova Zagora Fd
21 Novara Gd
35 Novaya Zemlya,
   Is. Hb
30 Nové Zámky Ed
32 Novgorod Fd
28 Novi Eb
21 Novi Ligure Ge
54 Novi Pazar Cd
31 Novi Sad Bc
28 Novigrad Bc
† 72 Novo Redondo Af
33 Novocherkassk Hf
54 Novokuznetsk Ld
35 Novomoskovsk Ge
33 Novorossivsk Gg
33 Novosibirsk Ld
33 Novorbkov Fe
34 Novy Port Kc
33 Nova Huta Fc
23 Nowemiastro Fd
61 Nowra Db
44 Nowshera Cb
23 Nowy Dwór Gb
22 Nowy Sacz Gd
3 Nowy Targ Fd
23 Nowy Tomysl Cb
71 Nsanje Eg
71 Nsawam Eg
71 Nsukka Gg
5 Nua Ec
96 Nubian Des. Cc
90 Nueva Rosita Db
45 Nuevitas Cb
33 Nuits Cb
20 Nuits St. George Cb
23 Nukha Jg
24 Nullagine Cc
65 Nullarbor Plain De
71 Numan Hg
55 Namazu Cc
44 Nuneaton Fe
51 Nunkiang Gb
82aNunivak, I. Bb
29 Nuoro Bd
35 Nurmes Fc
10 Nürnberg
   (Nuremberg) Cd
27 Nurri Bd
44 Nushki Bc
83 Nuweveldberge,
   mts. Cd
65 Nuyts Arch. Ee
65 Nuyts Pt. Bf
66 Nuhaka Fc
73 Nyahururu Fc
68 Nyala Cc

72 Nyamell Db
12 Nyborg Dd
33 Nyiregyhaza Cb
12 Nykobing Ee
75 Nylstroom Db
11 Nynashamn Dd
61 Nyngan Cb
22 Nysa Dc

54 O'Shima, I. Cd
57 Oahu I. Fb
68 Oak Ridge C.
81 Oakey Da
7 Oakham Ge
85 Oakland Bd
88 Oakland City Be
67 Oamaru Cf
70 Oasis, prov. Fc
96 Oates Coast Kc
54 Oaxaca Ed
34 Ob, G. of Kb
34 Ob R. Jc
81 Oba Ab
54 Obama Cc
39 Obbia Dd
34 Oberammergau Kd
18 Oberhausen Fc
27 Oberstdorf Jb
49 Obi Is. Dd
32 Obidos Dc
54 Obihiro Db
33 Oboyan Ge
32 Obozerskaya Hc
71 Obuasi Eg
69 Ocean City He
8 Ochil Hills Ed
28 Oconto Dc
35 October
   Revolution I Mb
54 Odate Db
54 Odawara Cc
27 Odemis Cb
72 Odendaaisrus Dc
12 Odense Dd
28 Oderzo Db
22 Odessa, U.S.A. Fe
33 Odessa, U.S.S.R. Ff
71 Odienne Dg
22 Odolanow Dc
40 Odorhei Eb
21 Odra, R. Cc
22 Odra Port Cb
75 Odweina De
18 Odzak Gb
21 Oeiras Ec
77 Offa Fg
9 Offaly, co. Dc
19 Offenbach Hd
21 Offenburg Fa
20 Oga, C. Cb
54 Ogaki Cc
77 Ogbomosho Fg
22 Ogden Dc
89 Ogdensburg Hd
21 Oglio, R. Jd
59 Ognon, R. Eb
69 Ogowe, R. De
68 Ogulin Eb
54 Ohakune Ec
87 Ohio, R. Cd
83 Ohio, st. Eb
22 Ohre, R. Bc
54 Oil City Fd
21 Oise, R. Be
54 Oita & pref. Bd
94 Ojos del Salado,
   mt. Be
32 Oka, R. Hd
74 Okahandja Bb
74 Okaputa Bb
54 Okarito Cf
54 Okavango R. Ba
54 Okavango
   Swamp Ca
55 Okayama &
   Pref. Bd
55 Okazaki Cd
87 Okeechobee, L. Df
27 Okehampton Dg
71 Okene Gg
54 Okha Rd
55 Okhotsk, & S.of Rd
54 Oki Shima Bc
54 Okiep Bc
83 Oklahoma, st. Dc
83 Oklahoma City Dd
33 Okulovski Gd
32 Okulovski Hb
77 Okuru Be
44 Okushiri, I. Cb
10 Oland Dd
29 Olbia Bd
26 Old Castle,
   prov. Ba
18 Oldenburg Ha
18 Oldenzaal Fb
6 Oldham Ed
18 Olean Fc
35 Olekminsk Pc

32 Olenya Fb
15 Oléron, Ile d' Cb
23 Oleśnica Dc
28 Olib Eb
94 Oilague Bd
22 Olonouc Dd
33 Olonets Fc
54 Olovyannaya Od
23 Olsztyn Fb
30 Olt, R. Ec
13 Otten Ba
33 Oltenito Fd
27 Olympus, mt. Ba
9 Omagh Db
84 Omaha Gc
54 Oman, st. Jd
43 Oman, G. of He
74 Omaruru Bb
49 Ombai str. Dd
54 Omdurman Cd
71 Omegna Gd
90 Ometepec Ed
54 Ominato Db
54 Omiya Cc
18 Ommen Fb
71 Omo, R. Fc
30 Omsk Kd
74 Omua Matako,
   R. Bb
55 Omuta Bd
71 Omuta Fg
74 Ondangua Ba
32 Onega Gc
54 Onega, G. of Gc
54 Onega, L. Gc
54 Onega R. Gc
54 Onehunga Eb
54 Oneida Hc
54 Oneonta Gc
54 Ongarue Ec
54 Ongerup Be
54 Onitsha Gg
54 Onoda Bd
55 Onomichi Bd
54 Onslow Ac
54 Onslow B. Ee
54 Onstwedde Fa
54 Ontake, mt. Cc
22 Ontario, I. Fc
71 Ontario, L. Fc
81 Ontario, prov. Jc
65 Oonadatta Ef
65 Ooldea Ee
18 Oosterhout Dc
54 Ootacamund Df
72 Opala Cd
22 Opalton Bd
22 Opava Dd
33 Opocno Fc
54 Opoitiki Aa
27 Opotiki Fc
54 Oppdal Be
72 Opua Ea
54 Opunake Dc
54 Oqair Gd
22 Oradea Cb
27 Orai Gf
70 Oran, Algeria Ea
94 Oran, Arg. Cb
20 Orange, France Ce
61 Orange, N.S.W. Cb
87 Orange, U.S.A. Bf
74 Orange, R. Bc
75 Orange Free State
   prov. Dc
16 Oranberurg De
33 Orany De
28 Orbetello Cc
21 Orbost Cc
32 Ordu Da
33 Ordzhonikidze Hg
32 Ore (Erz Gebirge)
   Mts. Bc
11 Orebro Cd
22 Oregon, st. Ab
23 Orekhovo
   Zvyevo Gd
33 Orel Ge
33 Orenburg Le
22 Orense Aa
67 Orepuki Ag
26 Orihuela Bb
68 Orilita Fa
22 Orinoco, R. Kh
47 Orissa, st. Kb
28 Cristano Bd
60 Orizaba Ed
8 Orkney, co. Ea
8 Orkney Is. Ea
87 Orlando Df
20 Orléanais, dist. Ab
54 Orléans Dd
54 Ormara Ac
49 Ormoc Db
66 Ormond Fc
2 Ormans Aa
10 Ornskoldsvik Dc
20 Oron Gh
54 Orontes (Asi) R. Db
22 Orosei Bd
21 Orsa Fe
33 Orsha Fe
33 Orsk 1e
28 Orte Dc

* Renamed Vanuatu

† Renamed Mucunda
† Renamed Ngunza

28 Ortona Ec
94 Oruro Bc
28 Orvieto Dc
21 Orzinuovi Hd
55 Osaka & pref. Cd
48 Oscoda Db
81 Oshawa, Canada Bb
89 Oshawa, U.S.A. Fc
71 Osnogbo Fg
30 Osijek Bc
86 Oskaloosa Bc
11 Osio & Fd.
27 Osmancik Da
27 Osmaneli Da
18 Osnabuch Hb
95 Osorio Ee
93 Osorno Ab
18 Oss Ed
18 Ostend
(Oostende) Bc
18 Osternoiz-
  scharunbeck Ha
10 Ostersund Cc
29 Ostia Dd
21 Ostrava Ed
23 Ostroda Eb
23 Ostroleka Fb
27 Ostrow Dc
23 Ostrow
  Mazowiecka Fb
23 Ostrowiec Swieto-
  krzyski Fc
22 Ostrzeszow Dc
55 Osumi Chan. Bd
89 Oswego Gc
7 Oswestry De
67 Otago, dist. Bf
54 Otaki Ed
54 Otaru Db
74 Otavi Ba
74 Otjiwarongo Bb
28 Otocac Gb
54 Otoineppu Db
28 Otoronanga Ec
29 Otranto Gd
54 Otsu Cc
51 Ottawa Bb
11 Ottenby Dd
86 Ottumwa Bc
23 Otwock Fb
21 Otztaler Alpen,
  mts. Jc
71 Ouagadougou Ef
71 Oualata De
70 Ouanda Djalé Cb
70 Ouango Cc
70 Ouargla Gb
70 Oubangi, R. Bc
71 Oudane, R. Db
74 Oudtshoorn Cd
72 Ouesso Bc
70 Ouezzane Db
70 Oulu & R. Fc
10 Oulujärvi, L. Fc
21 Ouro Preto Ee
7 Ouse, R., Beds Ge
6 Ouse, R., Yorks Gd
8 Outer Hebrides Ac
18 Outreau Ad
60 Ouyen Bc
13 Öv Tornea Eb
94 Ovalle Af
74 Ovamboland,
  dist. Ba
18 Over Flakkee, I. Dc
26 Oviedo Aa
33 Ovruch Ee
67 Owaka Bg
15 Owase Cd
66 Owatonna Bc
8 Owen Sound Ab
62 Owen Stanley
  Ra. Gh
88 Owensboro Bf
71 Owosso Ec
11 Oxelösund Dd
7 Oxford & co.,
  England Ff
67 Oxford, N.Z. Ce
72 Oyem Ac
71 Oyo Fg
20 Oyonnax Dc
49 Ozamiz Dc
77 Ozark Plat. Bd
28 Ozieri Bd
23 Ozorkow Ec

48 Pa Sak R. Bb
50 Paan (Batang) De
74 Paarl Bd
21 Pabianice Ec
18 Pabna Mf
62 Pachhadra Df
90 Pachuca Cd
56-57 Pacific Ocean
48 Padang Bd
48 Padang
  Sidimpuan Ac
18 Paderborn Hc
7 Padstow Cg
28 Padua (Padova) Db
87 Paducah Cd
66 Paeroa Eb

75 Pafuri Eb
28 Pag, I. Eb
49 Pagadian Dc
66 Pago Pago Dj
48 Panang R. Bc
66 Pahiatua Ed
7 Paignton Dg
11 Paijanne, L. Fc
88 Painesville Ed
8 Paisley De
51 Paiyin Ec
53 Paiyunpo Eb
10 Pajala Eb
44 Pakala Df
51 Pakhoi Ed
44 Pakistan, St. Bc
30 Paks Bb
72 Pala Bb
46 Palanpur Df
75 Palapye Db
49 Palau Is. Cc
44 Palawan, I. Cc
48 Palembang Bd
26 Palencia Ba
28 Palermo De
47 Palestine Ae
44 Palghat Df
46 Pali Df
44 Palitana Ch
44 Palianza Gd
48 Palma, Italy Df
31 Palma, Mozam. Gf
26 Palma, Spain Cb
70 Palma I. Bb
25 Palmares Ef
21 Palmarola, I. Dd
25 Palmas, C. Dh
26 Palmeria Ee
24 Palmeirinhas, Pta.
  das Ae
67 Palmerston Cf
74 Palmerston C. Cc
56 Palmerston I. Ed
56 Palmerston
  North Ee
28 Palmi Ee
42 Palmyra Dc
26 Palos Ab
26 Palos, C. de Bb
34 Pamirs, Mts. Kf
87 Pamlico Sd. Ed
25 Pampa Fd
30 Pampas, reg. Cc
16 Pamplona Ba
52 Panama Cc
52 Panama, rep. Ab
52 Panama Canal
  Zone Cc
49 Panay, I. Db
30 Pancevo Cc
44 Pandharpur De
72 Pangani Fe
48 Pangkalpinang Bd
48 Pangkiang Eb
44 Panjgur Ac
21 Pantelleria, I. Cf
90 Panuco, R. Ec
51 Paoki Ec
50 Paoshan Dd
15 Paoting Fc
15 Paotow Eb
18 Papa Ab
8 Papa Stour, I. Inset
66 Papakura Eb
90 Papantla de
  Olarte Dc
25 Paphos Dc
62 Papua & G. of Fh
62 Papua New
  Guinea Fh
42 Para, state Dc
95 Paracatú Fc
83 Paracel Is. Cb
54 Paraguarí De
42 Paraguay, rep. De
94 Paraguay, R. Dd
42 Paraiba, state Fc
33 Parana, Braz. Fb
25 Parana, Par. Cf
90 Parana, R. Cf
25 Parana, st. Ed
35 Paranaguá Fe
20 Paray le Monial Cc
46 Parbhani Fj
31 Parchim Db
23 Pardubice Cc
25 Parepare Cd
91 Paria, G. of Fd
21 Paris, France Ec
74 Paris, U.S.A. Ae
18 Parkersburg Fe
61 Parkes Cb
21 Parma Je
44 Parnaguá Gb
32 Parnu Dd
32 Pärös I, Fl
24 Parramatta Db
74 Parry Is. Ga
11 Parry Sd. Bb
87 Parsons Ad
29 Parrana Df
47 Parvatipuram Jj

85 Pasadena Ce
84 Pasco Cb
9 Passage West Ce
17 Passau Ed
21 Passo Fundo Ee
92 Pasto Bb
48 Pasuruan Cd
44 Peshawar Cb
93 Patagonia, reg. Cg
46 Patan Dg
66 Patea Ed
29 Paterno Ef
89 Paterson Hd
46 Patnankot Eb
46 Pati Cd
46 Patiala Ec
27 Patmos, I. Cb
47 Patna Kd
27 Patrai, & G. Bb
28 Pattani Bc
21 Pavia Hd
54 Pavlodar Kd
33 Pavlograd Gf
32 Pavlovo Hd
21 Pavullo nel
  Frignano Je
89 Pawtucket Kd
11 Paxoi, I. Bb
44 Payette Cc
54 Paysandu Df
31 Pazardzhik Ed
28 Pazin Db
80 Peace, R. Cb
80 Peace River Cb
65 Peak Hill Bd
22 Peak Ra. Cc
83 Pearl Harbor Ce
2 Peary I.d. Fa
52 Pechenga Fb
73 Pechora Lc
80 Pechora, G. Kb
74 Pecos, R. Ef
30 Pécs Bb
60 Peebinga Bb
37 Peebles Be
63 Peera Peera
  Poolana L. Ad
47 Pegu Je
45 Pegu Yoma,
  Mts. Hd
51 Pehpei Ec
87 Pekalongan Bd
86 Pekin Ec
61 Peking Fc
74 Peking, I. Ac
62 Pelican Pt. Ab
74 Pella Bc
78 Pelly, L. Gb
42 Peloponnese,
  dist. Bb
26 Pelvoux, Massif
  du, mt. Ee
74 Pemalang Bd
73 Pemba Fe
73 Pemba, I. Fe
32 Pemberton Ba
24 Pembroke, Can. Bb
7 Pembroke
  Wales Cf
7 Pembroke Dock Cf
44 Penang, I. Bc
30 Penas, G. de Bg
84 Pendleton Cb
72 Penedo Fd
28 Penetanguish-
  ene Fa
55 Pengpu Fc
48 Penida, I. Cd
51 Penki Gb
47 Penner R. Df
3 Pennine Ra. Ec
33 Pennsylvania,
  st. Fb
6 Penong Cc
61 Penrith Db
67 Pensacola Ce
20 Penticton Cc
8 Pentland Firth Eb
33 Penza Je
7 Penzance Bg
32 Penzberg Fd
86 Peoria Cc
48 Perak R. Bc
94 Pereira Bb
77 Perekop Ff
33 Pereyaslav-
  Khmelnitski Fe
62 Pergamino Cf
15 Périgueux De
46 Perim, I. Ga
32 Perm Jd
35 Pernambuco, st. Fc
55 Perpignan Ef
30 Persia, see Iran Jf
68 Perth,
  Australia Be
19 Perth, Canada Bc
31 Perth Ee
33 Perth
  Scotland Ed
94 Peru Bd

92 Peru, rep. Bc
28 Perugia Dc
33 Pervomaysk Ff
32 Pervouralsk Md
28 Pesaro Dc
28 Pescara Ec
44 Peshawar Cb
92 Pesqueira Fc
92 Petah Tiqva Bc
10 Petange Ae
81 Peterboro Bb
60 Peterborough,
  Australia Ab
7 Peterborough,
  England Ge
8 Peternead Gc
78 Peterman Pk. Pa
82a Petersburg,
  Alaska Ec
89 Petersburg, Va. Gf
46 Petlad Dg
90 Peto Gd
67 Petone Ed
88 Petoskey Cb
10 Petrich De
34 Petropavlovsk Jd
35 Petropavlovsk-
  Kamchatskiy Sd
95 Petropolis Gf
30 Petrosul, Mt. Eb
30 Petrovaradin Cd
30 Petrovsk Nd
32 Patrozavodsk Fc
19 Pforzheim Hf
66 Phagwara Ec
46 Phalodi De
48 Phan Rang Bb
48 Phan Thiet Bb
44 Phanom Dong
  Raek, mts. Bb
89 Philadelphia Hd
62 Philippi L. Ac
49 Philippines, Is. &
  Rep. Db
88 Phitsanulok Bb
85 Phoenix De
56 Phoenix Is. Ed
21 Piacenza Hd
28 Pianosa, I. Jc
30 Piatro Fb
72 Piaui, state Ec
94 Pica Bd
14 Picardy, reg. Ec
87 Picayune Ce
61 Picton, Austral. Db
71 Picton, N.Z. Ed
21 Pictou Gb
44 Pidurutalagala,
  Mt. Dg
29 Piedimonte Ed
90 Piedras Negras Db
11 Pieksämäki Fc
10 Pielinen, & L. Fc
21 Piemonte, prov. Fe
84 Pierre Fc
75 Pietermaritz-
  burg Ec
75 Pietersburg Db
28 Pieve Da
10 Pihtipudas Fc
7 Piketberg Bd
94 Pilar Df
64 Pilbara Bc
94 Pilcomayo, R. Cd
23 Pilica, R. Fb
84 Pilos Bb
11 Pilsen, see Plzen Bd
64 Pimba Fe
91 Pimenta Bueno Cb
91 Pinar del Rio Bb
21 Pinczów Fb
34 Pindus Mts. Bb
67 Pine Bluff Bc
32 Pine Creek Ea
32 Pinega Hc
32 Pinega R. Hc
21 Pinerolo Fe
48 Ping R. Ab
65 Pingelly Be
51 Pingliang Ec
65 Pingngup Be
53 Pingtung Gd
46 Pinjarra Be
60 Pinnaroo Bc
86 Pinos, I. de Bb
33 Pinsk Ee
32 Pinyug Jc
32 Piombino Cd
25 Pionsk Fb
23 Piorkov, R. Cc
88 Piqua Cd
92 Piraiévs Bb
48 Piran Db
95 Piray Ec
29 Pirgos Bb
19 Pirmasens Ge
31 Pirot Dd
33 Piryatin Fe
21 Pisa Cc
94 Pisagua Ac

22 Pisek Cd
28 Pistoia Cc
12 Pita Db
57 Pitcairn I. Ge
21 Pitea Eb
30 Pitesti Bd
87 Pittsburg Bd
81 Pittsburgh Fd
61 Pittsworth Da
48 Phuket Ac
28 Pizzo Fe
81 Placentia Db
93 Plata, Rio de la Df
99 Plattsburg Jb
17 Plauen Ec
66 Plenty, B. of Fb
28 Plesetsk Hc
22 Pleszew Dc
74 Plettenberg B. Cd
95 Pleven Ed
11 Pljevija Bd
23 Plock Eb
30 Ploesti Fc
31 Plomb du Cantal,
  mt. Ad
31 Plovdiv Ed
28 Pluj Ea
7 Plymouth, Eng. Cg
88 Plymouth, Ind. Bd
91 Plymouth, Mont-
  serrat Fc
74 Plymouth,
  Wisc. Bc
22 Plzen (Pilsen) Bd
46 Phom Penh Bb
21 Po, R. Jd
34 Pobeda Pk. Ke
84 Pocatello Dc
89 Pocomoke City He
53 Pocos de Caldas Fd
12 Podmokly Cc
32 Podolsk Gd
71 Podor Cc
30 Poduillouei Fb
44 Point Pedro Dg
99 Pointe à Pitre Fc
23 Poitiers Cd
53 Poitou Cd
46 Pokaran Ce
51 Pokataroo Ca
13 Poland, east. Je
27 Polatli Db
72 Poli Ab
29 Policastro Ed
10 Polmak Fa
32 Polotsk Ed
33 Poltava Ff
44 Ponce Fc
90 Pond Inlet Ka
44 Pondicherry Df
32 Pongoma Fb
32 Ponoi & R. Hb
19 Pont à Mousson Ff
84 Ponta Grossa Ee
25 Ponta Pora Dd
20 Pontarlier Ec
67 Pontchartrain,
  L. Be
23 Pontebba Da
29 Pontecorvo Dd
88 Pontiac Dc
84 Pontianak Bd
19 Pontine Is. Bd
19 Pontoise Be
31 Pontrémoli He
7 Pontypool Df
7 Pontypridd Df
29 Ponza, I. Bd
7 Poole Fg
94 Poopó, L. Bc
52 Popayan Bb
81 Poperinge Bb
87 Poplar Bluff Bd
90 Popocatepetl,
  mt. Ed
52 Popokabaka Be
46 Porbandar Bh
60 Pordenone Db
28 Porec Db
6 Pori Ec
67 Porjus Db
44 Porkkala Ec
27 Porsuk, R. Db
13 Port Aa
64 Port Adelaide Af
60 Port Alberni Bc
67 Port Albert Cc
6 Port Albert
  Victor Ch
75 Port Alfred Dd
57 Port Antonio Ce
51 Port Arthur-Dairen
  (Lü-ta) Gc
87 Port Arthur,
  U.S.A. Bf
91 Port au Prince De
60 Port Augusta Ab
91 Port aux Basques
  Db
45 Port Blair Gf
62 Port Bou Cb
60 Port Broughton Ab
81 Port Cartier Cb
67 Port Chalmers Cf

88 Port Colborne Fc
91 Port de Paix Dc
48 Port Dickson Bc
62 Port Douglas Cb
75 Port Elizabeth Dd
8 Port Ellen Be
68 Port Etienne Ac
60 Port Fairy Bc
72 Port Francqui, see Ilebo Cd
8 Port Glasgow Cb
71 Port Harcourt Gh
81 Port Hawkesbury Cb
64 Port Hedland Bc
88 Port Huron Dc
61 Port Jackson Db
48 Port Kelang Bc
9 Port Laoise Dc
65 Port Lincoln Fe
71 Port Loko Cg
75 Port Macquarie Db
62 Port Moresby Gb
82 Port Nelson Eb
74 Port Nolloth Bc
8 Port of Ness Bb
41 Port of Spain Fd
67 Port Pegasus Ag
75 Port Phillip B. Bc
60 Port Pirie Ab
78 Port Radium Eb
74 Port Roper Fa
41 Port Said (Bûr Sa'id) Ca
75 Port Shepstone Ed
38 Port Sudan Cd
7 Port Talbot Df
15 Port Vendres Ef
60 Port Wakefield Ab
80 Portadown Eb
80 Portage la Prairie Ec
26 Portalegre Ab
26 Portimao Ab
89 Portland, Me. Kc
61 Portland, N.S.W. Cb
84 Portland, Ore. Bb
60 Portland, Vic. Bc
8 Portland Bill Eg
26 Portlethen Fc
7 Portmadoc Ce
34 Portnaohnach Ec
26 Pôrto (Oporto) Aa
95 Porto Alegre Ef
95 Porto Anzio Dd
95 Porto Artur Bf
29 Porto Empedocle Df
94 Porto Esperanca Dc
94 Porto Murtinho Ld
95 Porto Nacional Fh
71 Porto Novo Fg
95 Porto Pfes Vargas Ed
95 Porto Recanati Dc
70 Porto Santo, I. Bb
92 Porto Seguro Fd
95 Porto Socompa Bd
29 Porto Torres Bd
95 Porto União Ee
92 Porto Velho Cc
28 Portoferrajo Cc
8 Portpatrick Cf
8 Portree Bc
8 Portrush Ea
7 Portsmouth, England Fg
89 Portsmouth, N.H. Kc
88 Portsmouth, Ohio Dc
89 Portsmouth, Va. Gf
9 Portstewart Ea
4 Portugal, Rep. Db
9 Portumna Cc
92 Posadas Ef
23 Poschiavo Eb
70 Poste Maurice Cortier (Bidon 5) Fd
74 Postmasberg Cc
75 Potchefstroom Dc
28 Potenza Ed
75 Potgietersus Db
33 Poti Hg
94 Potosi Bc
51 Potow Fc
16 Potsdam Eb
88 Pottsville Gd
89 Poughkeepsie Hd
9 Poulaphouca, Res. Ec
74 Pouso Alegre Dg
32 Povenets Gc
61 Powell Creek Eb
88 Powers Bb
De Powys, Co. De
30 Pozarevac Cc
94 Poznan Db
94 Pozo Almonte Bd
22 Praded, mt. Dc
12 Prades Ef
12 Praestö & co. Fd

22 Prague (Praha) Cc
62 Prairie Bc
9? Prata Fc
28 Prato Cc
85 Pratt Gd
16 Prenzlau Eb
22 Prerov Dd
85 Prescott De
95 Presidente Ispitacao Ed
95 Presidente Hermes Cb
95 Presidente Martinho Ec
95 Presidente Prudente Ed
85 Presidio Ff
23 Presov Fd
6 Preston Ed
8 Prestwick De
75 Pretoria Dc
27 Prévéza Bb
22 Pribram Cd
84 Price Dd
74 Prieska Cc
33 Prilep Ce
33 Priluki Fe
80 Prince Albert, Canada Db
78 Prince Albert Pen. Fa
79 Prince Charles I. Kb
3 Prince Edward Is. Jh
80 Prince George Bb
38 Prince of Wales, I. Ha
80 Prince Rupert Ab
82 Princess Charlotte B. Ba
7 Princetown Dg
69 Principe, I. Ce
69 Principe da Beira Cb
74 Prins Albert Cd
33 Pripyat, R. Ee
33 Pripyat Marshes Ee
31 Pristina Cd
31 Prizren Cd
90 Progreso Gd
34 Prokopevsk Ld
31 Proletarski Hf
45 Prome He
6 Proserpine Cc
22 Prostejov Dd
33 Provadiya Fd
20 Provence, dist. Df
20 Provence, reg. Ff
89 Providence Kd
91 Providencia, I. Bd
33 Provins Cf
90 Prudentopolis Ef
34 Prudhoe Bay Da
22 Prudnik Dc
33 Prut R. Ef
56 Prydz B. Ec
33 Przemysl Gd
33 Przeworsk Gc
34 Przhevalsk Ke
67 Psara, I. Cs
32 Pskov Ed
90 Puebla Ed
85 Pueblo Fd
50 Pueh Bd
90 Puerto Barrios Gd
91 Puerto Cabezas Bd
30 Puerto Cortés Ac
70 Puerto de Cabras Cc
93 Puerto Deseado Cg
94 Puerto Heath Bb
93 Puerto Madryn Cg
91 Puerto Montt Bg
90 Puerto Morales Gd
91 Puerto Plata Db
91 Puerto Princesa Cg
91 Puerto Rico, I. Ec
94 Puerto Suarez Dc
33 Pugachev Je
84 Puget Sd. Bb
29 Puglia, reg. Fd
20 Puisaye, Collines de la, mts. Bb
66 Pukekohe Eb
28 Pula (Pola) Db
23 Pulawy Fc
94 Puna, reg. Bc
94 Puna de Atacama Be
45 Punaka Gc
47 Punakha Me
94 Punata Bc
46 Punch Cb
46 Pune Dj
91 Pungue Ea
94 Puno Ac
93 Punta Arenas Bh
94 Puntarenas Bd
94 Puquios Bc
47 Puri Kj
47 Purisima Bb
47 Purnea Lf

47 Purulia Lg
31 Purvomai Ed
75 Pusan Bb
66 Pushkino Je
66 Putaruru Ec
34 Putih I. Kb
18 Putten Eb
12 Puttgarden Ec
20 Puy de Dôme, mt. & dept. Ad
84 Puyallup Bb
75 Pweto De
32 Pya L. Eb
45 Pyapon He
33 Pyatigorsk Hg
45 Pyinmana He
52 Pyongyang Bb
5 Pyrenees, mts. Df
15 Pyrenees-Atlan- tique, dépt. Cf
45 Pyu He

42 Quadhima De
42 Qualat at el Mudauwara Dd
42 Qalqiliyah Bc
38 Qamr B. Ed
41 Qasr Umm Ramad Fe
42 Qatana Cc
43 Qatar, pen. Gd
33 Qazvin Fb
38 Qena Cc
45 Qeshm, I. Hd
39 Qishn Ed
80 Quatsino Bb
*75 Que Que Da
41 Queanbeyan Cc
81 Quebec & prov. Bb
78 Queen Charlotte Is. Ab
80 Queen Charlotte Sd. Bb
96 Queen Elizabeth Is. Qb
96 Queen Mary Coast Fc
96 Queen Maud Land Bc
14 Queenborough He
60 Queenscliff Bc
59 Queensland, st. Cc
75 Queenstown, Cape Province Dd
67 Queenstown, N.Z. Bf
61 Queenstown, Tas. Cd
92 Queimados Fd
72 Queia Be
69 Quelimane Fg
90 Queretaro Dd
80 Quesnel Bb
44 Quetta Bb
42 Quezion City Db
48 Qui Nhon Bb
34 Quillagua Bd
20 Quillan Dg
63 Quilpie Bd
14 Quimper Ac
32 Quincy, Ill. Mf
30 Quincy, Mass. Kc
61 Quirindi Db
42 Quito Bc
43 Qum Gc
60 Quorn Ab
84 Quseir Cc

47 Rajshahi Mf
67 Rakaia De
75 Rakops Cb
89 Raleigh Fg
40 Ram Allah Bd
78 Ramah Lc
46 Ramgarh Ce
40 Ramle Bd
30 Ramnicu Sarat Fc
30 Ramnicu Vâlcea Ec
46 Rampur Bd
43 Ramree I. Ge
7 Ramsgate Hj
72 Ranaghat Mg
93 Rancagua Bf
47 Ranchi Kg
12 Randers Cc
45 Rangia Gc
67 Rangiora De
45 Rangoon He
47 Rangpur Mf
47 Raniganj Lg
46 Raniwara Df
46 Rann of Kutch Cf
49 Rantekombola, mt. Dd
21 Rapallo He
44 Rapid City Fc
13 Rapperswil Ca
56 Rarotonga I. Lee
41 Ras al Hadd, C. He
38 Ras Banas Cc
39 Ras Dashan, mt. Cd
25 Ras Lanuf Fd
43 Ras Rakan, C. Ge
43 Ras Tanura Fd
40 Rashayya Bc
45 Rasht Fb
33 Rasskazovo He
6 Rastatt Bb
46 Ratangarh Ed
9 Rathkeale Cd
9 Rath Luirc Cd
9 Rathdrum Ed
16 Rathenow Eb
9 Rathlin, I. Ea
9 Rathnew Ec
46 Ratlam Eg
86 Raukumara Ra. Fc
10 Rauma Ec
43 Ravar Hc
28 Ravenna Db
90 Ravensburg Hb
65 Ravensthorpe Ce
64 Ravenswood Cc
44 Rawalpindi Cb
76 Rawene Da
22 Rawicz Dc
84 Rawlins Ec
85 Rawson Cg
81 Ray, C. Db
80 Raymond Cc
50 Razgrad Fd
15 Ré, ile de Cd
9 Reading, Eng. Gf
89 Reading, U.S.A. Hd
26 Real de Antonio Ab
70 Rebun, I. Da
92 Recife Fc
18 Recklinghausen Gc
60 Red Cliffs Bb
80 Red Deer Cb
86 Red Oak At
87 Red R. Be
3 Red Sea Jd
84 Redding Bc
7 Redditch Fe
74 Redruth Bg
85 Redlands Cc
9 Ree, L. Cc
67 Reefton Ce
67 Regensburg (Ratisbon) Eb
30 Reghin Eb
29 Reggio di Calabria Ee
21 Regio nell Emilia Db
30 Regina Db
44 Registan, Dist. Ab
95 Registro do Araguaia Ec
74 Rehoboth Bb
40 Rehovot Bc
67 Reichenbach Cc
38 Reidsville Fi
7 Reigate Gf
16 Reims Fc
46 Reindeer L. Eb
29 Reinosa Eb
23 Rejowiec Gc
43 Remeshk Hd
22 Remiremont Ea
40 Remscheid Gc
16 Rendsburg Ca
8 Renfrew Dc
67 Renfrew U.S.A. Gb
46 Renkum Ec
60 Renmark Bb
14 Rennes Cc
84 Reno Cd

21 Reno, R. Je
94 Resistencia De
34 Resita Cc
79 Resolution, I. Lb
23 Reszel Fb
27 Rethimnon Bb
3 Réunion, I. Kg
26 Réus Ca
26 Réuss Ca
19 Reutlingen Jf
46 Revelstoke Cb
77 Revilla Gigedo Is. Gg
47 Rewa Hf
46 Rewari Ef
84 Rexburg Dc
26 Reykjanaes Ab
10 Reykjavik Ab
14 Rezayieh Eb
32 Rezekne Fd
21 Rhatikon, mts. Hb
18 Rheden Fb
18 Rhein, see Rhine R. Fc
18 Rheine Gb
13 Rheinfelden Ba
18 Rheydt Fc
18 Rhine (Rhein) R. Fc
86 Rhinelander Cb
21 Rho Hd
83 Rhode I., C. Hc
27 Rhodes, see Ródhos
*68 Rhodesia Eg
31 Rhodope Mts. Ee
7 Rhondda Df
20 Rhône, R. & dept. Cg
8 Rhum I. Bc
6 Rhyl Dd
46 Riasi Eb
48 Riau Arch. Bc
12 Ribe, co. & R. Bd
55 Ribeirão Preto Fc
62 Riccarton De
84 Richfield Dd
7 Richmond, Australia Bc
84 Richmond, Calif. Bd
88 Richmond, Ind. Ce
88 Richmond, Ky. Cf
76 Richmond, New Zealand Dd
89 Richmond, Va. Gf
87 Ridgway Fd
74 Rietfontein Cc
28 Rieti Dc
10 Rifstangi Ba
32 Riga, & G. of Dd
54 Riishti, I. Dab
28 Rijeka (Fiume) Db
18 Rijn, R. Db
18 Rijswijk Db
28 Rimini Db
31 Rimouski Cb
49 Rindjani, mt. Cd
12 Ringkôbing & co. Bc
12 Ringkobing Fjord Bd
12 Ringsted Ed
10 Ringvassoy Da
94 Rio Branco Ba
93 Rio Cuarto Cf
8 Rio de Janeiro, & st. Bd
93 Rio Gallegos Ch
95 Rio Grande Ef
85 Rio Grande, R. Fc
92 Rio Grande do Norte, st. Fc
95 Rio Grande do Sul, st. Ee
93 Rio Negro, prov. Cg
95 Rio Pardo Cg
95 Rio Verde Ec
52 Riobamba Bc
20 Riom Bd
29 Rionero Ed
13 Rioz Aa
6 Ripon Fc
11 Rísör Bd
10 Ristijârvi Fc
21 Riva Jd
20 Rive de Gier Cg
7 River Cess Dg
89 Riverhead Jd
74 Riversdale Cd
85 Riverside Ce
67 Riverton, Can. Eb
67 Riverton, N.Z. Bg
21 Riviera Ge
11 Rivière du Loup Cb
21 Rivoli Fd
43 Riyadh Fe
39 Rizan Dd
42 Rize Ea
56 Roanne Cc
89 Roanoke Ff
3 Roanoke I. Gf
89 Roanoke Rapids Gf

* Renamed Kwekwe
* Renamed Zimbabwe
† Renamed Urmia

60 Robe Ac
74 Robertson Cd
71 Robertsport Cg
60 Robertstown Ab
81 Roberval Bb
26 Roca, C. da Ab
93 Rocha Df
6 Rochdale Ed
15 Rochefort Ce
86 Rochester, Minn. Bc
89 Rochester, N.Y. Gc
86 Rock Island Bc
84 Rock Springs Ec
85 Rocky Ford Fd
91 Rocky Mount Gg
84 Rocky Mts. Db
86 Rockford Cc
62 Rockhampton Dc
62 Rockingham B. Cb
11 Rodberg Bc
12 Rodbyhavn Ec
15 Roder Ee
27 Ródhos (Rhodes), I. Cb
30 Rodna Db
64 Roebourne Bc
64 Roebuck B. Cb
81 Roermond Ec
18 Roeselare Cd
58 Rogers City Db
74 Roggeveldberge, mts. Cd
10 Rognan Db
46 Rohri Be
68 Rohtak Fd
90 Rojo, C. Ec
55 Rokugo, C. Cc
95 Rolandia Ed
2 Roma Cd
28 Romagna, reg. Cb
30 Roman Fb
22 Romanche, R. Ed
26 Romans Dd
8 Rome, Italy Dd
89 Rome, U.S.A. Hc
7 Romford Hf
12 Romo, I. Bd
24 Ronda Ab
92 Rondónia, st. Cc
12 Ronne Fa
18 Ronse Cd
18 Roosendaal Dc
96 Roosevelt I. Lb
92 Roraima, st. Cb
11 Røros Cc
13 Rorschach Da
10 Ros Vatn Eb
9 Rosario, Arg. Cf
90 Rosario, Mexico Cc
8 Roscommon, & co. Cc
9 Roscrea Dd
19 Roseau Fc
39 Roseires Cd
81 Rosedael Bc
77 Rosenheim Be
80 Rosenedom Db
16 Rosetock Da
5 Roskilde Fd
33 Roslavl Fe
7 Ross, England Ef
47 Ross, N.Z. Ce
94 Ross Dependency Lc
96 Ross I. Lb
96 Ross Sea Lb
96 Ross Shelf Ice La
80 Rossland Cc
9 Rosslare Ed
71 Rosso Be
33 Rossosh Ge
80 Rosthern Db
16 Rostock Ea
33 Rostov Gf
85 Roswell Fe
81 Rosyth Ed
18 Rotenburg Ja
7 Rother Hg
6 Rotherham Fd
8 Rothsay Fe
6 Roto Cb
66 Rotorua Fc
18 Rotterdam Dc
21 Rottweil Ga
12 Rottumeroog, I. Fa
14 Rouen Dc
8 Rousay, I. Fa
15 Roussillon Ef
11 Rouyn Jb
11 Rovato Jd
21 Rovereto Kd
21 Rovigo Cb
28 Rovinj Db
33 Rovno Ee
66 Roxburgh, N.Z. Bf
8 Roxburgh, & co., Scotland Fe
47 Royagada Jj
86 Royale, I. Ba
7 Royston Ge
23 Rožnava Fd
66 Ruapehu, Mt. Ec

39 Rub al Khali, des. Dd
32 Rudnichny Kd
50 Rudok Bc
17 Rudolstadt Cc
88 Rudyard Ca
73 Rufiji, R. Fe
71 Rufisque Bf
7 Rugby Fe
16 Rügen, I. Ea
18 Ruhr, R. Fc
72 Ruki, R. Bd
73 Rukwa, L. Ee
30 Rumania, st. Kf
73 Rumbek Db
54 Rumoi De
67 Runanga Ce
75 Rusape Ea
9 Rush Ec
6 Rushworth Cc
30 Ruse Fd
34–35 Russian Soviet Federal Socialist Republic Lc
75 Rustenburg Dc
17 Rutland, co., England Ge
89 Rutland, U.S.A. Jc
72 Ruvuma, R. Ff
41 Ruwenzori, mt. Dc
33 Ruzaevka Je
23 Ruzomberok Fd
73 Rwanda, st. Dd
33 Ryazan Ge
33 Ryazhsk He
32 Rybinsk Gd
32 Rybinsk Res. Gd
7 Ryde Fg
7 Rye Hg
32 Rynda Gd
23 Rypin Eb
55 Ryukyu Is. Bb
23 Rzeszów Fe
23 Rzhev Fd
19 Saarbrücken Fe
19 Saarburg Fe
2 Saaremaa, I. Dd
19 Saar, land Fe
19 Saarlouis Fe
46 Sabadell Ca
37 Sabah, st. Pj
91 Sabana Ec
29 Sabaudia Dd
75 Sabie Ec
90 Sabinas Hidalgo Db
81 Sable, C. Db
5 Sable I. Db
32 Sabzevar Hb
89 Sacramento Bd
39 Sa'da Dd
33 Sadiya Hc
54 Sado, I. Cc
12 Saeby Db
51 Saeki Bd
17 Saffron Walden Hf
70 Sari Db
32 Safonovo Jb
27 Safranbolu Ea
55 Saga & pref. Bd
55 Sagaing Hd
46 Sagar Gg
88 Saginaw & B. Cc
50 Sagli Da
91 Sagua La Grande Bb
26 Sagunto Bb
70 Sahara Des. Cc
70 Saharan Atlas, mts. Fb
46 Sahiwal (Montgomery) Dc
72 Sa'id Bundas Cb
32 Saida Guba Fb
43 Saidabad Hd
32 Saihut Ee
55 Saijo Bd
51 Saiki Bd
51 Sain Shanda Fb
7 St. Albans Gf
20 St. Amour Dc
67 St. Andrews, N.Z. Cf
8 St. Andrews, Scotland Fd
91 St. Ann's Bay Cc
26 St. Arnaud Bc
8 St. Augustin Bc
87 St. Augustine Df
7 St. Austell Cg
19 St. Avold Fe
3 St. Bernard, Col du Gd. Bc
80 St. Boniface Ec
14 St. Brieuc Bc
88 St. Catherines Cc
20 St. Chamond Cd
91 St. Christopher, see St. Kitts
88 St. Clair, L. Cc

20 St. Claude Dc
91 St. Cloud Bb
91 St. Croix, I. Fc
14 St. Denis Ec
20 St. Dié Df
20 St. Dizier Df
20 St. Eloy Ac
20 St. Etienne Cd
20 St. Florentin Ba
13 St. Gallen Da
20 St. George, Australia Ca
85 St. George, U.S.A. Dd
91 St. George's Fd
20 St. George's Chan. Ee
19 St. Germain Ee
20 St. Germain des Fosses Bc
13 St. Gotthard P. Cb
12 St. Heddinge Fd
74 St. Helena B. Bd
69 St. Helena, I. Bg
85 St. Helens Dd
81 St. Hyacinthe Jb
20 St. Ignace Cb
19 St. Ingbert Ge
7 St. Ives Bg
85 St. Jean Jb
20 St. Jerome Jb
17 Saint John Ee
91 St John's, Antigua Fc
81 St. John's, Can. Db
88 St. Joseph, Mich. Bc
86 St. Joseph, Miss. Bd
15 St. Juan Gf
15 St. Julien Ab
67 St. Kilda Cf
91 St. Kitts (St. Christopher), I. Fc
62 St. Lawrence Cc
81 St. Lawrence, G. of Cb
82 St. Lawrence I. Bb
81 St. Lawrence, R. Cb
14 St. Lô Cc
56 St. Louis, Sen. Be
86 St. Louis, U.S.A. Bd
91 St. Lucia, I. Fd
14 St. Maio Fc
91 St. Marc Ec
91 St. Martin, I. Fc
85 St. Mary's Fd
60 St. Mary's Pk. Ab
19 St. Maur Bf
13 St. Moritz Db
20 St. Nazaire Bd
7 St. Neots Gf
19 St. Nicolas Ff
14 St. Omer Eb
92 St. Paul, French Guiana Dc
86 St. Paul, U.S.A. Bc
2 St. Paul, I. Fe
87 St. Petersburg Df
8 St. Pierre I. Db
8 St. Pol-sur-Mer Ec
17 St. Polten Fd
8 St. Quentin Ec
55 St. Raphael Gf
74 St. Sebastian B. Cd
8 St. Thomas Ec
91 St. Thomas, I. Fc
18 St. Trond Ec
20 St. Tropez Gf
17 St. Veit Ff
84 St. Vincent, C. Ab
50 St. Vincent G. Ab
91 St. Vincent, I. Fd
69 Ste. Marie, C. Gh
53 Sakai Cd
53 Sakaiminato Bc
42 Sakaka Ed
73 Sakania Df
54 Sakarya, R. Da
54 Sakata Cc
35 Sakhalin I. Rd
43 Sakmara R. Ke
47 Sakskobing Ed
2 Sala Dc
39 Salala Ef
73 Salima Ef
91 Salina Cruz Ed
95 Salinas, Braz. Gc
85 Salinas, U.S.A. Bd
7 Salisbury, Eng. Ff

*75 Salisbury, Rhod. Ea
89 Salisbury, U.S.A. He
40 Salkhad Dc
32 Salla Eb
42 Salling, dist. Bc
39 Sallom Cd
84 Salmon Db
20 Salon Df
30 Salonta Ff
7 Salop, Co. Ee
33 Salsk Hf
21 Salsomaggiore He
40 Salt Bc
65 Salt L. Ac
84 Salt Lake City Dc
94 Salta Bd
7 Saltash Cg
8 Saltcoats De
12 Saltholm Fd
90 Saltillo Db
94 Salto Df
85 Salton Sea Ce
38 Salum Jj
47 Salur Jj
21 Saluzzo Fe
92 Salvador, R. Kg
45 Salween, R. He
33 Salyany Jb
17 Salzburg Ee
16 Salzgitter Db
52 Samar, I. Db
62 Samarai Hj
48 Samarinda Cd
34 Samarkand Jf
28 Samassi Bc
43 Sambalpur Jb
19 Sambre, R. Dd
52 Samchok Bb
73 Same Fd
43 Samnan Gb
56 Samoa Is. Ch
27 Sámos, I. Cb
48 Sampit, & B. Cd
51 Samshui Fd
12 Samsö, I. Ed
54 Samsun Ea
71 San Bd
23 San, R. Gc
91 San Andreas, I. Bd
90 San Andres Bd
85 San Angelo Fe
28 San Antioco, I. Bc
85 San Antonio Cd
94 San Antonio, C. Bb
72 San Antonio do Zaire Ge
21 San Benedetto Po Jd
85 San Bernardino Ce
90 San Carlos Db
93 San Carlos de Bariloche Bg
85 San Clemente, I. Ce
94 San Cristobal, Argentina Cf
90 San Cristobal, Mexico Fd
92 San Cristobal, Venezuela Bb
85 San Diego Ce
93 San Felipe Bf
90 San Fernando, Mexico Ec
26 San Fernando, Sp. Ab
84 San Francisco Bd
91 San Francisco de Macoris Ec
28 San Gimignano Cc
21 San Giovanni in Persecete Ke
94 San Ignacio Cc
90 San Jorge, B. Ba
93 San Jorge, G. de Cg
94 San José, Bol. Cc
91 San José, C. Rica
85 San José, Phil. Db
84 San José, U.S.A. Bd
84 San Juan, Arg. Bf
94 San Juan, Bol. Dc
91 San Juan, Puerto Rico Ec
91 San Julian Cg
90 San Lucas, C. Bc
93 San Luis & prov. Cf
85 San Luis Obispo Bd
90 San Luis Potosi Dc
28 San Marino, &, rep. Dc
8 San Martin Cc
94 San Matias Dc
93 San Matias, G. Cg
8 San Miguel Ad
28 San Nicandro Ed
93 San Nicolas Cf

49 San Pablo Db
91 San Pedro, Cuba Ec
90 San Pedro, Mex. Db
94 San Pedro, Par. Dd
71 San Pedro, Ivory Coast Dg
91 San Pedro Sula Ac
21 San Pelice sul Panaro Ke
28 San Pietro, I. Bc
90 San Quintin Aa
93 San Rafael Cf
21 San Remo Ff
77 San Sayador Kg
91 San Salvador (Watling) I. Db
26 San Sebastián Ba
28 San Sepulcro De
28 San Severo Ed
74 Sa'na Dd
11 Sanaga, R. Hh
43 Sanandaj (Sinneh) Fb
20 Sancerre Ab
93 Sancerrois, Collines du, mts. Ab
91 Sancti Spiritus Cb
49 Sandakan Cc
8 Sanday, I. Fa
74 Sandfish B. Ab
27 Sandikli Db
10 Sandnes Bd
10 Sandnessjön Cb
73 Sandoa Ce
11 Sandón Dd
6 Sandown Cb
74 Sandpoint Cb
7 Sandringham He
65 Sandstone Bd
88 Sandusky Da
12 Sandvig Allinge Fa
63 Sandy C. Dc
72 Sanga, R. Bc
72 Sangha Bc
49 Sangihe Is. Dc
72 Sangmelina Ac
52 Sangsang Cd
72 Sangwa De
53 Sanjo Cc
72 Sankuru, R. Cc
26 Sanúcar Ab
55 Sano Cc
52 Sanok Gd
8 Sanquhar Ed
94 Santa Ana, Bol. Bb
85 Santa Ana, U.S.A. Ce
94 Santa Bárbara, Brazil Dc
85 Santa Barbara, U.S.A. Ce
85 Santa Barbara I. Ce
85 Sta. Catalina, I. Ce
95 Santa Catarina, st. Ee
95 Santa Clara, U.S.A. Bd
91 Santa Clara, Cuba Cb
85 Santa Clara, U.S.A. Bd
93 Santa Cruz, Arg. Ch
94 Santa Cruz, Bol. Cc
68 Santa Cruz, Canary Is. Ac
85 Santa Cruz, U.S.A. Bd
94 Santa Cruz, I. Cd
93 Santa Cruz, prov. Bg
90 Santa Eugenia, Pt. Ab
94 Santa Fé, Arg. Cf
85 Santa Fé, U.S.A. Ed
94 Santa Isabel, Bolivia Cb
95 Santa Isabel, Brazil Eb
*71 Santa Isabel, Sp. Guin. Gh
21 Sta. Margherita Ligure He
95 Santa Maria, R. Ca
26 Santa Maria d'Ortigueira Aa
95 Santa Maria de Vitória Gb
92 Santa Marta Ba
85 Santa Monica Ce
93 Santa Rosa, Arg. Cf
95 Santa Rosa, Brazil Eb
91 Santa Rosa, Honduras Ad
84 Santa Rosa, U.S.A. Bd
85 Santa Rosalia Bc
26 Santander Ba
26 Santarém Ba
93 Santiago, Chile Bf

* Renamed Harare, Zimbabwe
† Renamed Soyo

* Renamed Rey Malabo

91 Santiago, Dom. Rep.
26 Santiago, Spain Aa
91 Santiago de Cuba Cb
94 Santiago del Estero Ce
90 Santiago Ixcuintla
95 Santo Angelo Ec
94 Santo Antonio Cb
94 Santo Corazón Dc
91 Santo Domingo Ec
26 Santona Ba
95 Santos Fd
75 Sanyati, R. Da
95 Sao Carlos Fd
75 São Domingos Fb
95 São Francisco Gc
95 São Francisco, R. Gb
95 Sao Gabriel Ef
95 São João Eb
95 São José do Norte Ef
95 São Lourenço Fd
92 São Luis Ec
95 Sao Paulo & st. Fd
95 São Sebastiãol Fd
69 São Tomé, I. Ce
22 Saône, R. Cc
20 Saone et Loire, dept. Cc
70 Saoura, prov. Fd
51 Sapele Gg
51 Sapporo Db
52 Saqota Fa
46 Saradiya Bh
28 Sarajevo Gc
33 Saraktash Le
33 Saransk Je
32 Sarapul Kd
89 Saratoga Springs Je
33 Saratov Je
91 Sarawak, st. Fj
46 Sardarsharh Ed
29 Sardinia, I. Bd
33 Sargans Da
46 Sargodha Db
68 Sarh De
51 Sark, I. Bc
27 Sarkisla Eb
33 Sarnia Aa
33 Sarny Fe
21 Saronno Hd
87 Sarosota Df
11 Sarpsborg Gf
70 Sarrebourg Gf
19 Sarreguemines Ge
71 Sarro Df
63 Sarupsa Dd
43 Sarur Hd
33 Sarych, C. Fg
47 Sasaram Kf
83 Sasebo Ad
78 Saskatchewan, prov. Gc
80 Saskatchewan, R. Db
80 Saskatoon Db
73 Sasobani Gb
73 Sasovo He
71 Sassandra & R. Dh
29 Sassari Bd
71 Satadougou Cf
46 Satara Dk
47 Satna Hf
33 Satoraljoujhely Ca
92 Satu Mare Cb
34 Saudi Arabia, King. Hg
81 Sault Ste. Marie, Canada Ab
88 Sault Ste Marie, U.S.A. Ca
15 Saumur Cd
89 Saugira B. Ed
10 Saurboer Ab
50 Sava, R. Bc
66 Savali, I. Ct
71 Savanna la Mar Cc
87 Savannah De
44 Savantvadi Ce
75 Save, R. Eb
71 Savigliano Fc
21 Savoie, dist. & dept. Ed
95 Savona Ge
55 Sawara Dc
49 Sawu Is.
40 Saya (Sidon) Bc
8 Scalasaig Bd
34 Scalloway Inset
10-11 Scandinavia
16 Scarborough Fc
13 Schaffhausen Ca
79 Schefferville Lc
89 Schenectady Hc
33 Schiedam Dc
33 Schiermonnikoog, I.
19 Schiltigheim Gf
28 Schio Hd

16 Schleswig Ca
13 Schopfheim Ba
49 Schouten Is. Ff
28 Schouwen, I. Cc
75 Schuckmann-burg Ca
21 Schwabischer Jura, mts. Ha
13 Schwanden Ca
48 Schwaner mts. Cd
51 Schwangyashan
13 Schwarzenburg Bb
21 Schwarzwald, mts. Gb
17 Schwaz De
17 Schweinfurt Dc
21 Schwenningen Ga
16 Schwerin Db
19 Schwetzingen He
13 Schwyz & cant. Ca
29 Sciacca Df
61 Scone Db
8 Scotland
96 Scott I. Lc
13 Scotts Bluff Fc
61 Scottsdale Cd
89 Scranton Hd
7 Seaton Dg
84 Seattle Bb
90 Sebastien Vizcaino B. Ab
44 Secunderabad De
62 Sedan Ab
67 Seddon Ed
67 Seddonville Cd
71 Sedhiou Bf
29 Seeheim Bc
16 Ségou Df
26 Segovia Ba
46 Séhore Fg
20 Seille, R. Dc
14 Seine, R. Ec
44 Seistan, Dist. Ab
12 Sejero, I. Ed
71 Sekondi-Takoradi Eg
21 Selestar Fa
21 Selibaby Ce
48 Selima Oasis Bc
33 Selitrenoye Jf
80 Selkirk, Canada Eb
8 Selkirk & co., Scotland. Ee
80 Selkirk Mts. Db
17 Selma Ce
7 Selsey Bill Gg
21 Selukwe Ea
42 Selvas, reg. Cc
62 Selwyn Bc
32 Samarange Cd
32 Semenovskoe Hd
48 Semeru, mt. Dc
34 Semipalatinsk Ld
47 Semna Cc
32 Sempach Ca
13 Sempacher See Ca
73 Sena Ea
55 Sendai, Honshu Dc
55 Sendai, Kyushu Bd
68 Senegal, rep. Ad
71 Senegal, R. Cf
71 Senekal Dc
33 Sengilev Je
28 Senigallia Dc
8 Senj Eb
10 Senja Db
39 Sennar Cd
81 Senneterre Bb
20 Sens Ba
30 Senta Cc
52 Seoul Bb
62 Sepik R. Fg
81 Sept Iles Cg
19 Seraing Ed
47 Serampore Mg
30 Serbia, dist. Cd
33 Serdobsk He
33 Seregno Hd
48 Seremban Bc
32 Sergipe, st. Fd
27 Sérifos, I. Bb
33 Serov Jd
33 Serpukhov Ge
92 Serra de Tumuc Humac Db
95 Serra do Espinhaco Gc
95 Serra do Mar Fe
94 Serra do Norte Db
95 Serra do Roncador Eb
94 Serra do Tombador Db
94 Serra dos Parecis Cb
27 Sérrai Ba
92 Serrania Fc
44 Sesfontein Aa
75 Sesheke Ca
29 Sessa Dd
21 Sesto Hd

21 Sestri Levante He
15 Sète Ef
70 Sétif Ga
55 Seto Uchi, see Inland Sea Db
70 Settat Db
26 Setúbal Ab
21 Setumo Fd
33 Sevastopol Fg
20 Séverac Be
7 Severn, R. De
35 Severnaya Zemlya, Is. Mb
26 Sevilla Ab
82a Seward Db
82a Seward Pen. Bb
76 Seychelles, Is. Jk
10 Seydisfjördur Ca
27 Seyham, R. Eb
33 Seym R
9 Sfantu Gheorghe Ec
9 Sfax Hb
79 Shaballe, Webi, R. De
† 75 Shabani Db
46 Shabkade Ae
47 Shahdol Hg
46 Shahgarh Be
68 Shahhat Eb
47 Shahjahanpur Ge
43 Shahreza Gc
‡ 43 Shahrud Gb
33 Shakhty Hf
52 Shakhunya Jd
73 Shala, L. Fb
43 Shamil Hd
73 Shambo, L. Fb
73 Shamva Ea
45 Shan States Hd
51 Shanghai Gc
51 Shangjao Fd
51 Shangkiu Fc
56 Shannon Ed
9 Shannon, R. Bd
51 Shansi, prov. Fc
51 Shantar Is. Qd
51 Shantung, prov. Fc
51 Shaohing Gc
54 Shari, B. Db
65 Shark Is. Ad
43 Sharka He
88 Sharon Ed
32 Sharya Jd
74 Shasi Fc
33 Shatsk He
51 Shaunavon Dc
81 Shawinigan Falls Bb
85 Shawnee Gd
88 Sheboygan Bc
7 Sheerness Hf
6 Sheffield, Eng. Fd
61 Sheffield, Tas. Cd
47 Shekhupura Dc
81 Shelburne Cc
48 Shelbyville Bg
35 Shelekhov G. Sd
30 Shemakha Jg
86 Shenandoah Ac
39 Shendi Cd
32 Shenkursk Hc
51 Shensi, prov. Ec
48 Shentsia Ke
50 Shenyang, see Mukden Gb
33 Shepetovka Ee
60 Shepparton Cc
7 Sheppey, I. of Hf
7 Sherborne Eg
71 Sherbro, I. Cg
81 Sherbrooke Cb
84 Sheridan Ec
80 Sherridan Db
18 's Hertogen-bosch Ec
6 Shetland,Co. Inset
8 Shetland Is. Inset
33 Shevchenko Kg
74 Shibam Db
54 Shibata Cc
54 Shibetsu Db
43 Shibin Dand Hb
62 Shignag, R. Cc

54 Shinjo Dc
72 Shinkolobwe Df
73 Shinyanga Ed
87 Shio, C., see
55 Shio, C. Dc
54 Shiogama Dc
55 Shirakawa Dc
54 Shiraoi Db
43 Shiraz Gd
54 Shiriya, C. Db
54 Shiukwan Fd
46 Shivpuri Ff
74 Shizuoka & pref.Cd
31 Shkoder & L. Bd
62 Shoalwater B. Dc
51 Shoayang Fd
54 Sholapur De
84 Shoshone Dc
87 Shreveport Be
7 Shrewsbury Ee
39 Shuqra Dd
75 Shushong Db
43 Shushtar Fc
32 Shuya Hd
45 Shweho Hd
45 Shweli R. Hd
47 Shyok R. Da
44 Siakwan Ed
61 Sialkot Eb
48 Siam, G. of Bc
51 Sian Ec
51 Siangfan Fc
51 Siangtan Fd
32 Siauliai Dd
28 Sibenik Ec
48 Siberut, I. Ad
43 Sibi Bc
51 Sibui Ec
51 Sibut Bb
48 Sibolga Ac
92 Sichang Ed
29 Sicily, I. Cf
27 Sidheros, C. Cb
51 Sidi bel Abbes Ea
7 Sidmouth Dg
44 Sidney Fc
40 Sidon, see Sayda
23 Siedlce Gb
18 Siegburg Gd
28 Siegen Hd
23 Siemiatycze Gb
28 Siena Cc
82 Sieradz Ec
94 Sierra de Cordoba
63 Sierra Leone, st. Ae
90 Sierra Madre,
84 Sierra Nevada Dc
37 Sifnos Bb
30 Sighet Db
50 Sighisoara Eb
46 Sikar Ec
44 Sikhote Alin Ra. Qe
47 Sikkim, st. Me
45 Silchar Gd
27 Silifke Db
47 Siliguri Me
30 Silistra Fc
12 Silkeborg Cc
13 Silvaplana Db
85 Silver City Ee
60 Silverton Bb
13 Silz Ea
48 Simeulue, I. Ac
18 Simferopol Fg
46 Simla Fc
30 Simleul Silvaniei Db
74 Simonstown Bd
13 Simplon P. & Bl
51 Sinkeborg Cc
49 Sinai (Sananadg) Fb
23 Sinoe, L. Gc
85 Sinoia Ea
27 Sinop Fa
51 Sinsiang Fc
51 Sintai Ec
48 Sintang Cd
29 Sinuiju Bb
51 Sinyang Fc
13 Sion Bb
86 Sioux City Ad
85 Sioux Falls Gc
60 Sioux Lookout Ec
51 Sir Edward Pellew Group Ab
29 Siracusa Ef
47 Sirajganj Mf

30 Siret, & R. Eb
46 Sirohi Df
27 Siros, I. Bb
46 Sirsa Ed
68 Sirte Db
28 Sisak Fb
47 Sitapur He
82a Sitka Ec
18 Sittard Ed
42 Sivas Db
27 Sivrihisar Db
38 Siwa Bc
47 Siwalik Ra. Jd
47 Siwan Ke
12 Sjaelland, I. Ed
12 Sjaellands Odde Ed
12 Skaelskor Ed
10 Skagafjördur Ba
12 Skagen Db
10 Skagerrak Bd
82a Skagway Ec
44 Skardu Db
6 Skegness Hd
50 Skelleftea Dc
9 Skerries Ec
11 Skien Bd
23 Skierniewice Fc
70 Skikda Ga
27 Skiros Bb
12 Skive Bc
12 Skjern & R. Bd
13 Skopije Cd
35 Skovorodino Pd
8 Skye, dist. I. Bd
12 Stagelse Ed
32 Slavgorod Fe
33 Slavyansk Gf
6 Sleaford Gd
23 Sliavnico Gd
18 Sliedrecht Dc
9 Slieve Mish, mt. Bd
9 Sligo & co. Cb
31 Sliven Fd
32 Slobodskoi Kd
7 Slough Gf
23 Slovakian Ore Mts. Ed
13 Slovenia, prov. Ea
28 Slupca Db
23 Slupsk Da
33 Slutsk Ee
9 Slyne Head Ac
70 Smara Cc
7 Smethwick Fe
79 Smith Sd. Ka
86 Smithfield Dd
61 Smithton Cd
10 Smöla, I. Bd
23 Smolensk Fe
27 Smólikas, mt. Ba
51 Smolyan Ec
18 Smyrna, see Izmir Cb
18 Sneek Ea
22 Snezka, mt. Cb
10 Snoksdalar Ab
9 Snow Mt. Ff
6 Snowdon, mt. Dd
80 Snowdrift Ca
60 Snowtown Ab
69 Soalalo Gg
73 Sobat, R. Eb
92 Sobral Ec
33 Sochi Ga
51 Society Is. Fd
85 Socorro Ed
39 Socotra, I. Ed
11 Soderköping Dd
78 Soest, Ger. Hc
81 Soest Hc
73 Sofia Eb
11 Sogndal Bd
11 Sogne fjord Bc
51 Sohag Cc
52 Sohagpur Gg
19 Soissons Ec
27 Söke Cb
52 Sokol Hd
23 Sokólka Gb
71 Sokoto Gf
33 Sol-Iletsk Le
10 Solangsverket Dc
32 Solikamsk Kd
18 Solingen, Lc
51 Solleftea Dc
49 Söller Cb
56 Solomon Is. Dd
6 Solomon S. Hh
13 Solothurn & cant. Ba
18 Soltau Ib
11 Sölvesborg Cd
6 Solway Firth Ep
21 Soma Cb
68 Somali Republic Ge
30 Sombor Bc
51 Sombrerete Dc
91 Sombrero, I. Fc
7 Somerset, co., England Df

* Renamed Shurugwi    * Renamed Masvingo    * Renamed Chinhoyi
† Renamed Zvishavane
‡ Renamed Qomsheh
** Renamed Tonekaban

88 Somerset, U.S.A. Cf
75 Somerset East Dd
74 Somerset West Bd
14 Somme, dept. & R. Db
12 Sönderborg Ce
48 Songkhla Bc
72 Songo Ca
32 Sonkovo Gd
44 Sonmiani Bc
90 Sonora, R. Bb
21 Sonthofen Jb
51 Soochow Gc
22 Sopot Ea
30 Sopron Ab
10 Sör Kvalöy Db
29 Sora Dd
81 Sorel Bb
29 Sorgono Bd
20 Sorgues Ce
12 Sorö & co. Ed
95 Sorocaba Fd
49 Sorong Ef
73 Soroti Ec
10 Söröya Ea
60 Sorrento, Australia Bc
29 Sorrento, Italy Ed
22 Sosnowiec Ec
80 Souris Dc
70 Sousse Ha
69 South Africa, Rep. of Eh
2 South America Df
36 South Arabia Hh
93 South Atlantic Ocean Ef
59 South Australia, st. Fd
88 South Bend Bd
83 South Carolina, st. Ec
3 South China S. Ne
61 South Coast Da
49 South Daja Is. Ed
82 South Dakota, st. Cb
7 South Downs Gg
2 South Georgia, I. Fh
7 South Glamorgan, Co. Df
88 South Haven Bc
67 South Invercargill Bg
88 South Milwaukee Bc
7 South Molton Df
96 South Orkney Is. Rd
48 South Pagai, I. Bd
84 South Platte, R. Fc
96 South Pole Ca
8 South Ronaldsay, I. Fb
2 South Sandwich Group Fh
96 South Shetland Is. Rd
6 South Shields Fc
8 South Uist, I. Ac
* 74 South West Africa (Namibia), mandate Bb
6 South Yorkshire, Co. Fd
7 Southampton Fg
79 Southampton, I. Jb
67 Southbridge De
7 Southend Hf
67 Southern Alps, mts. Ce
65 Southern Cross Be
80 Southern Indian L. Eb
2 Southern Ocean Hj
7 Southminster Hf
61 Southport, Australia Da
6 Southport, Eng. Ed
36 South Yemen Hh
75 Soutpansberge, mts. Db
35 Sovetskaya Gavan Re
54 Soya & C. Da
29 Spaccaforno Ef
4 Spain, Rep. Eg
23 Spala Fc
7 Spalding Ge
84 Spanish Fork Dc
71 Spanish Guinea Gh
91 Spanish Town Cc
84 Sparks Cd
27 Sparti Bb
87 Spartonburg Dd
74 Spencer B. Ac
67 Spenser Mts. De
8 Spey, R. Ec
17 Speyer Cd
18 Spiekeroog, I. Ga
23 Spirding L. Gb
2 Spitsbergen Hb
28 Split (Spalato) Fc
13 Splugen Db
84 Spokane Cb
28 Spoleto Dc
48 Spratly I. Cc
74 Springbok Bc
67 Springburn Ce
86 Springfield, Ill. Cd
87 Springfield, Miss. Bd
89 Springfield,N.Y. Jc
67 Springfield,N.Z. Ce
88 Springfield, Ohio De
81 Springhill Cb
75 Springs Dc
62 Springsure Cc
84 Springville Dc
80 Squamish Bc
65 Squires Mt. Dd
35 Sredne Kolymsk Sc
35 Sretensk Od
44 Sri Lanka, rep. Eg
46 Srikolayabji, *see* Kolayat De
44 Srinagar Cb
18 Stade Ja
11 Stadlandet Bc
8 Staffa, I. Bd
7 Stafford, & co. Ee
7 Staines Gf
7 Stamford, Eng. Ge
89 Stamford, U.S.A. Jd
75 Standerton Dc
80 Stanley, Can. Db
8 Stanley, Scot. Ed
35 Stanovoi Ra., Mts. Pd
61 Stanthorpe Da
28 Stara Gradiška Fb
31 Stara Zagora Ed
33 Starabelsk Gf
32 Staraya Russa Fd
22 Stargard Cb
22 Starogard Eb
7 Start Pt. Dg
89 Staunton Fe
11 Stavanger Bd
33 Stavropol Hf
60 Stawell Bc
23 Stebark Fb
65 Steep Pt. Ad
80 Steep Rock Ec
73 Stefanie, L.,(Chew Bahir) Fc
13 Stein Ca
18 Steinhuder Meer Jb
74 Steinkopf Bc
74 Stellenbosch Bd
16 Stendal Db
33 Stepanokert Jh
48 Stepok R. Bb
33 Sterlitamak Le
80 Stettler Cb
88 Steubenville Ed
86 Stevens Pt. Cc
80 Stewart Bb
67 Stewart I. Ag
17 Steyr Fd
86 Stillwater, Minn. Bb
85 Stillwater, Okla. Gd
31 Stip De
8 Stirling Ed
65 Stirling Ra. Be
10 Stjordalshalsen Cc
17 Stockerau Gd
11 Stockholm Dd
6 Stockport Ed
84 Stockton Bd
6 Stockton-on-Tees Fc
6 Stoke-on-Trent Ed
28 Stolac Fc
18 Stolberg Fd
8 Stonehaven Fd
80 Stonewall Eb
35 Stony Tunguska, R. Mc
10 Stora Lule-vatten Db
10 Stören Cc
75 Stormberge, Mt. Dd
8 Stornoway Bb
32 Storozhevsk Kc
10 Storsjön Dc
10 Storuman Db
7 Stour, R. Eg
7 Stourbridge Ee
7 Stow-on-the-Wold Ff
9 Strabane Db
16 Stralsund Ea
74 Strand, C. Prov. Bd
11 Strand, Nor. Bd
65 Strangeways Fd
9 Strangford & L. Fb
8 Stranraer Cf
14 Strasbourg Gc
81 Stratford, Can. Ab
66 Stratford, N.Z. Ec
7 Stratford-on-Avon Fe
60 Strathalbyn Ac
8 Strathclyde,Co. Ce
8 Strathdon Ec
8 Strathmore Ed
8 Strathpeffer Dc
8 Strathy Db
65 Streaky Bay Ee
86 Streator Cc
62 Strickland R. Fh
8 Stromness Eb
10 Ströms Vattudal Dc
11 Stromstad Cd
8 Stronsay Fa
7 Stroud Ef
12 Struer Bc
31 Struma R. De
7 Strumble Hd. Bf
31 Strúmica De
88 Struthers Ed
12 Stubbeköbing Fe
13 Stuben Ea
48 Stung Treng Bb
88 Sturgeon Bay Bb
88 Sturgeon Falls Fa
75 Stutterheim Dd
17 Stuttgart, Ger. Cd
87 Stuttgart, U.S.A. Be
39 Suakin Cd
51 Suanhwa Fb
30 Subotica Bb
30 Suceava Fb
51 Suchow Fc
94 Sucre Bc
68 Sudan, st. Fd
81 Sudbury, Can. Ab
7 Sudbury, Eng. He
34 Sudzhensk Ld
41 Suez (El Suweis) Dg
41 Suez Canal Cb
7 Suffolk, co., England He
89 Suffolk, U.S.A. Gf
51 Suihwa Fb
55 Suita Cd
48 Sukabun Bd
49 Sukarnapura, *see* Djajapura
32 Sukhona Hc
33 Sukumi Hg
46 Sukkur Be
49 Sula Is. Dd
53 Sulaiyil Fe
49 Sulawesi I. Dd
43 Sulaymaniyah Fb
22 Sulechów Cb
92 Sullana Ac
28 Sulmona Dc
49 Sulu Arch. & S. Dc
56 Suluq Eb
19 Sulzbach Ge
48 Sumatra, I. Ac
49 Sumba, I. Cd
49 Sumbawa, I. Cd
73 Sumbawanga Ee
54 Sumisu, I. Cd
81 Summerside Cb
87 Sumter De
33 Sumy Fe
48 Sunda Str. Bd
47 Sundarbans Mg
6 Sunderland Fc
11 Sundsvall Dc
51 Sungari, R. Fb
27 Sungurlu Da
10 Sunndalsora Bc
55 Suo, B. Bd
84 Superior, Neb. Gc
86 Superior Wis. Bb
86 Superior, L. Cb
40 Sur (Tyre) Bc
32 Sura Jc
48 Surabaja Cd
48 Surakarta Cd
46 Surat Dh
48 Surat Thani Ac
46 Surendranagar Cg
92 Surinam, Neth. terr. Db
7 Surrey, co. Gf
54 Suruyga, B. Cd
28 Sušak Eb
13 Susten P. Cb
46 Sutlej, R. Dd
66 Suva Gk
55 Suwa & I. Cc
23 Suwalki Ga
21 Suzzara Jd
34 Svalbard I. Db
33 Svatovo Gf
12 Svendborg Dd
34 Sverdlovsk Jd
78 Sverdrup Is. Ga
30 Svishtov Ed
22 Svitavy Dd
62 Swain Reefs Dc
74 Swakop, R. Ab
74 Swakopmund Ab
60 Swan Hill Bc
80 Swan River Db
7 Swanage Fg
7 Swansea Df
74 Swartberge Cd
44 Swat, Dist. Cb
51 Swatow Fd
69 Swaziland, prot. Fh
4 Sweden, King. Jc
85 Sweet Water Fe
41 Sweet Water Canal Cf
74 Swellendam Cd
22 Swindnica Dc
22 Swiebodzin Cb
80 Swift Current Db
9 Swilly, L. Da
7 Swindon Ff
13 Switzerland, st. Cb
9 Swords Ec
61 Sydney, Australia Db
81 Sydney, Can. Cb
32 Syktyvkar Kc
45 Sylhet Gd
34 Syr Darya R. Je
89 Syracuse Gc
36 Syria, st. Gf
45 Syriam He
42 Syrian Des. Dc
33 Syzran Je
30 Szârvas Cb
22 Szczecin (Stettin) Cb
22 Szczecinek Db
50 Szecnwan, prov. Ec
30 Szeged Cb
30 Szekesfehervar Bb
30 Szekszárd Bb
50 Szemao Ed
30 Szentes Cb
51 Szeping Gb
30 Szolnok Cb
30 Szombathely Ab
23 Szydlowiec Fc

70 Tabarka Ga
43 Tabas Hc
22 Tábor Cd
73 Tabora Ee
43 Tabriz Fb
49 Tacloban Db
94 Tacna Ac
94 Taco Pozo Ce
84 Tacoma Bb
94 Tacuarembó Df
70 Tademait, plat. Fc
67 Tadmor Dd
81 Tadoussac Bb
34 Tadzhikistan Kf
52 Taegu Bb
52 Taejon Bb
68 Tafassasset, Wadi Cc
11 Tafjord Bc
47 Taga-Dzong Me
33 Taganrog Gf
80 Tagish Aa
95 Taguatinga Fb
62 Tagula I. Hj
26 Tagus, *see* Tajo, R.
67 Tahakopa Bg
48 Tahan mt. Bc
70 Tahat, mt. Gd
50 Tahcheng Cb
43 Taheri Gd
57 Tahiti Fd
51 Taichung Gd
66 Taihape Ec
60 Tailem Bend Ac
21 Tailfingen Ga
35 Taimyr, L. Nb
51 Tainan Gd
27 Tainaron, C. (Matapan) Bb
51 Taipei Gd
48 Taiping Bc
55 Taira Dc
35 Taishet Md
51 Taitung Gd
10 Taivalkoski Fb
51 Taiwan (Formosa) I. Gd
51 Taiyuan Fc
26 Tajo (Tagus) R. Ab
48 Tak Ab
55 Takada Cc
66 Takaka Dd
55 Takamatsu Bd
55 Takaoka Cc
66 Takapuna Eb
55 Takasaki Cc
73 Takaungu Fd
55 Takayama Cc
55 Takefu Cc
50 Takla Makan, des. Cc
49 Talaud Is. Dc
93 Talca Bf
93 Talcahuano Bf
51 Tali Ec
40 Tall Kalakh Cb
87 Tallahassee De
32 Tallinn Ed
94 Taltal Ae
71 Tamale Eg
55 Tamano Bd
70 Tamanrasset (Ft. Laperrine) Gd
† 69 Tamatave Gg
33 Tamboy He
72 Tambura Db
71 Tamchakett Ce
71 Tamgak Mts. Ge
44 Tamil Nadu, st. Df
87 Tampa Df
11 Tampere Ec
90 Tampico Ec
51 Tamsag Bulak Fb
70 Tamsagout Dd
61 Tamworth Db
39 Tana, L. Cd
73 Tana, R., Kenya Gd
10 Tana & Fd., Norway Fa
49 Tanahgrogot Cd
33 Tanalitskaya Le
82a Tanana Cb
* 69 Tananarive Gg
21 Tanaro, R. Fe
9 Tanderagee Eb
93 Tandil Df
48 Tandjung Pandan Bd
48 Tandjung Selor Cc
46 Tando Adam Bf
66 Taneatua Fc
55 Tanega Shima Bd
70 Tanezrouft Fd
73 Tanga Fe
73 Tanganyika, L. De
70 Tanger (Tangier) Da
51 Tangshan Fc
49 Tanimbar Is. Ed
46 Tank Cb
12 Tannis Bay Db
71 Tanout Gf
38 Tanta Cb
40 Tantura (Dor) Bc
68 Tanzania Ff
51 Taonan Gb
69 Taoudenni Bc
70 Taourirt Eb
67 Tapanui Bf
92 Tapuruquara Cb
40 Tarabulus (Tripoli) Bb
49 Tarakan Cc
66 Taranaki, dist. Ec
26 Tarancon Bb
46 Taranga Hill Dg
29 Taranto, & G. Fd
20 Tarare Cd
66 Tarawera Fc
26 Tarazona Ba
8 Tarbert Bc
15 Tarbes Df
65 Tarcoola Ee
50 Tardin Dc
61 Taree Db
20 Tarentaise, dist. Ed
70 Tarfaya Cc
30 Targoviste Ec
30 Târgu-Jiu Dc
30 Targu Mures Eb
30 Targu Neamt Fb
94 Tarija Cd
39 Tarim Dd
33 Tarkhankut, C. Ff
71 Tarkwa Eg
49 Tarlac Db
23 Tarnobrzeg Fc
23 Tarnów Fc
22 Tarnowskie Góry Ec
63 Taroom Cd
26 Tarragona Ca
27 Tarsus Db
35 Tartary, G. of Re
32 Tartu Ed
40 Tartus Bb
81 Taschereau Bb
50 Tashigong Bc
34 Tashkent Je
50 Tashkurgan Bc
48 Tasikmalaja Bd
67 Tasman Bay Dd
3 Tasman Sea Pg
59 Tasmania, st. Hg
30 Tatabanya Bb
34 Tatarsk Kd
55 Tateyama Cc
50 Tatsaitan Dc
46 Tatta Af
51 Tatung Fb
66 Taumarunui Ec
45 Taunggyi Hd
7 Taunton Df
66 Taupo Fc
66 Tauranga Fb
27 Taurus Mts. Db
33 Tauz Jg
73 Taveta Fd
66 Taveuni, I. Hk
26 Tavira Ab
45 Tavoy & I. H
27 Tavsanli Cb
88 Tawas City Db
85 Taylor Ge


* *Renamed Namibia*

* *Renamed Antananarivo*
† *Renamed Taomasina*

42 Tayma Dd
8 Tayside, co. Ed
8 Tayport Fd
73 Tayulehsze Dd
34 Taz R. Lc
70 Taza Eb
38 Tbilisi Jg
22 Tczew Ea
6 Te Aroha Eb
6 Te Awamutu Ec
66 Te Hora Ed
66 Te Kuiti Ec
66 Te Puke Fb
79 Teano Ed
70 Tébessa Ga
30 Tecuci Fc
48 Tegal Bd
43 Tegucigalpa Ad
43 Tehran Gb
76 Tehtsin (Atuntze) Dd
90 Tehuantepec Dd
7 Teignmouth Dg
72 Teixeira de Sousa Cf
26 Tejo, R. Ab
27 Tekirdağ Ca
40 Tel Aviv-Jaffa Bc
91 Tela Ac
48, Telanaipura Bd
33 Telavi Jg
70 Telegraph Creek Ab
7 Telford Fe
44 Tellicherry Df
48 Telok Anson Bc
51 Teluk Betung Bd
48 Telukdalam Ac
71 Tema Eg
56 Temax Gd
27 Temora Cb
29 Tempio Bd
85 Temple Ge
9 Templemore Dd
93 Temuco Bf
67 Temuka Cf
45 Ten Degree Chan. Gg
5 Tenasserim, & Dist. Hf
7 Tenby Cf
71 Tenda, Col di, P. Fe
6 Tenerife, I. Ac
50 Tengchung Dd
72 Tenke Df
64 Tennant Creek Eb
87 Tennessee, R. Ce
83 Tennessee, st. Cc
55 Tenryu, R. Cc
7 Tenterden Hf
61 Tenterfield Da
95 Teófilo-Otoni Gc
90 Tepic Dc
72 Teplice Bc
28 Teramo Dc
90 Terang Bc
33 Terek Jg
92 Teresina Ec
70 Terhazza Ec
34 Termez Jf
29 Termini Df
90 Terminos, Laguna de Fd
47 Ternate Dc
18 Terneuzen Cc
28 Terni Dc
18 Ternopol Ef
92 Terracina Dd
28 Terralba Bc
88 Terre Haute Be
87 Terrell Ae
18 Terschelling, I. Ea
28 Teruel Ba
76 Tešanj, Fb
70 Tessalit Fd
39 Tessenei Cd
27 Tetbury Ef
75 Tete Ea
70 Tetuan Da
72 Teutoburger W., mts. Cb
7 Tewksbury Ef
87 Texarkana Be
82 Texas, st. Cc
18 Texel, I. Da
90 Tezpur Gc
75 Thabana Ntlenyana, mt. Dc
48 Thailand (Siam) Bb
7 Thame Gf
66 Thames Eb
7 Thames, R. Hf
44 Thana Dj
46 Thar Desert, see Gt. Indian Des.
46 Tharad Cf
46 Thargomindah Ba
27 Thasos, I. Ba
45 Thaton He
85 Thazi Hd
84 The Dalles Bb
7 The Fens Gf

18 The Hague ('s Gravenhague) Db
43 The Gulf Fd
80 The Pas Db
12 The Skaw Db
12 The Sound Fd
38 Thebes Cc
63 Theodore Dc
27 Thérmaikos, G. of Ba
27 Thermopylai, pass. Bb
27 Thessaloniki Ba
27 Thessaly, dist. Bb
81 Thetford Mines Bb
65 Thevenard Ee
14 Thianville Gc
20 Thiers Bd
6 Thiès Bf
73 Thika Fd
19 Thionville Fd
27 Thira, I. Cb
12 Thisted Bc
62 Thomson R. Bc
20 Thonon Ec
47 Thor Ke
10 Thorshöfn Ba
27 Thrace, dist. Ca
81 Three Rivers Bb
12 Thun Bb
70 Thunder Bay Fc
13 Thurgau, cant. Da
9 Thurles Dd
62 Thursday I. Ba
8 Thurso Eb
23 Thysville Ae
70 Tiaret Fa
72 Tibati Ab
40 Tiberias Bc
40 Tiberias, L. (S. of Galilee) Bc
50 Tibet, Aut. Reg. Cc
90 Tiburon, I. Bb
73 Tichit Cb
13 Ticino, R. & cant. Cb
18 Tielt Cd
50 Tien Shan, mts. Cb
18 Tienen Dd
72 Tienshui Dd
51 Tientsin Fc
54 Tierra del Fuego Cf
88 Tiffin Db
81 Tignish Cb
43 Tigris, R. Fc
51 Tijuana Aa
33 Tikhoretsk Hd
51 Tiksi Pb
18 Tilburg Ec
71 Tillabéry Ef
18 Tillsonburg Ec
27 Tilos, I. Cb
50 Tímaru Cf
71 Timbédra De
70 Timiris, C. Be
30 Timisoara Ab
48 Timmis Ab
49 Timor, I. & S. Dd
70 Tindouf Dc
61 Tingha Da
27 Tinos Cb
60 Tintinara Bc
9 Tipperary & co. Cd
71 Tirane Be
23 Tiraspol Ef
47 Tirat Karmel Bc
8 Tiree, I. Bd
13 Tirol, prov. Ea
29 Tirso Bc
44 Tiruchchirappalli Df
44 Tirunelveli Dg
44 Tiruvannamali Df
80 Tisdale Db
44 Titicaca, L. Bc
47 Titlagarh Jh
31 Titograd Bd
13 Titov Veles Ce
13 Titovo Uzice Bd
72 Titule Cc
7 Tiverton Dg
23 Tivoli Dd
70 Tizi-Ouzou Fa
14 Tjilatjap Bd
44 Tjirebon Bd
90 Tlaxcala Ed
90 Tlaxiaco Ed
70 Tlemcen Eb
48 Toba L. Ac
91 Tobago, I. Fd
83 Tobermory Eb
29 Tobol R. Jd
27 Tobolsk Jd
83 Tobruk Eb
55 Tochigi & pref. Cc
88 Toco Bd
94 Tocopilla Ad
40 Tocumwal Cc
6 Todcaster Fd
20 Toghral Ombo Cc
44 Togian Is. Dd
68 Togliatti Jd
68 Togo, rep. Ce

54 Tōhoku, dist. Dc
73 Toinya Db
30 Tokaj Ca
67 Tokanui Bg
39 Tokar Cd
63 Tokara Str. Ad
67 Tokarahi Cf
27 Tokat Ea
56 Tokelau Is. Ed
66 Tokoroa Ec
57 Tokushima & pref. Bd
55 Tokuyama Bf
55 Tokyo & pref. Cc
66 Tolaga Gc
30 Tolbukhin Fd
26 Toleao & Sa. de, Bb
88 Toledo, U.S.A. Dd
72 Tolo Ed
49 Tolo, G. of Dd
90 Toluca Ed
54 Tomakomai Db
26 Tomar Ab
25 Tomaszów Ec
71 Tombouctou (Timbuktu) Ee
85 Tombstone Ee
49 Tomini, G. of Dd
34 Tomsk Ld
90 Tonala Fd
7 Tonbridge Hf
12 Tönder Be
93 Tonga (Friendly) Is. Hk
66 Tongatabu, I. Hk
18 Tongeren Ed
94 Tongoy Af
48 Tonkin, G. of Ba
2 Tonle Sap L. Bb
85 Tonopah Cd
11 Tönsberg Cd
61 Toowong Da
61 Toowoomba Da
32 Top I. Fb
86 Topeka Ad
94 Topolobampo Cc
7 Torbay Dg
16 Torgau Ec
18 Torhout Cc
54 Tori-shima I. Cd
34 Tornio (Turin) Fd
10 Torne, R. Eb
50 Torokina Jh
22 Toronaios, G. Ba
7 Toronto, Australia Db
81 Toronto, Can. Bd
32 Toropets Fd
73 Torori Ec
17 Torquay Dg
50 Torre Annunziata Ed
26 Torrelavega Ba
90 Torreon Db
95 Tórres, Brazil Fe
56 Torres, Mexico Bb
26 Torres Vedras Ab
99 Torrington Jd
62 Torrowange Bb
28 Tortoli Bc
21 Tortona Ce
26 Tortosa & C. Ca
22 Torun Eb
55 Tosa, B. Bd
28 Toscana, reg. Cc
27 Tosya Da
74 Toteng Cb
32 Totma Hd
7 Tottenham Gf
56 Tottori & pref. Bc
70 Toubkal, Dj., mt. Db
71 Tougouort Gb
70 Tougué Cf
19 Toul Gf
75 Toulon Gf
20 Toulouse Df
48 Toungoo He
19 Tournai Cd
15 Tours Dd
94 Towada, L. Db
7 Towcester Ge
62 Townshend C. Dc
82 Townsville Cb
49 Towson Ge
65 Toyama & pref. Cc
55 Toyama, B. Cc
55 Toyohashi Cd
55 Toyooka Bc
70 Tozeur Gb
42 Trabzon Da
50 Tracy Cd
26 Trafalgar, C. Ab
80 Trail Cc
9 Tralee Bd
44 Tranás Cc
29 Trangie Cb
29 Trani Fd
70 Transkei Cc
75 Transvaal, prov. c
30 Transylvania, dist. Eb

30 Transylvanian Alps Dc
29 Trapani De
60 Traralgon Cc
32 Traverse City Cb
34 Travnik Fb
21 Trebnia, R. He
32 Trebic Cd
28 Trebinje Gc
52 Trebon Cd
7 Tregar Df
11 Trelleborg Cd
95 Tremadal Gc
28 Tremiti Is. Ec
12 Trencin Ed
21 Trentino, prov. Kc
28 Trento Ca
89 Trenton Hd
81 Trepassey Db
93 Tres Arroyos Cf
95 Três Lagôas Ed
21 Treviglio Hd
28 Treviso Db
19 Trier Fe
28 Trieste Db
27 Trikkala Bb
9 Trim Ec
44 Trincomalee Dg
7 Tring Gf
94 Trinidad Cb
85 Trinidad, I. Cd
81 Trinity B. Db
68 Tripoli, Libya Db
40 Tripoli(Tarabulus), Syria Bb
27 Trípolis Bb
45 Tripura, St. Gd
2 Tristan da Cunha, I. Fg
44 Trivandrum Cd
22 Trnava Dd
74 Troia Ed
32 Troitsko-Pechorsk Lc
10 Trollforsen Db
19 Trombudo Fe
10 Tromsö Db
10 Trondheim Cc
87 Troodos, Mt. Dc
18 Troon De
7 Trowbridge Ef
72 Troy, Turkey Cb
10 Troy, U.S.A. Jc
21 Troyes Ca
70 Trujillo, Hond. Ac
92 Trujillo, Peru Bc
7 Truro, Canada Cb
1 Truro, England Cg
22 Trutnov Cc
20 Truyere, R. Be
51 Tsamkong Fd
74 Tsane Cb
74 Tselinograd Kd
51 Tsetserleg Eb
33 Tshikinali Hg
51 Tsiaotso Fc
51 Tsinan Fc
50 Tsinghai, prov. Dc
51 Tsingshih Fd
51 Tsingtao Gc
51 Tsining Fb
74 Tsitsihar Gb
51 Tsu Cd
54 Tsu Shima Ad
72 Tsuchiura Dc
74 Tsugaru Str. Db
74 Tsumeb Ba
51 Tsunyi Ec
74 Tsuruga Cc
74 Tsuruoka Cc
52 Tsushima, & Str. Bb
55 Tsuyama Bc
51 Tuam Cc
57 Tuamotu Arch. Gd
33 Tuapse Gg
67 Tuatapere Ag
48 Tubarb Fe
51 Tubarão Fe
70 Tübingen Jf
57 Tubuai Is. (Austral. Is.) Fe

87 Tulsa Ad
35 Tulun Nd
48 Tulungogung Cd
92 Tumaco Bd
72 Tumba, L. Bd
61 Tumbarumba Cc
65 Tumby Bay Fe
44 Tumkur Df
61 Tumut Cc
7 Tunbridge Wells Hf
51 Tungchow Fc
51 Tungchuan Ec
51 Tunghwa Gb
51 Tungking Gc
51 Tungliao Gb
70 Tunis Ga
68 Tunisia, king. Cb
92 Tunja Bb
81 Tunki Fd
45 Tuntai Nf
47 Tura Nf
42 Turaba Ed
30 Turda Db
22 Turek Eb
50 Turfan Cb
31 Turgovishte Fd
27 Turgutlu Cb
21 Turin, see Torino
73 Turkana, L. Fc
36 Turkey, rep. Cd
34 Turkmenistan Hf
91 Turks, is. Db
11 Turku (Åbo) Ec
90 Turneffe, I. Gd
18 Turnhout Dc
31 Turnovo Ed
30 Turnu Magurele Ed
30 Turnu Severin Dc
49 Turtle Is. Cc
32 Turya Kc
87 Tuscaloosa Ce
44 Tuticorin Dg
30 Tutrakan Fd
21 Tuttlingen Gb
6 Tutuila, I. Dj
45 Tuvalu, Is. Dd
50 Tuxtla, I. Cd
32 Tuymazy Ke
50 Tuyun Ed
27 Tuz, L. Db
30 Tuzla Bc
8 Tweed, R. Ee
11 Twillingate Db
50 Two Harbors Bb
88 Two Rivers Bb
87 Tyler Ae
6 Tyne & Wear, Co. Fc
6 Tynemouth Fb
40 Tyre (Sur) Bc
37 Tyrol, mts. De
9 Tyrone, co. Db
29 Tyrrhenian Sea De
34 Tyumen Jd
7 Tywyn Ce
51 Tzekung Ed
51 Tzepo Fc

95 Uba Gd
46 Ubauro Bd
55 Ube Bd
51 Uberaba Fc
72 Uberlandia Fc
48 Ubon Bb
54 Uchiura B. Db
16 Udaipur Df
10 Uddjaur Db
46 Udhampur Eb
28 Udine Da
75 Udzi Mts. Eb
55 Ueda Cc
16 Uelzen Db
72 Uere, R. Cc
32 Ufa & R. Ld
73 Ugalla, R. Ee
68 Uganda, st. Fe
8 Uig Bc
75 Uitenhage Dd
70 Ujda Eb
73 Ujiji Dc
49 Ujjain Eg
49 Ujung Pandang Cd
73 Ukerewe Ed
32 Ukhta Kc
33 Ukraine Ef
51 Ulan Bator Eb
50 Ulan Ude Nd
51 Ulanhot Gb
46 Ulhasnagar Dj
61 Ulladulla Dc
55 Ullung Do, I. Bc
21 Ulm Ha
8 Ulmarra Da
9 Ulster, prov. Db
22 Ultava, R. Cc
60 Ultima Bc
27 Ulukisla Db
61 Ulverstone Ad
33 Ulyanovsk Je
50 Ulyasutai Db
51 Uman Ff
46 Umarkot Bf
75 Umata Db

* Renamed Toliara

32 Umba Fb
62 Umboi I. Gh
28 Umbria, reg. Dc
30 Ume, R. Dc
10 Umeå Ec
42 Umm Lajj Dd
73 Umm Ruwaba Ea
43 Umm Said Ge
83c Unimak, I. Eb
* 75 Umtali Ea
† 75 Umvuma Ea
75 Umzimvubu Dd
75 Umzinto Ed
83c Unalaska, I. Eb
94 Uncia Bc
31 Unecha Fe
79 Ungava B. Lc
52 Unggi Ca
95 União da Vitoria Ec
83c Unimak, I. Eb
5 Union of Soviet Socialist Reps. Pd
88 Uniontown Fe
43 United Arab Emirates Gd
4 United Kingdom Ee
77 United States of America He
47 Unnao He
8 Unst, I. Inset
13 Unter Walden, cant. Cb
32 Unzha Hd
72 Upemba, L. De
78 Upernavik Ma
74 Upington Cc
66 Upolu, 1. Dj
67 Upper Hutt Ed
73 Upper Nile, prov. Eb
11 Uppsala Dd
35 Ural Mts. Lc
35 Ural, R. Hd
34 Uralsk Hd
80 Uranium City Db
55 Urawa Cc
82 Urbana Dd
24 Urbino Fc
90 Ures Bb
42 Urfa Db
82 Uri, cant. Cb
43 Urmia, L. Fb
34 Urosevac Cd
94 Uruguaiana De
8 Uruguay, rep., & R. Df
50 Urumchi Cd
33 Uryupinsk Ne
32 Usa R. Lb
24 Usak Cb
74 Usakos Bb
8 Useko Ee
42 Usfan De
14 Ushant, I. Ac
78 Usküdar (Scutari) Cb
33 Usman Ge
55 Ust-Izhma Kb
35 Ust Kamchatsk Td
52 Ust Port Lb
52 Ust-Shchugar Lc
52 Ust Tsilma Kb
55 Ust-Usa Lb
34 Ust Urt Plat. He
52 Usti Cb
52 Ustka Da
32 Ustyug Jc
52 Usuki Bd
34 Utah, L., Dc
82 Utah, st. Bc
73 Utete Fb
89 Utica Hc
73 Utrecht, Nat. Ec
18 Utrecht & prov., Netherlands Eb
55 Utsunomiya Cc
47 Uttar Pradesh, st. He
48 Uttaradit Bb
10 Uusikaarlepy Ec
85 Uvalde Gf
73 Uvinza Ee
55 Uwajima Bd
34 Uyuni Bd
34 Uzbekistan Je

93 Valdivia Bf
26 Valenca Aa
20 Valence Cc
26 Valencia & G. of, Spain Bb
92 Valencia, Ven. Ca
9 Valentia I. Ae
21 Valenza Gd
32 Valga Ed
30 Valjevo Bc
18 Valkenswaard Ec
90 Valladolia Gd
26 Valladolid Ba
21 Valle d'Aosta, prov. Fd
78 Valleyfield Bc
84 Vallejo Bc
94 Vallenar Ac
84 Valley City Gb
24 Vallombrosa Cc
13 Vallorbe Ab
93 Valparaiso, Chile Bf
85 Valparaiso, U.S.A. Bd
21 Valtellina, dist. Hc
42 Van, L. Eb
64 Van Diemen C., & G. Ea
92 Vancluse, dept. Df
32 Vancouver, Can. Bc
84 Vancouver, U.S.A. Bb
80 Vancouver I. Bc
32 Vänern, L. Cd
32 Vanersborg Cd
73 Vanga Fd
62 Vanimo Fg
30 Vännäs Dc
10 Vannöy Da
66 Vanua Levu, I. Gk
47 Varanasi (Banaras) Jf
32 Varangeren Ga
20 Varanger Pen. Fa
21 Varazdin Fa
21 Varazze Ge
31 Vardar, R. De
21 Varde & R. Bd
12 Vardingborg Ee
10 Vardö Ha
21 Varel Ha
21 Varese Gd
31 Varna (Stalin) Gd
31 Varnamo Cd
10 Vaslui Fb
31 Vatna Jökull Bb
33 Vatra-Dornei Eb
31 Vattern, L. Cd
13 Vaud, cant. Ab
18 Vechte, R. Fb
30 Vega, L. Cb
80 Vegreville Cb
12 Vejle & co. Cb
20 Velay, Mts. du, Be
24 Velebit Planina, mts. Eb
33 Veliki Dd
26 Vélez Málaga Bb
32 Veliki Hc
32 Veikie Luki Fd
32 Velizh Fd
18 Velsen Db
32 Veisk Hc
12 Vendsyssel, dist. Db
28 Veneto, reg. Db
22 Venezuela, rep. Cb
22 Venice, Gulf of Db
28 Venice Db
18 Venlo Fc
21 Ventimiglia Ff
7 Ventnor Ff
20 Ventoux, mt. De
32 Ventspils Dd
94 Vera Ce
90 Veracruz Ed
32 Vercelli Gd
10 Verdalsöra Cc
90 Verde, R. Ed
14 Verden Cb
14 Verdun Fc
32 Verdun, R. Ef
75 Vereeniging Dc
71 Verga, C. Cf
35 Verkhoyansk, & Ra. Qc
32 Vermilion Cb
37 Vermont, st. Fb
74 Verneukpan, L. Cd
90 Vernon, Can. Cb
85 Vernon, U.S.A. Ge
37 Veroia Bd
21 Verona Jd
14 Versailles Ec
14 Verviers Ed
13 Vesoul Gd
10 Vesteralen, I. Cb
82a Valdez Cb

12 Vesterøhavn Db
10 Vestfjorden Cb
10 Vestmannaeyjar, I. Ab
29 Vesuvio, vol. Ed
50 Vesprem Ab
32 Vetluga, & R. Jd
13 Vevey Ab
21 Viadana Cg
92 Viana Ec
26 Viana do Castelo Aa
28 Viareggio Cc
12 Viborg & co. Cc
28 Vicenza Cb
20 Vichy Bc
87 Vicksburg Be
80 Victor Harbor Ac
80 Victoria, Can. Bc
93 Victoria, Chile Bf
71 Victoria, Guin. Cf
85 Victoria, U.S.A. Gf
80 Victoria Beach Eb
75 Victoria Falls Da
73 Victoria, L. Ed
96 Victoria Land Kb
45 Victoria Pt. He
64 Victoria River Downs Ec
59 Victoria, st. Cf
74 Victoria West Cd
89 Victoriaville Ka
30 Vidin Dd
52 Viedma Cg
17 Vienna (Wien) Gd
20 Vienne Cd
48 Vientiane Bb
18 Viersen Fc
18 Vierwaldstatter See, L. Ca
48 Vietnam, st. Bb
21 Vigevano Gd
90 Vigia Chico Gd
26 Vigo Aa
45 Vijayavada Ee
13 Vikna I. Cc
72 Vila Cabral Ff
24 Vila de Cangamba Bg
* 75 Vila de Manica Ea
* 75 Vila Fontes Ea
** 72 Vila Henrique de Carvalho Ca
* 75 Vila João Belo Ec
† 72 Vila Luso Bf
* 75 Vila Machado Ea
‡ 72 Vila Mariano Machado Af
26 Vila Nova de Gaia Aa
94 Vila Vila Bc
75 Vilanculos Fb
94 Vilhena Cb
90 Villa Ahumada Ca
93 Villa Bella Cd
94 Villa Maria Cf
93 Villa Mercedes Cf
94 Villa Montes Cd
21 Villafranca di Verona Jd
90 Villahermosa Fd
26 Villanueva y Geltru Ca
28 Villaputzu Bc
21 Villarosa Ef
94 Villarrica De
20 Villefranche Cd
22 Villena Bb
20 Villeneuve Df
20 Villerupt Fe
20 Villeurbanne Cd
21 Villingen Ga
73 Vimiea Ec
18 Vilvoorde Dd
35 Vilynisk Pc
93 Vina del Mar Bf
22 Vinaroz Ca
88 Vincennes Be
48 Vinh Bb
33 Vinnitsa Ef
46 Viramgam Dg
80 Virden Dc
51 Virgin Is. Fc
86 Virginia Bb
83 Virginia, st. Fc
89 Virginia Beach Hf
28 Vis, I. Fc
71 Visby Dd
78 Viscount Melville Sd. Cg
45 Vishakhapatnam Ee
28 Vishera Ee
28 Visoko Gc
13 Visp Bb
75 Vistula (Wista) R. Eb
32 Vitebsk Fd
28 Viterbo Db
66 Viti Levu, I. Gk
93 Vitoria, Braz. Ec
75 Vitoria, Spain Ba
32 Vitoria da Conquista Ed

19 Vitry le François Df
20 Vitteaux Cb
28 Vittorio Db
29 Vittoria Ef
47 Vizianagaram Jj
18 Vlaardingen Dc
32 Vladimir Hd
35 Vladivostok Qe
18 Vlieland, I. Da
31 Vlone Be
49 Vogelkop, mts. Ee
14 Voges, mts. Gc
24 Voghera Ge
73 Voi Fd
20 Voiron Dd
11 Volda Bc
21 Voldagno Kd
32 Volga R. Jf
32 Volgograd Hf
32 Volkhov Fd
32 Völklingen Fe
75 Volksrust Ec
32 Vologdo Hd
27 Vólos Bb
33 Volovo Ge
32 Volsk Je
70 Volta, L. Eg
68 Volta, rep. see Upper Volta Bd
28 Volteri Cd
78 Voorburg Db
10 Vopnafjördur Ca
10 Vopnajökull Bb
21 Voralberg, prov. Hb
13 Vorderrhein. R. Cb
32 Vorkuta Mb
35 Voroshilovgrad (Lugansk) Gf
33 Vyatka Kd
32 Vyazma Fd
32 Vyborg Ec
32 Vychegda Kc
32 Vyshni Fd
32 Vytegra Gc

71 Wa Ef
18 Waal, R. Ec
88 Wabash Cd
22 Wabrzezno Eb
35 Wachock Fc
85 Waco Ge
92 Wad Medani Cd
18 Wadden Zee Ea
80 Waddington, Mt. Bb
44 Wadi De
42 Wadi ar Rima Dd
42 Wadi as Subai, R. Ee
42 Wadi Dawasir, R. Ee
42 Wadi Hauran, R. Ec
42 Wadi Sabha, R. Fe
42 Wadi Sirhan, R. Dc
18 Wageningen Ec
72 Wager B. Hb
65 Wagga Be
61 Wagga Wagga Cc
86 Wahpeton Ab
49 Waigeo, I. Ed
66 Waihi Eb
86 Waikaia Bf
60 Waikari Ec
60 Waikerie Ab
66 Waikokopu Fc
60 Waikouaiti Cf
66 Waimarino Ec
47 Waimate Cf
49 Waingapu Dd
40 Wainwright Cb
66 Waiouru Ec
66 Waipara Ec
66 Waipawa Fc
66 Waipiro Gc
66 Waipu Ea
66 Waipukurau Fc
66 Wairoa Fc
66 Waitara Ec
66 Waiuku Eb
66 Wajima Cc
35 Wakamatsu Cc
54 Wakasa, B. Cc

55 Wakayama & pref. Cd
56 Wake I. Dc
67 Wakefield Dd
78 Wakeham Bay Kb
54 Wakkanai Da
73 Walcheren, I. Cc
61 Walcott Pt. Bc
7 Wales De
61 Walgett Ec
88 Walkerton Eb
84 Walla Walla Cb
84 Wallace Cb
84 Wallaceburg Dc
30 Wallachia, dist. Ec
61 Wallsend Db
7 Walsall Fe
85 Walsenburg Fd
85 Walvis Bay & B.A.B
26 Wana Bb
75 Wanaaring Ba
75 Wanaka Bf
63 Wandoan Cd
66 Wanganui Ec
60 Wangaratta Cc
33 Wangen Da
18 Wangeroge, I. Ga
51 Wanhsien Ec
* 75 Wankie Da
91 Wanks, R. Bd
7 Wantage Ff
73 Warandab Gj
46 Warangal Gk
66 Waratah Cd
60 Warburton Cc
63 Warburton R. Ad
67 Ward Ed
46 Wardha Gh
7 Wareham Eg
18 Warendorf Gc
69 Warkworth Eb
74 Warmbad, S.W. Afr. Bc
75 Warmbad, Trans. Dc
7 Warminster Ef
60 Warragul Cc
60 Warrego R. Ca
7 Warren, Australia Cb
88 Warren, U.S.A. Ed
9 Warrenpoint Eb
75 Warrenton Ad
7 Warri Warri Ba
65 Warrina Fd
6 Warrington Ed
66 Warrnambool Bc
23 Warsaw (Warszawa), Poland Fb
88 Warsaw, U.S.A. Cd
22 Warta, R. Cb
61 Warwick, Australia Da
7 Warwick & co., England Fe
85 Wasatch, Mts. Dd
6 Wash, The He
89 Washington, D.C. Ge
88 Washington, Ind. Bb
88 Washington, Ohio De
88 Washington, Pa. Ed
82 Washington, st. Ab
18 Wasseraar Db
87 Water Valley Cd
74 Waterberg Bb
39 Waterbury Jd
7 Waterford & co. Dd
9 Waterford Hr. Dd
86 Waterloo, Iowa Bc
71 Waterloo, Sierra Leone Cg
89 Watertown, N.Y. Hc
86 Watertown, Wis. Cc
80 Waterways Cb
7 Watford Gf
9 Watling I. (S. Salvador 1.) Db
80 Watson Lake Eb
8 Watten Eb
7 Watton Ho
33 Wattwil Da
92 Wau, Australia Gh
73 Wau, Sudan Db
86 Waukegan Bc
88 Wauwatosa Bc
44 Wave Hill Eb
66 Waverley Ec
45 Waw He
88 Waycross He
85 Waynesboro Fe
46 Waziristan, West Pakistan Eb

* Renamed Mutare
† Renamed Mvuma

* Renamed Caia
** Renamed Saurimo
† Renamed Luena
‡ Renamed Ganda

* Renamed Hwange

38 Wazirabad, Afghanistan Fb
7 Weald, The Gf
86 Webster City Bc
2 Weddell Sea Ej
61 Wee Waa Ca
18 Weert Ec
13 Weesen Da
13 Weggis Ca
51 Weifang Kb
21 Weilheim Kb
17 Weimar Dc
13 Weinfelden Ca
21 Weingarten Hb
19 Weinheim He
42 Wejn Dd
22 Wejherowo Ea
65 Weld Spring Ea
88 Welland Fc
62 Wellesley Is. Ab
7 Wellingborough Fe
74 Wellington, Cape Province Bd
61 Wellington, N.S.W. Cb
67 Wellington, New Zealand Ed
6 Wellington, dist., New Zealand Ed
85 Wellington, U.S.A. Gd
93 Wellington I. Bg
7 Wells Ef
88 Wellsville, Ohio Ed
89 Wellsville, N.Y. Gc
17 Wels Fd
7 Welshpool De
51 Wenchow Gd
13 Wengen Bb
60 Wentworth Bb
18 Werne Gc
61 Werris Creek Db
16 Wesel Bc
7 Weser, R. Ha
22 West Beskids, mts. Ed
88 West Bend Bc
47 West Bengal, st. Lg
7 West Bromwich Fe
49 West Daja Is. Dd
32 West Dvina, R. Ed
18 West Frisian Is. Ea
7 West Glamorgan, Co. Df
7 West Ham Hf
67 West Harbour Cf
49 West Irian, prov. Ff
8 West Lothian, co. Ee
75 West Nicholson Db
87 West Palm Beach E.Cc
18 West Schelde, R.Cc
7 West Sussex, Co. Gg
83 West Virginia, st. Ec
61 West Wyalong Cb
6 West Yorkshire, Co. Fd
89 Westbrook Kc
61 Westbury Cd
58 Western Australia, st. Cc
44 Western Ghats, mts. Ce
8 Western Isles, Co. Bc
68 Western Sahara Ab
46 Western Samoa Is. Ch
67 Westland Bight Be
67 Westland, dist. Ce
9 Westmeath, co. Dc
49 Weston, Sabah Cc
88 Weston, U.S.A. Ee
7 Weston-super-Mare Ef
7 Westport, Ire. Bc
67 Westport, N.Z. Cd
4 Westray, I. Fa
49 Wetar, I. Dd
18 Wetteren Cc
19 Wetzlar Hd
65 Wewak Fg
7 Wexford, & co. Ed
80 Weyburn Db
81 Weymont Bb
7 Weymouth Eg
66 Whakatane Fb

66 Whanga-momona Ec
66 Whangarei Ea
88 Wheeling Ed
65 Whidbey Pt. Ed
7 Whitby Gc
7 Whitchurch Ff
22 White Nile (Bahr el Abiad) R. Cd
39 White Russia Dc
32 White Sea Gb
33 White Volta Gf
67 Whitecliffs Ce
86 Whitefish B. Db
7 Whitehaven Dc
78 Whitenorse Db
8 Whithorn Df
66 Whitianga Eb
7 Whitstable Hf
82a Whittier Pc
60 Whitton Cb
88 Wiarton Eb
85 Wichita Ge
85 Wichita Falls Ge
6 Wick Eb
9 Wicklow, & co. Ed
9 Wicklow, mts. Ed
22 Wielun Ec
17 Wiener Neustadt Ge
19 Wiesbaden Hd
23 Wierzonik Fc
6 Wigan Ed
13 Wil Da
61 Wilcannia Bb
21 Wildspitze, mt. Jc
18 Wilhelmshaven Ga
13 Wilhelmsburg Ja
21 Wilkie Da
89 Wilkes Barre Hd
9b Wilkes Land Hc
11 Willemstad Ed
25 Wilham Mt. Be
89 Williamsburg Gf
88 Williamson Df
89 Williamsport Gd
88 Williamstown Bc
84 Williston Fd
14 Willmar Bb
74 Willowmore Cd
18 Wilmette Bc
60 Wilmington, Australia Ab
87 Wilmington, N.C. Ec
89 Wilmington, N.J. He
7 Wimborne Fg
93 Wilson Gg
7 Wilton Ff
7 Wiltshire, co. Ff
65 Wiluna Cd
72 Winburg Dc
7 Winchester, England Ff
18 Winchester, Ind. Cd
89 Winchester, Wash. Fe
6 Windermere Ea
74 Windhoek Bb
63 Windorah Bd
81 Windsor, Can. Ab
7 Windsor, Eng. Gf
91 Windward Is. Fd
91 Windward Passage Dc
61 Wingham Db
31 Winisk Aa
44 Winnemucca Cc
87 Winnfield Be
80 Winnipeg & L. Ec
80 Winnipegosis, L. Db
61 Winona Bc
23 Winslow Dc
88 Winston-Salem Ed
18 Winterswijk Fc
13 Winterthur Ca
90 Winton, Australia Bc
32 Winton, N.Z. Bg
7 Wisbech Hf
86 Wisconsin Rapids Cc
83 Wisconsin, st. Db
8 Wishaw Ee
16 Wismar Db
22 Wista (Vistula) R. Eb
18 Witten Gc

16 Wittenberge Db
75 Witwatersrand Dc
51 Wloclawek Eb
23 Wlodawa Gc
11 Wloszczowa Ec
29 Wolfsberg Fe
22 Wolin, R. Gb
80 Wollaston L. Db
78 Wollaston Pen. Fb
24 Wollongong Db
25 Wolmaransstad Dc
23 Wolomin Fb
7 Wolverhampton Ee
52 Wonsan Bb
60 Wonthaggi Cc
7 Woodbridge Je
62 Woodlark I. Hh
85 Woodroffe Mt. Ed
81 Woods, L. of the Ec
81 Woodstock, Canada Cb
7 Woodstock, England Ff
85 Woodville Ed
85 Woodward Gd
62 Woolgar Bb
65 Woomera Fe
89 Woonsocket Kd
86 Wooramel & R. Ad
60 Wooroorooka Ca
56 Wooster Dd
74 Wootton Bassett Ff
7 Worcester, Cape Province Bd
7 Worcester, England Ee
21 Worcester, U.S.A. Kc
7 Yeovil Ef
17 Wörgl Jf
10 Workington Dc
16 Worms Fc
7 Worthing Gg
16 Wrangel I. Vb
7 Wrigley Fc
16 Wroclaw (Breslau) Dc
51 Wuchang Ec
51 Wuchow Fd
51 Wuhan Fc
51 Wuhu Fc
16 Wuppertal Ec
17 Würzburg Cd
16 Wurzen Dc
16 Wusih Gc
70 Wusu Cc
88 Wyandotte Dc
63 Wyandra Cd
7 Wye, R. De
7 Wyndham, Australia Db
61 Wyndham, N.Z. Bg
61 Wynnum Da
63 Wynyard Cd
42 Wyoming, st. Cb
75 Xai-Xai Fb
7 Xanthi Ba
48 Xieng Khouang Bb
95 Xingu, R. Eb
95 Xique-Xique Gb

72 Yangambi Cc
51 Yangchuan Fc
22 Yangtze Kiang, R. Gc
7 Yaqui, R. Bb
33 Yar Je
63 Yaraka Bc
32 Yarensk Jc
50 Yarkand Bd
81 Yarmouth, Can. Cb
7 Yarmouth, England Fg
40 Yarmuk, wadi Bc
32 Yaroslavl Gd
8 Yarrow Ee
61 Yass Cb
94 Yati Cc
55 Yatsushiro Bd
68 Yaunde De
55 Yawatahama Bd
45 Yazd Dc
87 Yazoo R. Be
51 Yenisen Fc
3 Yelets Ge
38 Yell, I. Inset
52 Yellow Sea Bb
40 Yellowhead P. Cb
80 Yellowknife Ca
84 Yellowstone, R. Eb
36 Yemen, st. Hh
45 Yenangyaung Gd
42 Yenloa De
35 Yenisei, R. Lc
65 Zanthus Cc
87 Yenki Cb
33 Yeqodayevsk Jf
32 Yeotmal Gh
7 Yeovil Ef
33 Yerevan Hd
33 Yershov Je
27 Yesil, R. Éa
55 Yeu, Ile de Bd
33 Yeviakh Jg
33 Yevpatoriya Fc
38 Yeysk Gf
51 Yiian Gd
51 Yinchwan Ec
51 Yingkow Gb
51 Yiyang Fd
10 Yli Kitka Fb
52 Ylivieska Ec
85 Yoakum Gf
7 Yobe, R. Hf
55 Yokkaichi Cd
55 Yokohama Cc
55 Yokosuka Cc
54 Yokote Dc
7 Yonago Bc
54 Yonezawa Dc
89 Yonkers Jd
7 Yonne, R. & dept. Ee
65 York, Austral. Be
7 York, England Fd
89 York, U.S.A. Gd
55 York C. Ba
80 York Factory Eb
7 York Moors Fc
64 York Sd. Ca
80 Yorkton Db
32 Yoronezh Ge
54 Yosemite National Park Cc
54 Yoshiwara Cc
7 Youghal Ce
41 Young Cb
88 Youngstown Ed
27 Yozgat Db
17 Ypres Bd
33 Yuanyang Ed
51 Yubari Db
54 Yubetsu Db
90 Yucatan, pen. Gd
91 Yucatan Str. Ab
65 Yugoslavia Jg
51 Yumen Db
51 Yungas reg. Bc
51 Yungera Bb
35 Yungtsi Fc
54 Yunnan, prov. Ed
51 Yunndaga Cd
60 Yunta Ab
32 Yurevets Hd
50 Yushu Dc
55 Yutze Fc
55 Yuzhno-Sakhalinsk Re
14 Yvelines, dept. Re
13 Yverdon Ab
18 Zaandam Db

40 Zabdani Cc
39 Zabid Dd
40 Zabiah Bc
43 Zabol Jc
12 Zabrze Ec
90 Zacapa Gd
90 Zacatecas Dc
90 Zacoaico Dc
28 Zadar Eb
40 Zafed Bc
2 Zagan Cc
20 Zagharta Eb
28 Zagreb Eb
43 Zagros, mts. Fc
43 Zahedan Jd
72 Zaire, rep. Cd
72 Zaire, R. Cc
32 Zajecar Dd
72 Zakinthos Bb
23 Zaklikow Gc
35 Zalau Db
43 Zambesi, R. Fg
72 Zambia Eg
72 Zamboanga Dc
30 Zamegerzeg Ab
90 Zamora, Mex. Dd
26 Zamora, Spain Aa
23 Zamosc Gc
57 Zanaga Ad
23 Zandvoort Db
35 Zanesville Ee
43 Zanjan Fb
73 Zanzibar & I. Fe
74 Zaouiet El-Kahla (Fort Flatters) Dc
70 Zaouiet Reggane Ec
93 Zapala Cf
35 Zaporozhye Gf
26 Zaragoza Ba
31 Zaria Cd
64 Zarqa, wadi Bc
42 Zary Cc
35 Zastron Dd
53 Zawada Cc
23 Zawichost Fc
23 Zawiercie Ec
12 Zdunska Wola Ec
18 Zeebrugge Cc
22 Zeehan Cd
72 Zeerust Dc
39 Zeila Dd
28 Zeist Eb
36 Zeitz Dc
53 Zelechów Fc
64 Zelenodolsk Jd
68 Zella Dc
30 Zemun Cc
28 Zepce Gb
16 Zerbst Ec
13 Zermatt Bb
13 Zernez Db
25 Zile Ea
33 Zhdanov Gf
35 Zhigansk Pc
33 Zhitomir Ee
44 Zhob R. Bb
25 Zgorzelec Cc
75 Zimane Eb
75 Zimbabwe Eb
30 Zimmicea Ed
33 Zimovniki Hf
71 Zinder Gf
23 Zira Gd
27 Zivarik Db
52 Zlatoust Ld
22 Zlin (Gottwaldov) Dd
22 Znamenka Ff
22 Znojmo Dd
13 Zofingen Ba
69 Zomba Fg
27 Zonguldak Da
30 Zrenjan Cc
13 Zuid Holland, prov. Db
30 Zug Ca
33 Zugdidi Hf
75 Zululand, dist. Cc
72 Zungeru Gd
13 Zürich, & cant. Ca
13 Zürichsee, L. Ca
15 Zutphen Fb
75 Zwai, L. Bd
19 Zweibrücken De
23 Zweisimmen Bb
17 Zwettl Fd
17 Zwickau Dc
18 Zwischenahn Ga
18 Zwolle Fb
23 Zyrardów Fb
23 Zyrzyn Fb